L. M. RULLA S.J. - F. IMODA S.J. - SR. J. RIDICK S.S.C.

PSYCHOLOGICAL STRUCTURE AND VOCATION

a study of the motivations for
entering and leaving the religious life

EDITRICE PONTIFICIA UNIVERSITÀ GREGORIANA
ROMA 1995

1978 - First Edition - VILLA BOOKS, DUBLIN
1985 - First Printing
1988 - Second Printing
1995 - Third Printing

ISBN 88-7652-586-6

EDITRICE PONTIFICIA UNIVERSITÀ GREGORIANA
Piazza della Pilotta, 35 - 00187 Roma, Italia

CONTENTS

PART ONE: THEORETICAL AND METHODOLOGICAL BACKGROUND

PART TWO: ISSUES

PART THREE: EPILOGUE

Chapter 10

APPENDICES

Appendix A:

PREFACE TO THE PRESENT EDITION

Since this book came out in 1978 all the available copies have been sold out. The first reprint made available in 1985 has also been sold out and we have received many requests for a reprint.

New developments have taken place concerning this research both in terms of the anthropological reflection and the empirical observations.

The results of these developments have been published in *Anthropology of the Christian Vocation, voll. I and II* (Editrice Pontificia Università Gregoriana).

The Institute of Psychology, where the research was pursued and where it continues to be confronted with our ongoing formative and therapeutic experience, is now approaching its 25th Anniversary (1971-1996).

We are persuaded however that the presentation of the data with the introduction, comments and implications as they appear in this *Psychological Structure and Vocation* are still valid and can be considered as a complement and even a foundation of what will follow. This is so first of all because — as is explained in the text — the approach followed is fundamentally 'transtemporal' and 'transcultural'. Furthermore, the work undertaken after the first publication of *Psychological Structure and Vocation* has not only expanded on these findings, adding new information, but has also confirmed the earlier conclusions. The reader who will be interested in studying vocation and personality will find a real complementarity between the initial and the later steps taken toward understanding the various aspects of the person called to the Christian vocation. This complementarity will be indicated by frequent reference in the more recent works to the basic data presented in this book.

L.M.R. F.I. J.R.

Rome, June 1995

PREFACE

On April 11, 1976, the International Commission for the Scientific Psychology of Religion conferred on the authors of the present book the prize which it offers every five years for research in the psychology of religion.

A scientific presentation of the results has already appeared in the book *Entering and Leaving Vocation: intrapsychic dynamics* (Gregorian University Press, Rome, and Loyola University Press, Chicago, 1976). However, the International Commission, in awarding the prize, also strongly recommended the preparation of a further publication addressed to a wider readership, to help those responsible for priestly and religious formation (and indeed others) in reaching a deeper understanding of certain factors involved in the present crisis of vocations.

The present volume is our response to this recommendation. The major findings presented are the same as in the earlier *Entering and Leaving Vocation;* here, we have modified the form of presentation, and to some extent the content.

This contribution is part of the work of the Institute of Psychology of the Gregorian University in Rome, which, in addition to preparing students to work in priestly and religious formation, also attempts to reach a deeper and more scientific understanding of the complex problems of formation, with a view to better solutions.

The title of the present publication calls attention to an important aspect of the approach adopted. The vocation of each individual, as explained in the second Chapter, is studied by means of a structural method, which permits the results obtained in one nation and culture to be applied to other cultures and other social settings; there emerges a general understanding of the psychological structures which underlie the decision to enter on a vocation, as well as perseverance and growth in vocation, in different places and at different times. The observations and reflections presented here are applicable to the problems encountered in formation throughout the world.

The book has an introduction, by Roger Champoux S.J., which offers a synthetic view of the work as a whole. Each subtitle of the introduction makes reference, in parentheses, to the corresponding Chapters of the text.

The authors wish to express particular gratitude to Father André Godin S.J. for his invaluable cooperation in preparing this book for publication; also to Father David Barnes and Father Paul Crowe for their work in translating the original text.

The Authors.

Rome, February 1978

AN INTRODUCTORY OVERVIEW [1]

by Roger Champoux, S.J.

Psychology has been giving its attention to the problems of religious life for a number of years. As Father Godin points out in a recent book,[2] there has been a constantly increasing amount of research into vocation to the priesthood and the religious life in the last 25 years. One fact, however, emerges: notwithstanding the great quantity and the variety of research completed in various countries, there are as yet very few consistent and definite results. On the one hand, there are few research projects that have followed an approach suited to specifically religious vocation; on the other hand, almost all the research has had serious methodological or conceptual gaps (anthropological and theological).

In this context, the work of Luigi M. Rulla, S.J., and of his associates in the Institute of Psychology of the Gregorian University in Rome merits close attention. It purports to be the first formulation of· a psychosocial theory of the priestly and religious vocation,[3] a theory whose hypotheses have been systema-

---

[1] This article was published as *Nuove prospettive nella formazione religiosa. Una integrazione della spiritualità e della psicologia del profondo.* (New Perspectives in Religious Formation. An Integration of Spirituality and of Depth Psychology), in *La Civiltà Cattolica.* July 17, 1976. This translation, by Sister Regina Dubickas, S.S.C., B. Kiely, S.J. and A. Flannery, O.P., is published by kind permission of the editor.

[2] A. Godin. *Psychologie de la Vocation. Un Bilan.* Paris, Ed. Du Cerf, 1975. This book has already appeared as an article with the same title in Le Supplément, n. 113 (May, 1975), 151-236.

[3] The first work containing a general presentation of the theory appeared in English: L.M. Rulla, *Depth Psychology and Vocation: A Psychosocial Perspective*, Rome, Gregorian University Press; Chicago, Loyola University Press, 1971.

1

tically subjected to scientific research.[4]

This article offers, first of all, a concise overview of the theory of vocation developed by Father Rulla. The second part presents the main results obtained by his research up to now, results that are mainly concerned with the motivation of the initial choice of the religious life and with the motivation for leaving religious life. Finally, it considers some implications of these results, primarily in so far as they relate to the problem of religious formation.

The Inadequacy of Existing Theories (Premises)[5]

There are already in existence a good number of theories of personality, such as the psychoanalytic theory of Freud, the behavior theory of Skinner, the self-fulfillment theory of Rogers, etc.; but none of these theories is formulated with enough clarity and precision to permit the formulation of hypotheses that may then be subjected to an empirical verification. It is impossible to take as a basis for research on religious vocation a theory of personality that itself has not been tested: the results of such research and their interpretation would be open to the same

---

4 The first two articles of research were published in 1972: L.M. Rulla —R.S. Maddi, 'Personality and the Catholic Religious Vocation, I. Self and Conflict in Female Entrants', in *Journal of Personality*, 40 (March, 1972), 104-122; II. 'Self and Conflict in Male Entrants', ibid., 40 (December, 1972), 564-587. More informative and recent is the volume: L.M. Rulla—J. Ridick—F. Imoda, *Entering and Leaving Vocation: Intrapsychic Dynamics*, Rome, Gregorian University Press; Chicago, Loyola University Press, 1976. This research won the international quinquennial award of the International Commission of Scientific Religious Psychology, Brussels, 1976. Obviously, in our context, the word *theory* is not to be understood in the sense of 'a speculative knowledge that is ideal and independent of applications', but in the scientific sense of 'a combination of rules and laws, organized systematically, that serve as a base for knowledge, and that explain a large number of facts' (see French Dictionary of *Grand Larousse*, art.: 'theorie'). In this scientific sense the *theory* does not place itself in opposition to, but in relation to, a dynamic and heuristic *praxis*. A scientific theory has constantly to redefine itself in the service of the facts it seeks to explain.

5 In this Introductory Overview, the reader will find that the various subtitles are accompanied by indications in parentheses which refer to the corresponding parts of the present book where the topic is discussed at length.

scientific uncertainty as the theory on which it was based. Moreover, none of these theories takes *religious values* into consideration, and these are the fundamental features of the religious vocation.

There also exist a certain number of *specifically vocational theories* that set out to interpret the choice of a career or a profession by means of some of the attributes of personality. These theories have one factor in common: they see self-actualization, or self-fulfillment as the fundamental motivation at the root of every choice of vocation. At this point we can rightly question whether such motivation respects the reality of the religious vocation; on the contrary, is not the choice of a life according to the Gospels based on the call to renounce all, including oneself, in order to follow Christ? It would be a contradiction to place self-fulfillment as a primary motivation for a vocation whose principal orientation is self-transcendence.

These are the more significant reasons that have inspired Father Rulla to develop a theory that endeavors to integrate spiritual values and psychological insight into a logical and coherent whole. Such a conceptualization has to permit the formulation of hypotheses or axioms, and their translation into concrete terms that may in turn permit experimental verification, without which the theory, however logical and solid in itself, would risk remaining simply 'theoretical'.

Father Rulla's theory proposes as a principal aim the clear presentation of the motivational predispositions that may influence *entrance, perseverance,* and *effectiveness* in vocation. The English subtitle of his first book is: *A Psychosocial Perspective;* it deals in the first place with the *individual psychodynamics,* that is, with the set of motivational forces that operate within a person and that direct and capture his attention, but this individual dynamic view is then seen in relation to social and cultural factors.[6]

Theological Premises

A theory that sets out to respond to the question set out above

---

6 In the present article we will limit ourselves to the intrapsychic dimension, that is, in so far as it concerns the dynamics of the individual. The *interpersonal* aspect of the theory is developed in the English volume of 1971.

regarding motivation to the religious life has first to define the essential characteristics of such a vocation. From a theological point of view, based primarily on the documents of Vatican Council II, we can isolate the three following elements common to the priestly and religious vocation.[7]

First of all is the fact that a religious vocation is primarily an invitation by God: 'A religious vocation is an internal grace (therefore gratuitous) by which God calls, invites a person to consecrate himself to the mission of a priest or to the life of the evangelical counsels, through the three vows of poverty, chastity, and obedience (in the religious life).'[8]

This call of God *lays claim to the total existence of the person.* It is a call not merely to a job or function or to a part-time existence. It is a call to a new existence, in which the religious element has to be the dominant motivation that integrates and unifies the whole person. It is this religious element that confers on the religious vocation its characteristic of transcendence: the religious and the priest choose to witness, as a full-time commitment, to the absolute value of the kingdom founded in Jesus Christ.

The religious vocation entails, for him who is called, *a new obligation,* over and above the call to holiness already included for every Christian in baptism. This new obligation concerns the permanent choice of a particular form of life in the Church.

A central point emerges from these brief considerations: the essential function that *spiritual values* play in the vocation to religious life. It is around these fundamental values that the personality will have to be unified. It is not being implied, however, that what has just been said is true of the religious life exclusively. There is no essential difference, in this regard, between the religious and the baptized Christian. Consequently, the theory presented here is also valid, *mutatis mutandis,* for the

---

7 It is the presence of these common elements that allows us to consider the two forms of life, religious and priestly, together. In this article, therefore, the term *religious life* or *religious vocation* will be used to indicate both the religious life proper and the priestly vocation. Father Godin, in the book cited above, also includes the priesthood and the religious life under the same term *vocation.* This (the vocation) is understood as a commitment of life, religious or priestly, which entails celibacy and is oriented toward the service of others or to the apostolic activity of the Church' (p. 8).

8 L. M. Rulla: *Depth Psychology and Vocation,* p. 24.

christian life, which fundamentally is a life lived for God and for others.

Psychological Premises (Chapter 1)

From the psychological point of view, how can we approach the study of the personality in a way that will integrate these essential theological data on the religious vocation with the many dimensions of the personality itself? Among these latter dimensions there is one of particular importance, that of the subconscious.[9] As is indicated by the title itself of the work referred to earlier, Father Rulla's theory makes use of the contributions of depth psychology. It deals with realities that, even though unknown to a great majority of superiors and subjects, influence to an important degree the life of an individual and of the community.[10]

There has been, and still is, a tendency when considering a person's suitability for the religious life to be satisfied with ascertaining whether he or she is acting freely and is of good character, and is free of mental illness. The religious community that makes use of a psychologist for the selection of its candidates aims above all to exclude the psychopathological cases, for there is little awareness that other psychological factors can affect a person's suitability for the religious life.[11] Outside of these cases of mental illness, people tend to presuppose in the subject the capacity to persevere and to grow in the religious life. Conse-

---

[9] The subconscious taken in the whole field of psychic experience that is not present to the actual consciousness of the individual and, in turn, consists of: the *preconscious,* which comprises those psychic contents that can be recalled to consciousness through ordinary rational methods (such as reflection, examination of conscience, introspection, meditation, etc.) and of the *unconscious,* which takes in those psychic contents that can be brought to consciousness only by special means, as for example, psychotherapy (see *Glossary* of the book, *Entering and Leaving Vocation: Intrapsychic Dynamics,* p. 400).

[10] L.M. Rulla, *Depth Psychology and Vocation,* p. 8.

[11] In the book already cited, Father Godin traces some 'historical features' of the contribution of psychology to the study of religious life. He points out that at first psychologists were asked to provide 'at least some contraindications, related primarily to the psychological balance (mental health) of the candidates, at times to their intelligence (. . .) and a little later, some positive indications related to their interests, to their capacity for adaptation, or to certain attitudes'. p. 13.

5

quently, of those who leave it would be said that they had used their freedom poorly and had not responded sufficiently to the grace that God was offering them. But is it not necessary, perhaps, to introduce another dimension between a pathological state so severe as to destroy a person's free will, on the one hand, and a state where the person is totally free, on the other hand, with no psychological factors curtailing freedom? Is there not deep interpenetration between the conscious and the unconscious? If there is a subconscious, and if this subconscious influences — at least to a certain degree, difficult to determine with precision — the conscious life, do we not then have to take into consideration, in the evaluation and selection of candidates, not only their possible pathological symptoms, not only their wishes, interests, and attitudes, not only their consciously formulated desires, but also the unconscious motives that may influence, in various degrees, their capacity to internalize[12] and personalize the spiritual values that will be presented to them in the course of their formation? Outside of the evident good will and the sincere proclamation of authentic values, there is at the origin of behavior, a complex being, whose unconscious needs may sometimes stifle conscious desires.[13]

As a means of keeping in mind the diverse and complex elements that make up the personality, we approach the study of the personality from two points of view: *structure* and *content*. From *the point of view of structure,* the personality may be considered at two levels: the *ideal-self* which is conscious, and the *actual-self* which may be either conscious or subconscious. On the one hand, therefore, there is what the individual desires to be or to become; on the other hand, there is what he really is, which he may or may not know, and also the way in which

12 We prefer to use the term 'to internalize' in order to emphasize that we are dealing with a technical term of the theory that we are presenting, and not the pure and simple 'to interiorize' of common parlance. Further in the article we will also meet other uncommon words (such as 'consistency' and 'inconsistency', 'compliance', 'transference' . . .); their technical significance will be explained each time. For greater clarification we recommend the *Glossary* of the 1976 book *(Entering and Leaving Vocation: Intrapsychic Dynamics)* whose terminology we are using in this article.

13 It is for this reason that, as Father Godin has noted, 'the practical duty of the psychologist ought to be that of fostering a personal decision at this point of intersection between the influences coming from the past and the foreseeable obstacles of the future' (p. 9).

he acts habitually.

The principal *contents* within these structures are *values, attitudes,* and *needs.* By *values* we mean the ideals of life that a person proposes to live. For example, for the religious life, these would be: union with God, imitation of Christ, and the three vows of poverty, chastity, and obedience. The *attitudes* are also, like the values, tendencies towards action, but they are more specific and numerous than the values. So a value, such as obedience, may be expressed in many different attitudes, such as respect for superiors, apostolic availability, etc. In such a case, the attitudes carry out an *expressive function* in relation to the values and serve as the mediators between them and behavior. Thus, the *ideal-self* is constituted of a combination of values and of attitudes which characterize every single person.

The *actual-self,* besides the habitual behavior of the person, also includes conscious or subconscious *needs.* The needs are predispositions to action that inhere in the very nature of the human person in his organic, emotional, and spiritual dimensions. Modern psychology has developed a list of about twenty needs which are considered fundamental; for example, the need of affective dependence, the sexual need, the need for autonomy, the need for knowledge, etc. The needs, like the values, find expression through the attitudes; for example, the need to be aggressive may manifest itself in a refusal to accept authority, in reluctance to cooperate with others, in a tendency to criticize others, etc.

The attitudes function as the fulcrum of the personality; in fact, because of their central position, they may come from the values and/or from the needs. They may serve to satisfy and express these needs, or on the contrary, to defend the self from these needs (for example, when one develops attitudes of gentleness and of deference as a self-defense against a profound aggressive need).

Consistencies and Inconsistencies (Chapters 1 and 2)

There are some needs that give rise to attitudes which can be described as 'dissonant' from — one might say 'in conflict with' — values which are fundamental in a religious vocation. Such needs are for example, aggression, affective dependence, the sexual need, etc. These needs may be called 'vocationally dissonant'. Others, on the other hand, are neutral or 'consonant', for example the need to overcome obstacles and difficulties, the need for order, for knowledge.

If the *attitudes* were simply the expression of the values of an individual, it would be easy to discern the suitability of the candidate for the religious life. It would be enough to ascertain the presence of the fundamental values of religious vocation and to verify their expression at the level of attitudes and behavior. Formation could then be limited to helping a person understand and accept these values, and to explaining their logical translation at the level of attitudes and actions.

The existence of the *latent-self* complicates the situation. The attitudes of the subject are not only the expression of his values, but may also come from his conscious or subconscious needs. In other words, the *ideal-self* may be, in part, the projection of the *latent-self*. An example will clarify what we mean. The christian value of charity may express itself in many ways: in the service of others, in apostolic prayer, in humble respect for the opinions of others, etc. Each of these concrete expressions or attitudes, however, may have a motivation very different from charity. The service of others may have as an end the satisfaction of a strong need for affective dependence, and so, may be in reality, the opposite of charity: to give in order to receive is not the expression of an altruistic love. Or again, humble respect for the opinions of others may come from a feeling of inferiority that hinders the individual from expressing himself freely. Now, such a motivation may easily escape the consciousness of the individual. He dedicates himself in total good faith to the service of others, without being aware that he is still somehow self-centered. He believes that he is showing respect for others by being deferential in any dialogue in which he is engaged, but the reality is that, in the last analysis, he lacks the courage of his own convictions.

The possibility exists, then, of *inconsistency* between the *ideal-self* and the *actual-self,* and this inconsistency may be conscious or *unconscious*. The theory presents four general types of consistency or inconsistency, based on the dynamics that may exist between the values, the attitudes, and the needs:

> *Social consistency:* when a need, conscious or subconscious, is compatible with both the values and the attitudes of the individual. Thus, a need to help others may be in harmony with a generous attitude, oriented towards the

8

realization of charity. This consistency is called social because the individual is well-adapted socially, in contrast to what appears in the other type of consistency.

Psychological consistency: when a need is compatible with the values, but not with the attitudes of the individual. Thus a need to help others may be in harmony with the ideal of charity, but the individual has developed, more or less consciously, *some* attitudes that are contrary to it, for example, aggressive or egoistic attitudes. However much he is socially maladjusted, he is still fundamentally, or psychologically consistent.

Psychological inconsistency: when a subconscious need is not in harmony with values and attitudes. For example, someone may have a subconscious need to be helped by and to depend on others, but this need is incompatible with his attitudes, which are oriented more in the opposite direction (to help others). This individual, exteriorly a good religious, is psychologically inconsistent. He manifests a tendency to help others, but in fact has a need of a defensive nature, since in the last analysis, he wants to give in order to receive.

Social inconsistency: when a subconscious need is not in harmony with the values of vocation, and the attitudes obey the need more than the values. Thus a need of affective dependence may produce some attitudes that are not in conformity with vocation, such as the constant and continuous search for friendship, the rejection of private prayer, etc. This individual is inconsistent not only psychologically, but also socially.

In evaluating these consistencies or inconsistencies it is necessary to consider also several other aspects: in particular, whether they are *conscious* or *unconscious,* and their *centrality.* An inconsistency, recognized as such by the subject, makes possible a free decision and growth. The unconscious inconsistency, on the other hand, risks bringing about either a defensive adaptation to religious life, or departure from religious life, in which case the needs have reached the point of overcoming the values.

It is necessary to keep in mind the working together of the needs and attitudes and to seek a person's central motivation. Inconsistencies and consistencies may in fact coexist in the same person, and according to various needs and various degrees of intensity. Still, it is possible to evaluate the dynamic forces present in a person and to determine the central nuclear motivation, that is, the movements that influence, also unconsciously, entrance, departure, or growth in vocation.

Self-Transcendent Consistency

The expression, *self-transcendent consistency,* expresses and summarises well the central elements of the theory. The religious vocation is based on the transcedence of self since it is an invitation to pursue transcendent values whose direct aim is not self-fulfillment. The religious seeks first of all 'the kingdom of God and his justice', both in others and in himself, 'and everything else will be given to him besides'. The life of the Gospel, which is a way of love, demands the gift of self to others and the renouncement of one's own life. Therefore the values that make up the 'ideal-self' of the religious should be based on charity.

The religious commitment, because of these personal and ecclesial demands, presupposes, besides the divine call, the capacity to respond and to grow in this response. Such a capacity is based on the consistency of the self, that is, on the presence in the actual-self of attributes consistent with the ideal-self. The proclaimed values, then, seem to be insufficient to guarantee the perseverance and the vocational effectiveness of a person if they are not supported by a personality sufficiently free of unconscious needs.

The Capacity to Internalize Values (Chapters 7 and 9)

One of the fundamental notions of the theory is this: growth in vocation, or vocational growth, presupposes the capacity to internalize spiritual values and to live them. In psychology the process of maturation is often presented in terms of integration of the different components of the personality. A person is mature if he or she engages all the dynamic forces of the personality, both conscious and unconscious, in a freely chosen project of life. The same is true of vocational maturity, which may be presented as the integration of affective maturity and spiritual maturity. It is this fundamental idea that is expressed by the

10

notion of consistency between the emotional needs and the spiritual values. The *internalization of values* is precisely the process of maturation that allows a person to integrate into a consistent system of motivation the values of his new vocation presented in the course of formation.

As has been seen with regard to the notion of inconsistency, there is the possibility of a split between the ideal-self and the actual-self. The values may be inconsistent with the needs, and therefore, not integrated into the motivational system of the individual. In such a case, adherence to the vocational values will remain merely exterior, having been chosen, at least primarily, as a defense of the self against its unconscious conflicts, and/or to gratify some of its needs. The values will be kept for as long as they serve such an end. The individual will believe in all good faith that he has really grown and matured, but it is possible that this apparent growth may be the result either of a *compliance* that is purely exterior (if he accepts the influence of the institution, the superior, or the group, not out of an interior conviction, but in order to obtain a reward, such as admission to the vows, or priesthood, or to avoid a punishment), or of *identification* with the institution (if the individual, because of his insecurity, seeks to reinforce his wavering personality by identifying himself with another person or group and, therefore, accepts the norms and the values of the group for the gratification and stability that this relationship provides for him).

Internalization, however, presupposes that the candidate accepts the vocational values that have been presented on the basis of their intrinsic value and because of the harmony between them and his own consistent ideal. Only this kind of internalization permits a vocational decision that is truly free and not dependent on the pressures of the family, group, institution, or the unconscious needs of the candidate himself. The capacity for internalization is therefore directly proportioned to the degree of consistency of the personality. Now, a religious formation of the traditional type, constituted primarily on the presentation of the religious values by means of conferences, retreats, etc., presupposes the presence of this capacity to internalize, and is not prepared to increase this capacity in those who do not already possess it. Thus, one is able to understand the well known phenomenon of the enthusiastic conversion during the novitiate, followed shortly by a sometimes painful reversal when neither the Novice Master nor an environment favorable to sustaining enthusiasm are any longer present. The explanation is that the visible change was mostly at the level of external behavior or of the conscious ideal, but was not reaching the true motivational forces of the personality.

The Trans-cultural Character of the Theory (Chapter 2)

When these essential elements are considered, it is clear that the theory presented is both trans-cultural and trans-situational. The current questioning of values may make us lose sight of the unchangeable aspects of the Gospel and religious lift across the ages and cultures. This trans-situational character may be seen both under the aspect of the *contents* and, above all under the aspect of the *structures* considered.

The fundamental *contents* considered in the theory are the *values* and the *needs*. The five values that the theory affirms as fundamental for the religious life are:

terminal values: union with God and the imitation of Christ;
instrumental values: poverty, chastity, and obedience.

The way of living these values concretely will vary according to the age and the culture, but they are in themselves as unchangeable as the essential meaning of the religious life. With reference to the *needs*, these are by definition intrinsic to human nature, and therefore, they also are unchangeable. The tendency toward aggression, affective dependence, sexuality, knowledge, overcoming of obstacles and difficulties, etc., have been and will always be present in man, though their exterior expression will vary enormously according to the historical and social situation.

The *structures* considered, the ideal-self and the actual-self, as well as the consistency between the one and the other, are also, precisely because they are structural characteristics of the personality, independent of the concrete conditions of time and place. The images and values of the ideal-self will undoubtedly be different for an African and for an American; similarly, the fantasies and the needs of the *subconscious* actual-self will not be the same in a young religious as in an old contemplative woman . . . ; but the theory is not concerned with these diverse contents. It concentrates on the elements that, within these structures, are essential to human nature and to the religious vocation. It, therefore, permits us to reach some conclusions that are valid outside of historical changes, social relativism, and the varieties of spirituality.

The Results of Research: Entrance and Perseverance in the Religious Life

Having discussed the essentials of the theory, we can pose some more specific questions regarding the factors that may influence entrance and perseverance in the religious life. Father Rulla's research and that of his associates has until now been directed to the following five questions:[14]

Do candidates choose the religious life more on the basis of what they believe themselves to be or on what they would like to become?

Is it necessary to take at face value the declared motivations of the candidate, or should one rather consider also the possibility of subconscious motivation?

If the conscious motivation is not the *entire* motivation, what is its part in the psychodynamics of the individual? And what is the part played by subconscious motivation? What contents characterize both the conscious and the subconscious motivation?

Do the psychodynamics at the moment of entrance *tend to persist* in those who remain in the religious life?

Can the dynamics of entrance influence *leaving* the religious life, or be detrimental to vocational growth?

Without entering into the details of the methods followed for the collection and analysis of data, we will now briefly present the answers to these five questions, based on the results already obtained in the course of research carried out on several hundred seminarians, male and female religious, and American lay students.

The Conscious Motivation for Entrance (Chapter 5)

There is a clear tendency in the candidates to choose the religious

---

14 These questions are formulated and studied in L.M. Rulla, et al., *Entering and Leaving Vocation: Intrapsychic Dynamics*, cit., 61ff.

13

institution on the basis of *personal ideals,* that is, more on the basis of what they would like to become, than on the basis of what they consciously are. This choice is accompanied by a quite idealized conceptualization of the institution to which they belong. They seem to attribute to the institution the qualities of their *ideal-self.*

This prevalence of the ideal-self over the actual-self manifests a tension of growth that may be valuable for the development of vocation since it may favor openness to the influence of grace as well as self-transcendence in the fulfillment of a mission. However, man is not motivated solely by his ideals.

The Subconscious Motivation for Entrance (Chapter 6)

There is a strong tendency in candidates to idealize either their own personality or the religious institution, and therefore, there is a lack of realism in the choice. This is confirmed by the presence of *unconscious inconsistencies* within the personality. The lack of reality seen in these candidates seems related, at least in part, to the presence of unconscious needs in dissonance with the proclaimed vocational ideals. In other words, the choice of a vocation and the decision to enter a religious order are not only the fruit of an ideal freely chosen, but are also the result of unconscious needs. Certain individuals may, without knowing it, choose a religious vocation with the aim of gratifying some of their needs, or in a defensive effort to resolve their conflicts or inconsistencies. Despite the undoubted sincerity and the evident generosity of the candidates, the way they consciously describe themselves and their motivation is not to be accepted as completely valid. It is also necessary to keep the unconscious factors in mind, since the ideals formulated consciously may be the result of subconscious forces.

As has already been said, a certain idealization of self and of the religious institution is normal and also desirable in those entering, since it expresses the desire of the individual for growth and his openness to grace, but only on the condition that there is not an unconscious inconsistency between this ideal and the true self.

On this point, it has become a common practice to *delay the entrance* of candidates to houses of formation. The usefulness of such a measure seems evident, especially in cases in which the candidate has not yet resolved certain normal problems of development. But we may ask if this measure is useful when the candidate presents some unconscious inconsistencies. Will the mere acquisition of a broader experience of life truly influence the individual, and to what degree? It is more to be foreseen that the individual who presents some unconscious inconsistencies will continue to act in accordance with them in whatever environment he finds himself by developing defensive or gratifying attitudes. These attitudes, in their turn, will produce the concrete results of perpetuating the unrealistic idealization of self and of the institution.

The Prevalence of Subconscious Motivation (Chapter 7)

The results of this research invite us to reflect seriously on the following point: the vocational motivation of a great majority of the candidates, between 60 and 80%, was marked by attitudes in the service of subconscious needs: attitudes maintained either to defend the self against these needs or to satisfy them. Therefore, the subconscious motivation seems to be an important element in the decision to enter the religious life.[15] Moreover, within this subconscious motivation, *the dissonant needs,* such as aggression, the need for abasement, the need to justify oneself, are of particular relevance. Thus, one can expect these inconsistencies to have a negative influence on perseverance and vocational effectiveness.

---

15 These results, however difficult to accept at first sight, are similar to the results obtained in other research. According to Baars and Terruwe: 10-15% of the priests in the U.S. and Western Europe are psychologically mature, 60-70% are emotionally immature, and 20-25% present serious psychiatric difficulties (*How to Treat and Prevent the Crisis in the Priesthood,* Chicago, Franciscan Herald Press, 1972). The research of Kennedy and Heckler has produced the following results for 271 U.S. priests (the sample, however, is not scientifically representative of the population): 19 'developed' (7%), 50 'developing' (18%), 179 'underdeveloped' (66.5%), 23 'maldeveloped' (8.5%), *The Catholic Priest in the United States: Psychological Investigations,* Washington D.C., U.S. Catholic Conference, 1971). However, it is necessary, to note that religious are not 'worse' than others. Research completed on the 'lay' population in various countries give results that are fundamentally similar to these. The methodological differences among these researches make the agreement of the results more noteworthy.

Such results do not speak of *psychopathology* — even though, in fact among the less 'mature' psychologically, some cases of this may be present — but more of the lack of maturity, be it affective or vocational. These insufficiencies of the personality are already present at the moment of entrance before the individuals begin their religious formation. Therefore, they are not caused by the centers themselves of formation.

The Persistence of Vocational Inconsistencies (Chapter 8)

By its very nature, unconscious conflict tends to persist since it is not recognized for what it is. The mechanisms of defense used by the individual have precisely the aim of hiding from him the true nature of his difficulties and the true source of his frustration so that he is not able to learn from experience as it is offered. He will seek various solutions here and there — changing his environment, experimenting with new forms of retreats, of prayer, seeking courses and conferences . . . — but without lasting results, since none of these solutions is based on a true grasp of the basic problem.

In fact, the results of the research show that four years of formation have not brought about any significant increase in the degree of affective maturity of the group of male and female religious studied: only 2% of the male religious and 2% of the female religious profited from the formation offered them for growth in affective maturity. Similarly, it seems that there was little progress in in-depth knowledge of self: at the moment of entrance 86% of the male religious and 87% of the female religious were ignorant, totally or in part, of their central conflict (or their central conflicts), and after four years of formation, 83% of the men and 82% of the women were still ignorant of such conflicts.

An interesting phenomenon, that of *transference,* also manifests the persistence of unconscious inconsistencies. The subject, in his relation with authority or with his peers, relives a relationship he had with members of his family during infancy or adolescence. This regressive repetition of a past experience reveals and also

16

reinforces the inconsistencies already present.[16] As a matter
of fact, the results show that 69% of the male religious and
67% of the female religious seem to establish some transferential
relationships in the course of their formation. Moreover, these
transferential relationships are related to either the *family conflicts*
or the *personal conflicts* of the candidates. The personal conflicts
tend to be expressed in the adoption of the transferential relationships that are, in their turn, the repetition of the original family
conflict. Thus one is faced with a *vicious circle,* since the
transferential relationship not recognized as such perpetuates the
original conflict and reinforces the defenses of the individual
against it.

These results pose a very important problem, that of the real
usefulness of formation, if four years have not produced some
significant in-depth change in the sense of a greater maturity. It
is important to note that the subjects studied have completed
these four years of formation between 1969 and 1972; they have,
therefore, profited from the new methods following Vatican
II.

Every man always has the intrinsic strength, with the help of
God, to change himself and to perfect himself, but these results
seem to indicate that, in fact, this strength is not effective in the
great majority of individuals affected by unconscious inconsistencies.

The Motivation for Leaving Religious Life (Chapter 9)

The striking phenomenon of the numerous priests and male
and female religious who have left the religious life and the
priesthood in these last ten years can be explained on the basis
of various factors: divine grace and human co-operation, the
pressure of the group or the community on the individual, factors
dealing with the norms, constitutions, and structures of the
religious institution, the influence of the historical and socio-
cultural environment in general, and of the structural functioning

---

16 The person is generally conscious of his feelings, but lacks awareness
as to 1. *what* they are a repetition of (e.g., earlier familial experiences),
2. *that* they are being re-enacted, or 3. *why*. There is, thus, a perpetuation of his conflicts' (*Entering and Leaving Vocation*) *Intrapsychic
Dynamics,* p. 151).

of the Church in particular, and the characteristics of the individual personality. The research with which we are dealing considers only the last factor: the possible influence of the individual psychodynamic, evaluated at the moment of entrance, on an eventual leaving of vocation.

The results show that the internal forces of the personality at work at the moment of *entrance* and at the moment of *leaving* are not necessarily the same ones. The set of forces that seem to prevail at the moment of entrance into the religious life consists of the values and the attitudes of the subject, his ideal-self. This ideal proclaimed by the subject, however, is not a guarantee of perseverance.

To explain at least in part the phenomenon of leaving, it is necessary to refer to a second set of forces: the balance or imbalance of the consistencies and the inconsistencies, or what in this theory is called *'predictable internalizing capacity'*. The greater the prevalence of the consistencies over the inconsistencies, the greater is the capacity for internalization, and the greater is the likelihood of perseverance in the religious life. The results show a significant correlation between the prevalence of vocational inconsistencies and subsequent leaving of vocation. Therefore, the greater or lesser capacity for internalization of values, determined by the consistencies and inconsistencies, seems to be one of the decisive elements for perseverance in a person's vocation.

One obvious explanation for this is that, if vocational values are not internalized, religious commitment itself will gradually be called in question. A second explanation is based on a less direct effect of the unconscious inconsistencies. The more they predominate in a person, the more they determine unrealistic personal ideals and false expectations with regard to future vocational roles. The discrepancy between the ideal-self and the actual-self tends to increase, and with that the profound dissatisfaction of the subject. The *source* of the increasing dissatisfaction cannot be recognized because of the unconscious character of the inconsistencies present in the individual, and because the realistic perception of his real conflictual needs presents a too serious threat to his self-esteem. This dissatisfaction is, therefore, 'projected' onto the structures of the institution or of the Church. There follows the phenomenon of 'perceptive distortion' that hinders the individual from making an objective judgement on the exterior world and forces him gradually to reinterpret in his own peculiar way the authentic significance of vocational values and attitudes. Thus the day comes when the religious discovers himself irremediably isolated and alienated within his religious group. The logical conclusion is to leave.

However, it is not necessary to conclude that all who are inconsistent leave the religious life after some time. On the one hand, it is very possible that *consistent* candidates may also leave after some time of probation. If, for example, a more profound knowledge of the institution shows them that it does not respond to the ideal that they were proposed, they are able to make the mature and objective decision to seek another way. On the other hand, *inconsistent* candidates may remain in the religious life despite their unconscious conflicts. For example, if the religious life offers them a security that they could not find in another form of life. In such a case, it will be the area of apostolic effectiveness that will suffer the lack of vocational maturity.

The true question that should be asked with regard to those who leave is not primarily *why they leave,* but more so, what are the *expectations,* above all the unconscious expectations, that have influenced their decision to enter the religious life. It is the *total psychodynamic* of the candidate at *entrance* that can influence in a relevant way the later decision to leave.

Some Conclusions and Consequences. Sanctity and Human Maturity (Chapter 10)

The main results of the research that we have briefly presented raise very serious questions, above all with regard to formation. We will try to clarify some of the principal consequences that emerge; these are discussed at greater length in the volume that appeared in English in 1976. In the first place, we are able to offer a more adequate understanding of the relationship between sanctity and human maturity.

Sanctity is the fruit of the presence of divine love in man. It depends, therefore, on the gratuitous action of God and on the free response of man, independently of the psychological dispositions of the individual, presupposing obviously that there is a minimum of personal freedom present. However, it is possible that subconscious factors may limit the field of freedom through which man welcomes the action of grace, and so diminish his availability to the action of grace. *Subjective* sanctity, therefore, does not depend on the degree of psychological maturity of the person; *objective* sanctity, on the other hand, which consists in the affective and human maturity of the person.

Certainly, grace may overcome the subconscious limitations of a person to transform him in depth; but such a 'therapeutic' action of grace seems to be the exception rather than the rule. It is this that the results of the research show: God respects the freedom of man and the dynamic laws of his development. On the other hand, it is difficult to see why God ought not in general to respect the psychodynamic laws he himself created.

The human and vocational maturity of the religious is also very important for *apostolic effectiveness*. It makes a person a better instrument in the hands of God, more sensitive to the needs of the ministry, and a more convinced witness to the values of Jesus Christ. If the religious is barely able to internalize spiritual values, his basic attitudes will tend little by little to conform to his needs more than to his transcendent ideals. His capacity to hear objectively and to transmit the word of God, in the scriptures, the liturgy and the Church, his ability to understand the profound sense of reality will be seriously jeopardised. He will have difficulty in mastering himself and will be incapable of losing himself in order to abandon himself generously in love.

The Actual Crisis of Vocations (Chapter 10)

What do the theory and the results of the research tell us with regard to the actual crisis of vocations? This crisis can be considered under the aspect of the large number of those who have left, and also the very small number of those who enter. The theory and the results of the research throw an interesting light on the problem of those leaving. Although it is also necessary to consider the numerous other socio-cultural factors, the fact that they leave seems, in part, attributable to the existence of unconscious inconsistencies in a great number of religious, and to the increasingly negative influence that these inconsistencies exercise on the vocational ideal.

Such inconsistencies are not limited to a particular country or to our age.[17]   Why then has the number of those leaving increased so much in the last ten years?   It is here that the *socio-cultural* factors enter, among which institutional structures have an important function.   These structures have notably lost importance in the last ten years, leaving a greater freedom and responsibility to the individual, and demanding on his part a greater adaptability.   But it is not enough to be given a greater freedom in order to become capable of using that freedom with maturity.   If inconsistencies are prevalent in a person, the presence of institutional structures reinforce the process of *compliance,* and thus support his wavering freedom and help him to persevere; but all this is done in an attitude of rigid and defensive adherence to the rules and to the norms of the institution.   When the structures disappear, the dissonant needs, until now kept under control by the environment, seek to express themselves and risk damaging seriously the freedom and the vocational choice of the religious.   The lack of vocational maturity could be, therefore, one of the causes that has made a certain number of religious incapable of accepting the challenge of this new freedom.

It is necessary to add that a return to the structures of the past is not the solution to the problem of leaving vocation.   A perseverance that is both creative and effective depends on the capacity of the individual for internalization of vocational ideals, rather than on the external imposition of rules, or the simple proposal of values, however authentic and valid.

Selection and Formation of Candidates to the Religious Life (Chapter 10)

What, then, can be done in selecting and forming candidates for the religious life?   Is it necessary to turn away all those who

---

17 The research indicates the presence of inconsistencies in around 60-80% of the candidates in a particular environment (across the United States).   Theoretically the number could be lower in another environment; although, in fact, from the results of other research this does not seem to be the case.   The trans-situational character of the theory is not in regard to this number, but to the ideas themselves of consistency and inconsistency and the consequences that are derived for perseverance and effectiveness.

have inconsistencies? According to the data obtained, in such a case, only 10% or 15% of the actual number of candidates would remain, which would reduce the numbers in a community almost to zero. Are inconsistencies an indication that the candidate does not have a vocation, or can they be seen instead as one of the possible ways chosen by the Lord to call to himself whom he wills? In this hypothesis it becomes very important not only to *discern* these vocational inconsistencies, but above all to help the religious to *resolve* them.

It is evident that it is necessary to preserve the *didactic* element in formation: the presentation of the fundamental values of the religious life by means of conferences, retreats, study groups, etc. According to the results obtained, such formation remains clearly insufficient when the capacity to internalize the values is weak, and this, we repeat, is the case in the majority of the candidates.

For some years there has been much emphasis on the value of *experience,* that is, on the need to offer to religious the opportunity to experience different roles by becoming university students or teachers, by participating in social activities for the poor, by working in new apostolic endeavors, by participating in prayer groups, etc. But what will be the real benefit of these experiences if the subject is incapable of profiting from them because of his inconsistencies? To experience roles does not lead automatically to a greater maturity; it presupposes, on the contrary, the capacity to profit from them and, therefore, the capacity to internalize values. It is obvious that experiences will permit a person to achieve a greater capability: a university diploma will enable a person to teach successfully, practice in social work will enable a person to know the problems of the poor and to discover solutions, etc. But are the experiences in themselves a guarantee of a greater apostolic *effectiveness?* Apostolic effectiveness is not to be confused with *efficiency.* The former, which is the visible manifestation of the christian values, depends primarily on the orientation toward such values, while the latter is tied to the orientation toward the roles in themselves.[18] In other words, if the experiencing of roles is not rooted in the pre-existing capacity

---

18 In technical terms, *role-orientation* consists in the fact of considering the role or the function as an end in itself, instead of using it as a means to realize some values that transcend it and that also transcend the individual. *Value-orientation,* on the other hand, consists in the adoption and utilization of behaviors and roles as a means towards the expression and actualization of values.

to internalize vocational values, it will not have any effect on the spiritual or apostolic maturation of the subject. It will be instead the role in itself that will become for him a value, so that he will identify his apostolic effectiveness with the role or with the profession and will become fixated on this. He will not be able to serve the Kingdom without teaching this particular subject in this particular university, or having this particular occupation in this particular city.

As for the *transmission of values,* so also for the *experience of life:* in order to be effective, the religious must have the capacity to internalize. But how is it possible to develop this capacity for internalization?

The Role of Psychology in Formation (Chapter 10)

The more common vocational difficulties may be grouped into four types: spiritual problems (for example, doubts of faith, morals, etc.); problems resulting from the normal difficulties of psychological development; subconscious vocational inconsistencies not directly reducible to psychopathology; and psychopathology.

The solution to the first two types of problems should not present particular difficulties. However, these can be the expression of inconsistencies or of pathology. In such a case, their resolution presupposes a prior resolution of the inconsistencies or of the pathological disturbance. But, as the results of the research indicate, the means commonly used (spiritual direction, examination of conscience, group dynamics, experience of life) seem insufficient to bring about a lasting resolution of inconsistencies and unconscious conflicts. Therefore, new methods of formation, which utilise the contributions of psychology are necessary.

Until now communities have limited the contribution of the psychologist to the following two functions: the *selective* and the *therapeutic.* The screening of undesirable candidates remains necessary, but this should take place before entrance to the religious life. With regard to therapeutic treatment of cases of psychopathology, that is not, strictly speaking, a function of vocational formation. The role of psychology in formation should be defined on the basis of the following three functions:

23

pedagogical, preventative, and *integrative.* The contribution of psychology should aim, first of all, to develop in the religious the capacity to internalize vocational values and attitudes; that is, it has more to do with *preventing* than with healing. In fact, it is already possible to discover at the time of entrance the sources of the future difficulties that the religious will meet in his vocational commitment. Why then wait for such difficulties to develop and become, at times, irreversible? It seems much more preferable to intervene from the beginning with the aim of allowing the individual to recognize in himself and to overcome the inconsistencies that hinder his human and spiritual growth. Therefore, one should not make a dichotomy between psychology and spirituality. Formation has to present to the candidate the necessary spiritual nourishment, but it has to also assure him the capacity to assimilate and to internalize this nourishment. Without this integration between the human and the spiritual, the ideals proposed, instead of favoring growth, may become a source of frustration and alienation.

Such formation evidently demands new types of *'formators'* properly prepared for their work. With regard to this, we can formulate the following two *new* qualifications. In the first place, they ought to have already recognized and overcome in themselves their psychological difficulties and their inconsistencies, to avoid projecting them on the subjects for whom they are responsible, either under the form of a peculiarly subjective interpretation of the constitutions and the spirit of the institution, or by favoring, in a more or less explicit way, attitudes of compromise in disaccord with fundamental religious values. These new formators would also be able to avoid the frequent trap of transferential relationships that keep the subjects in their unconscious conflicts. In the second place, these formators would be capable of perceiving in the subjects indications, at times subtle, of subconscious motivation, above all when it concerns vocational inconsistencies, and of helping the subjects to see this in themselves.

Besides this first category of educators, capable of *discerning* and *helping others to discern* the presence of vocational inconsistencies, a second category of formators would be necessary who would be capable of *helping the subject himself to resolve his difficulties.* The unconscious nature of such difficulties demands that these educators have a serious formation in depth-psychology.

We are speaking of 'new' educators. However, their role does not differ from the traditional role of the 'spiritual director' or the director of formation. The new element is that, besides the help offered to the person for developing a conscious spiritual life, they would be able first of all, to *add* to this and to *integrate* into it the help necessary to free the candidates from the negative influence of their subconscious life; secondly, they would be able to increase in the candidates their capacity to internalize and to live vocational values. The results of this research of Father Rulla and of his associates show the necessity and urgency of this responsibility.

PREMISES

In the parable of the sower (Mt 13:1-23) the Lord tells us that his message and his call, are received by men having different dispositions, and that there are therefore different results.

Why do these differing personal dispositions exist? It is true that the parable is concerned with the call to everyone becoming a Christian, but as regards the disposition to accept that call, or 'the knowledge of those inclinations involved in responding to that call,'[1] it would seem to be applicable also to the religious life characterized by vows.

Why do a considerable number of young people, who accept a vocation, then present signs of insufficient growth in their vocational commitment during the years which immediately follow the beginning of formation at vocational centers?

Why do some of the young people who enter — and indeed there are many more of them in recent times — then abandon the vocational commitment?

Why do a considerable number of priests and religious of both sexes, who at the beginning do not show the above-mentioned signs of insufficient growth in vocation, then later finish in what might be called 'early retirement'; they make a 'nest', and then 'nest' in their vocation while living in a state of more or less apathetic routine where only a fraction of their potentiality is used for the Kingdom?

There is a huge number of complex elements involved in any attempt to find points of reference to reply to these questions. The import of supernatural factors, for example, will be neither denied nor diminished in what follows here. Likewise, the orientation, function, and structures of vocational institutions will not be overlooked. We simply ask ourselves the question: What can be said about the personal dispositions about which our Lord speaks?

This book will study some dispositions, at both the conscious and subconscious level, of young people who enter on a vocation to the priesthood or the religious life. These two terms, apart from a few clearly defined places, will be included under the

---

[1] Godin, 1975.

single word 'vocation'.

The research, presented in a simplified form in this book, was begun some ten years ago by the first author. It was a matter of studying the personality of candidates for the priesthood and the religious life with the intention of learning how better to select candidates, but above all how to improve their formation.

With this aim, their personality was evaluated at three points: on entry, which usually took place after their secondary education (i.e., after American high school), then again towards the end of the second year of formation, and finally at the end of the fourth year. Each time the evaluation was made by means of questionnaires, tests and depth interviews; all of these were done in the light of the objectives which will be presented here.

There were also lay students, male and female, who were evaluated in the same way so as to have a comparison.

Those invited to take part in the research belonged to the various institutes of formation for priests and religious from the mid-West, East and West of the United States of America. Table I (Appendix B) shows the groups studied, the dates the tests were taken, and those used. This table will be explained fully in Chapter 3; in fact, each Chapter will give exact details of the sampling and of the tests used in the corresponding analyses.

So far as the total number of subjects is concerned, there were 257 seminarians or male religious, and 107 male lay students (control group); there were 446 female religious, and 136 female lay students (control group). There are, then, 946 subjects, of which 703 are members of religious institutes, and 243 of lay institutes.

When the research began, our approach was a purely positivistic one; we wanted to gather the data, find the facts and let them speak for themselves. However, after some years working in the field, we came to realize that this approach could not really bring us to a right understanding of many of the central factors in vocation to the religious and priestly life, such as self-transcendence and growth in vocation. Was it possible to discover those aspects of personality which favor entering the seminary or religious community, as well as perseverance and growth in vocation? Was it possible to identify the motivational tendencies which could explain the psychodynamics of entering, persevering, and growing in or abandoning the vocation? Was it possible to find motivational structures which might be trans-cultural, independent of situations and therefore perhaps inherent

27

in human nature? If the psychodynamic of the motivation were known, would it be possible to predict the possibility of adapting to the groups or institutions to which the candidate wanted to commit himself? Was it possible to work out conflict models which are typically 'vocational', and which might be bound neither to particular situations nor be the same as the well-known conflicts of psychopathology? Are these the conflicts which influence entry, or vice-versa? What is their relation to perseverance or dropping out, to growth in vocation, to adapting or failing to adapt to the groups and ambience?

The answer to these questions could not come from the rather positivistic method with which we had at first undertaken our research project. The general theories of personality did not appear able to answer our questions. Above all, they 'are generally lacking in clarity and explicitness, and they have not been sufficiently formalized to allow for the generation of hypotheses by formal axiomatic deduction'.[2] Thus, it is difficult to subject these theories to empirical tests. Furthermore, current personality theories do not offer a thorough examination of the rational and empirical links between their conceptualization and the measuring operations directed toward it.[3]

Similar considerations are valid, at least in part, also for some of the psycho-social theories of non-religious vocations.[4] Even when the limitations discussed about the general theories of personality are not found in theories of non-religious vocations, it is nevertheless true that all of these theories show a common factor: self-actualization, self-fulfillment is the basic motivation underlying all vocational choices. We have gradually discovered[5] that priestly and religious vocations go beyond self-actualization and specifically stress also self-transcendence. Any conceptualization about a vocation requires that its core be explicitly identified.

Considering the present lack of a theoretical and psychological formulation of religious vocation, and the need felt for one especially since the impact of Vatican II, we have attempted to formulate some theoretical propositions and at the same to develop ways of empirically testing them by means of new measuring operations. After all, given the present needs there is nothing

---

2   Wiggins, 1973, p.447.
3   Fiske, 1971.
4   Super, 1963; Tiedeman and O'Hara, 1963; Holland, 1966; Roe, 1956, 1964; Ginzberg et al., 1951; Bordin, Nachmann and Segal, 1963; Sartre (in Simons, 1966).
5   Rulla, 1971.

more useful than a theory arising from the topic under study and verifiable experimentally. Earlier research had formulated a certain number of theoretical propositions about religious vocation and subjected them to the beginnings of empirical verification by ways of measurement worked out in accordance with the theory.[6] The results of this pilot study were encouraging, at least in so far as concerned those propositions dealing with the process of entering the seminary or novitiate. This fact encouraged further thinking which led to the writing of a psycho-social theory of priestly and religious vocation,[7] with implications and applications for vocational perseverance, effectiveness, celibacy, group dynamics, leadership and various facets of institutional life and community renewal. Further empirical findings seem to support this theoretical frame of reference.[8]

The present book adopts the same frame of reference and aims to make further contributions toward finding answers to some of the previously outlined questions. It focuses on the personality of vocationers, defining personality as 'the way the person interacts with the world outside him and the world inside him'.[9] We will distinguish between two types of processes or dispositions; transitory dispositions, which reflect the various stages a person goes through at different times and situations, and then the enduring dispositions which prevail over the transitory ones and determine a certain continuity in the behavior of individuals. This distinction, which at first sight may appear purely theoretical, does in practice have some very widespread implications. For instance, only if it is possible to recognize the enduring dispositions of a person will it be possible to predict with some reliability the perseverance and effectiveness of entering vocationers as well as their potentialities of adapting themselves to different vocational environments or differing groups. Thus, it will be possible to consider, on a scientific basis, the nature of the help that could be offered to them.[10]

---

6 Rulla, 1967.
7 Rulla, 1971.
8 Imoda, 1971; Maddi and Rulla, 1972; Rulla and Maddi, 1972; Ridick, 1972.
9 Fiske, 1971, p. 3.
10 For work done on the project in its initial phase we are grateful for the collaboration of Professor S.R. Maddi of the University of Chicago; also for the grants from the Social Science Research Council of the University of Chicago, from the Foundations' Fund for Research in Psychiatry, and from the National Science Foundation of the U.S.A.

The theory followed in this book seeks to estimate the enduring dispositions of the subjects and to separate them from the transitory ones. This is the theme of the first two Chapters of the book.

PART ONE

THEORETICAL AND METHODOLOGICAL BACKGROUND

CHAPTER 1

THEORETICAL FRAMEWORK: THE THEORY OF SELF-TRANSCENDENT CONSISTENCY

When the psychological problems of religious vocation have been tackled (especially in the United States) by precise methods such as questionnaires and tests, then the complexity of variables involved is often overlooked. One of the results of this has been that the psychometric approach in vocation selection has been somewhat discredited. Yet the tests used were not only based on categories taken over from psychopathology (and therefore had the limitation of simply providing contra-indications), but also the axiomatic frame of reference of the variables used was not sufficiently taken into account.

This Chapter presents the different concepts, which are operationalized in the research; they are used in our research and in the analysis of the results. These concepts are presented and discussed in detail in a book already mentioned.[1]

In so far as is possible in this abbreviated version of our work, each concept will be illustrated by examples taken from the instruments used to measure them.

The personality or self of the vocationer should be considered at least according to the following components:

Ideal-self:[2]
— *Institutional ideals* (II): the perceptions a person has of the ideals his vocational institution values for its members; therefore, the II represents the individual's role concept.

— *Self-ideals* (SI): the ideals a person values for himself, i.e., what he would like to be or do.

---

1 Rulla, 1971.
2 Ideal-self: this concept is used to emphasize the contrast between the Actual-self and the Ideal-self. Thus the typically psychoanalytic meaning of Ideal-self which always has a narcissistic connotation, is avoided (Laplanche and Pontalis, 1967, pp.255-256).

Actual-self:

— *Present behavior* (PB) or manifest self-concepts: the subject's cognitions about his own or present behavior, i.e., what he thinks he usually is or does.

The content of these three levels (II, SI, PB) can be obtained by means of questionnaires, or even by a single questionnaire answered at these three levels.

— *Latent-self* (LS): the personality characteristics revealed by projective tests. It is assumed that this type of test reveals what characterisitics (conscious or subconscious) a person actually possesses, not merely those which he thinks he has or would like to have.

— *Social-self:* the self considered as a social object, i.e. as seen by others. This part of the self will be dealt with only briefly in this book.

The *ideal-self,* as already seen, includes the institutional ideal (II) and the self-ideal (SI). It can be described as the self-ideal-in-situation (SI-II). It is important to note that we are concerned with the institutional ideal as perceived by the individual; this can be (at least in part) the result of group pressure.[3]

The *ideals* consciously proclaimed by the individual come out as either values or attitudes.

Values are enduring abstract ideals of a person, which may be ideal end-states of existence (terminal values or ends) or ideal modes of conduct (instrumental values or means) which are the ideal ways of conduct for attaining the terminal values.[4] In religious vocation, examples of terminal values are union with God and the imitation of Christ, which are common to all Christians; poverty, chastity and obedience (the evangelical counsels), whether considered as vows or as virtues, are instrumental values.

Attitudes are dispositions expressing a state of readiness to respond.[5] They differ from values: values are relatively general action tendencies, while attitudes pertain to the more specific and changeable activities. A grown person probably has hundreds of

3   Allen, 1968.
4   Rokeach, 1966, a, b; 1973; Lovejoy, 1950; Hilliard, 1950.
5   Allport, 1935, 1954; McGuire, 1969.

attitudes, but only dozens of instrumental values and perhaps only a few terminal values.

Thus, attitudes may stem from and serve values: e.g., attitudes of nurturance may stem from and serve the value of christian charity. However, seemingly positive attitudes may become values for the individual, especially in the form of instrumental values which may be poorly compatible with religious vocation; for instance, nurturance may be motivated by succorance, by affective dependency; i.e. the attitudes of nurturance do not stem from and serve the value of charity but the *need* of succorrance. In such a case, the individual gives but in order to receive through the affective dependency; he values 'to be with people' because, in the final analysis, he *needs* to get from them more than to give to them.

The attentive reader by now has realized that attitudes may stem from values or from needs, or from both at the same time. Another example will clarify this point. A value like 'self-discipline . . . overcoming my irrational and sensuous desires' can be an expression of love for chastity, but could be motivated (at least in part) by a conflictual fear of sexuality.[6]

These examples will also assist the reader in understanding the following possibility: the values and specific attitudes of religious vocation which novices and seminarians ascribe to themselves in self-descriptive questionnaires, and which represent their personal ideals and their motives for entering the religious life, could be (at least in part) the *unconscious* expression of some *underlying* need which is in opposition to the personal ideal proclaimed. 'To be with others' and 'self-discipline' have been given as two examples. Another, which is frequently encountered and also uses the variables taken from the tests adopted for this research, would be that of the vocationer who proclaims the orientation of deference characteristic of obedience and endorses values like 'doing my duty' and 'having good relations with other people'; however, it may be that he is driven to proclaim such an obedient orientation as a defense against a strongly repressed, unacceptable

---

6 'Self-discipline' is a value taken from Modified General Goals of Life Inventory. See Appendix A-2.

The variables such as 'poverty', 'chastity' are taken from the Modified Activities Index (MAI): cf. Appendix A-1, or from the needs used in the projective tests (TAT and Rotter ISB), cf. Appendix A-3.

33

orientation of rebelliousness stemming from a subconscious need of aggressive autonomy. In such a case there is an *inconsistency* between the values and attitudes proclaimed and the subconscious needs, i.e. there is a subconscious inconsistency between the ideal-self and the actual-self of that person, between what he would like to be as a vocationer and what he actually is. Research has shown that such lack of awareness may be unawareness of the existence of the inconsistency itself, or unawareness of any associated stress or unawareness of the inconsistency-resolving activity.[7]

These *subconscious inconsistencies* between the actual-self and the ideal-self are present when the individual is prompted subconsciously to respond simultaneously in different and incompatible ways because of the opposition between the needs of his latent self (LS) and the vocational attitudes and/or values of his ideal-self. Similarly, *conscious inconsistencies* are present when the opposition is between the conscious part of the actual-self, i.e. the present behavior or PB, and the ideal-self. Parallel with the inconsistencies, there can be conscious or subconscious vocational consistencies between the actual-self and the ideal-self.

In the theory which we have presented, four types of intra-personal, intrapsychic vocational consistencies and inconsistencies have been differentiated.[8] They are based on the relationships among three basic elements of personality: the vocational *values* (terminal and instrumental) of a person, his *attitudes* and his needs. *Vocational* values are assumed to be always present in a person who enters a religious vocation; if they are not present, the strength of the vocational inconsistencies is even greater. The same can be said when the individual has pseudo-values, i.e., subjective values (which he may have created) inconsistent with the objective vocational values. Such inconsistencies are easily discovered at the conscious level; however some of those responsible for admission or even formation take into consideration only this aspect.

We now describe briefly the four types:

    1) *Social consistency* (SC): when a need (conscious or

---

7   See Tannenbaum, 1967 and 1968, and Brock, 1968, who review also the research of McGuire, 1960, Brock, 1963, Brock and Grant, 1963, Cohen Greenbaum and Mansson, 1963.
8   Rulla, 1971.

subconscious) is consonant with vocational values and with its corresponding attitude. So for example, a need for 'achievement' is consonant with a generous attitude directed towards the fulfilment of charity. This consistency can be defined as 'social' because the individual is socially well adapted, contrary to what happens in the other type of consistency.

2) *Psychological consistency* (PsC): a need (conscious or subconscious) is consonant with vocational values, but dissonant with its corresponding attitude. Thus the need for nurturance can be consistent with the ideal of charity, but the individual may develop (consciously or subconsciously) contrary attitudes, for example aggressive attitudes. Even though these may not be adaptive socially, he is basically consistent psychologically.

3) *Psychological inconsisten*cy (PsI): when a *subconscious* need is dissonant with values and attitudes. For example, when a person completely lacks the subconscious need for nurturance, and yet shows the values and attitudes typical of charity, even though maybe socially fitting in to the setting of religious vocation, psychologically he is inconsistent. Or again, (and this is even more frequent), when someone has a subconscious need for affective dependency, for succorrance, and this need is incompatible with his attitudes which are rather directed toward the opposite pole (i.e. to nurture). This individual, who has the signs of a 'good' vocationer, is psychologically inconsistent. This type of person generally shows a great need for nurturance, even though it may be subconscious; and even if it is consistent with the values and attitudes, this need is by its very nature defensive, as we shall show further on.

4) *Social inconsistency* (SoI): when a *subconscious* need is dissonant with vocational values but not with its corresponding attitude. For example, a subconscious need for affective dependency, for succorrance, which then creates attitudes which are inconsistent with vocation. This individual is not only psychologically inconsistent, but also socially.

These four types are at the two extreme, opposite poles of a continuum where there are other intermediate types. These extreme types of the continuum are considered to be particularly important for vocational adjustment or growth when they are *central,* i.e. functionally significant for vocational commitment and the development of the vocation.[9]

According to the common tenets of depth psychology and the results of relevant research, our theory claims that *subconscious inconsistencies* exercise a particularly negative influence upon the vocational commitment, especially when the dominant motivation (which is unknown to the individual) is incompatible with vocation.

From the theoretical tenets presented up to this point, it is seen that the theory has two basic elements: 1) the *self-transcendence* of the self-ideal, especially of the vocational terminal and instrumental values; 2) a pursuit of these ideals which is accomplished and supported by a *consistent* self. Thus, this theoretical framework can be identified as a theory of self-transcendent consistency. Self-transcendence and consistency in turn will dispose to and foster self-fulfillment, effectiveness and perseverance. The relationships among these elements is schematically represented in chart 1:

CHART 1

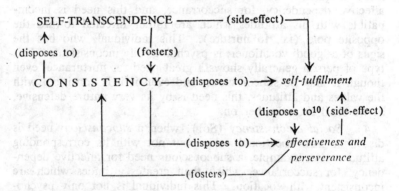

---

9 The concept of the *centrality* of the *inconsistencies* will be presented in Chapter 2 of this book. The intermediary types are discussed in greater detail in Chapter III of the original English book.

10 Self-fulfillment will lead to effectiveness and perseverance according to whether or not the *part* of the self fulfilled may be integrated with objective vocational values. Chapter 7 will be given over to this aspect of the problem. Here, effectiveness will not be explicitly dealt with.

Up to this point, the theory has developed the intrapsychic aspects of personality, i.e., the ways in which the individual reacts to the world within him. However, the way he interacts with the world outside him is very important also. We have already discussed elsewhere[11] the question of the individual's relationship with his vocational institution and his peer groups.

Here it suffices to state that mere gratification of vocationally dissonant needs, both in the intra- and interpersonal dimension, may have a 'positive' influence on perseverance, but it does not have a positive influence on effectiveness: people may remain in vocation prevailingly because some of their vocationally dissonant needs are gratified, e.g., their need for security or power; but this will not have a positive influence on their 'effectiveness' as priests or religious, that is, on their visible manifestation of the values of Christ. At most, this will support their 'efficiency' as administrators, as teachers, etc.

Vocational effectiveness, however, is fostered when both vocationally consonant needs and vocational values and attitudes are fulfilled. Several theories and research findings seem to confirm this.[12]

Returning now to the intrapersonal dimension, we now present five basic propositions for the intrapersonal aspect of the vocational theory of self-transcendent consistency.

Proposition 1

Religious vocation is an implementation of the self-ideal rather than of the self-concept.

Proposition 2

Religious vocation is an implementation of the self-ideal-in-situation.

Proposition 3

The self-ideal implemented in the commitment to a religious vocation is characterized more or only by instrumental and terminal values rather than by attitudes, and the content of this self-ideal is made up of normative variables to a greater extent than is true of the self-concept.

Proposition 4

Perseverance and effectiveness of religious vocation correlate with the type, degree and number of aware or unaware central

---

11   Rulla, 1971.
12   Winch, 1955 a,b, 1958; Thibaut and Kelley, 1959; Miller, 1963; Fouriezos, Hutt and Guetzkow, 1950; Rokeach, 1968 b.

consistencies and inconsistencies of the actual-self with the vocational attitudes and/or vocational values.

Proposition 5

At the beginning of vocational crises, some central inconsistencies are present at the level of attitudes more than among instrumental or terminal values. The number of inconsistencies can increase and gradually bring about a deterioration in the instrumental values essentially related to one of the three evangelical counsels of poverty, chastity and obedience.

Propositions 1, 2 and 3 will be dealt with in Chapters 5 and 6, and propositions 4 and 5 in Chapters 6 (in part), 7, 8 and 9. The various tests used for verification will be indicated in the relevant Chapters.

This brief presentation of the theory necessarily involves a certain *philosophical* and *anthropological* vision of man.

That the social sciences can be neutral in their philosophical and anthropological stance is a complete myth, and is not conducive to an adequate understanding of the reality studied;[13] a psychology without presuppositions does not exist.[14] This is why the formulation of a number of anthropological, philosophical and theological premises is inevitable. Then on follow up it has to be seen whether these premises are confirmed by the scientific results.[15]

Our premises and basic presuppositions from the anthropological point of view can be put in the following way.

1) There are at least five values which can be considered as the objective basis for the roles assumed by young people entering vocation. Their legitimacy and strength of attraction are grounded in the Gospel, and they transcend the norms made by individuals or vocational groups of different cultures or social settings. These five values are represented in the theory by the two terminal values of union with God and the imitation of Christ, (which are common to all Christians), and by the three instrumental values of the evangelical counsels — poverty, chastity and obedience.

2) Taking these five values as the ultimate points of reference for self-transcendence, psychological observation reveals

---

13 De Waelhens, 1958.
14 Wyss, 1973.
15 Fiske, 1971.

consistencies or inconsistencies between a person's actual-self and the ideal-self. These consistencies or inconsistencies exist *in spite of* the difference of content or presentation that the vocational institutions or groups adopt for these five values as norms or that the individuals take on as their ideals. For example, aggression and exhibition *are not* consonant with the five values.

It is, then, to these five normative parameters that we refer so as to discover the consistencies and inconsistencies rather than to the norms adopted by the individuals or groups of a particular culture. This prepares the reader to take account of the structural aspect of our theory.

3) For a proper appreciation of this anthropology, the reader is referred to the results of the Chapter which deals with the predictive internalizing capacity on perseverance in vocation. The predictive internalizing capacity, which is based on the interplay of consistency-inconsistency, appears to be, broadly speaking, a 'causal' factor in the prediction of dropout or non-dropout of the vocation. This comes out in the three groups of young vocationers: male religious, female religious, and seminarians, representing three different sorts of institution.

4) These same results also seem to confirm the use of seven needs or attitudes which can be considered as dissonant or not neutral as regards to vocation, and of another seven needs or attitudes thought to be less dissonant or more neutral in respect to vocation.[16]

What criteria are used in order to decide the dissonance or neutrality of these fourteen needs/attitudes?

To decide this, two questions should be answered:

1) *First question:* Are there some variables which are less compatible with union with God, the examples and values proclaimed by Christ, and the commitment represented by the three evangelical values of poverty, chastity and obedience? Perhaps two examples might help to illustrate the possibility of this distinction with regard to the consistency of the different needs/attitudes with the two instrumental values of obedience and poverty.

---

16 These are Murray's (1938) needs. The seven needs/attitudes considered as vocationally dissonant, or not neutral, are: aggression, sex, abasement, harm avoidance, exhibition, succorrance, defendence.

The seven needs/attitudes considered as vocationally neutral are: achievement, affiliation, nurturance, understanding, domination, order, counteraction.

The need/attitude of 'achievement'[17] (to accomplish something difficult, to overcome obstacles and attain a high standard, to excel, etc.,) or the need/attitude of 'counteraction' (to strive persistently to overcome difficult, frustrating, humiliating or embarassing experiences and failures etc.) seem to be compatible with *obedience*. On the other hand, obedience seems less compatible with the need/attitude of *aggression* (to overcome opposition forcefully, to revenge and insult, to attack, to slander, to maliciously make fun of and to depreciate etc.), or with the pride expressed in the need/attitude of *'avoid censure of failure'* (avoid the situations which could bring about a sense of inferiority, to conceal or justify a misdeed, failure or humiliation etc.).[18]

The same applies to *poverty:* it seems to be compatible with the need/attitude of *affiliation* (to adhere and remain loyal to a friend, to cooperate or reciprocate with another) or the need/ attitude of nurturance (to give sympathy and gratify the needs of a helpless object, to help an object in danger, to feed, help, console etc.). On the other hand, poverty seems less compatible with the need/attitude of succorance (to have one's needs gratified by the sympathetic aid of an allied object, to be nursed, supported, sustained, indulged, to always have a supporter) or the need/ attitude of *exhibition,* (to make an impression, vanity in dress, to attract attention, to shock, intrigue, entice others), or again, the need/attitude of *harm avoidance* (to take precautionary measures involving expense in order to avoid pain, physical injury, illness, to escape from a dangerous situation, to look for comfort in order to avoid stressful situations).

2) *Second question:* How, at the conscious or subconscious level, can one discover the presence of these fourteen variables, and then measure them adequately? At the *conscious level,* the needs and attitudes can be measured by means of the answers

---

17 When one speaks here of needs/attitudes, one refers always to the system of variables developed by H. Murray (1938, pp. 152-226) which has the advantages 'of conveying broadly, if not exaustively, the spectrum of personality needs, states, and dispositions, of possessing a carefully worked out and polished definition and of having a good deal of theoretical and empirical underpinnings' (Jackson, 1970, p.67; Wiggins 1973, p.410).

18 The reader should note the difference between the self-affirmation with a connotation of aggressiveness present in the need/attitude defined by Murray as 'aggression', and the absence of this aggression in the needs/attitudes such as 'achievement' or 'counteraction'.

given by the individual to the questionnaire devised by Stern, Activities Index, which was used in this research (Modified (Activities Index), MAI, see Chapter 3).

This test translates Murray's system into measurable terms and is validated by extensive empirical analyses.[19] In his works, Stern also tends to use words and terms which reveal at a more subconscious level the presence of needs and attitudes defined by Murray. The use of words which would be more clearly expressive of needs/attitudes is not thought to be desirable by Stern if a defensive style of answering is to be avoided; in fact if the defensive style prevails, it is impossible to measure the needs and attitudes of the individual objectively.

On the *subconscious level,* the classification of the subject's answers to the projective tests (TAT and Rotter ISB, see Chapter 3) is made on the basis of the definitions given by Murray. Thus it becomes possible to compare the two levels, conscious and subconscious.

Do the observations of this research confirm the anthropological premises already put forward above? It seems that they do. Two sets of results emphasize that the prevalence of inconsistencies (especially of vocationally dissonant variables) is in direct relationship with: 1. dropping out of vocation (compare Chapter 9, hypotheses 2 and 4), and 2. The possibility of growth in values and vocational attitudes (see Chapter 9, hypothesis 6). These results are valid for religious of both sexes, as well as for seminarians.

---

19 Stern, 1958, 1970, 1961, 1966 a,b: cf. also the numerous researches of authors quoted in the introduction to Chapter 5.

CHAPTER 2

THE THEORY AS A STRUCTURAL APPROACH
TO THE STUDY OF VOCATION

It has already been stated that our research started with an exploratory, positivistic approach. Later on,[1] our desire to break through the enormous number of problems bound up with religious vocation brought us to formulate a theoretical frame of reference and to adopt a method of structural analysis. The reader will find here the main points of this formulation.

Personality theorists and researchers offer different models for the study of personality. The dispositions of the self, enduring and transitory, which we pointed out previously and which can also account for the regularity and changes observable in human behavior,[2] can be studied by analyzing not only the *content* but also the *structure* of personality.

1. Content and structure

A well known example of the *content typology* is the one proposed by Erikson,[3] with its eight stages of ego development. Examples of the *structural typology* are the logical-developmental stages described by Piaget,[4] and the moral-developmental stages proposed by Kohlberg.[5] Let us discuss in more detail this distinction between a typology of content and a typology of structure by using the models theorized by Erikson and Kohlberg.

Erikson characterizes successive stages of ego-development by eight successive nuclear conflicts: basic trust versus mistrust;

---

1 Rulla, 1971.
2 Dahlstrom, 1972.
3 Erikson, 1959, 1963.
4 Piaget, 1963.
5 Kohlberg, 1958, 1969, 1971, 1973.

autonomy vs. shame and doubt; initiative vs. guilt; industry vs. inferiority; identity vs. role diffusion, intimacy vs. isolation, generativity vs. stagnation, and ego integrity vs. despair (see Appendix A-3). These stages describe the focal concerns of persons in different periods of their development; thus, trust-mistrust is the central concern in infancy, identity-role diffusion the central concern in adolescence, etc. Here, the content, the *what*, is what characterizes the developing person, and what characterizes his developmental period. Each stage is defined by its content.

Kohlberg, who is in the Piaget tradition, presents six universal stages of development in moral thought. These six stages of moral development are divided into three major levels, the preconventional, the conventional, and the postconventional or autonomous. What interests Kohlberg is not so much the content of thought during the different stages, but rather the structure of the thought. The series of structural changes in the way of thinking is what defines Kohlberg's stages. The quality of development is seen in terms of a *structure,* of a *'how'*, rather than of *content,* of a *what.*

While the stages proposed by Erikson tell us *what* a person thinks about, whether he is preoccupied, for instance, with trust or autonomy or guilt, Kohlberg's moral stages tell us *how* that person thinks concerning autonomy or guilt and so forth. That is: in the content or 'what' typology, stages tell us what is in the person's mind; in the structural of 'how' typology, stages tell us only how he thinks about what is on his mind (for example, on a conventional or post-conventional level). In the structural typology, each new stage of development implies a complete reorganisation of the various elements, leading to the formation of a new structural unity functioning as a whole: for example, from a conventional level to a post-conventional level.

2. *Content and structure of our research*

The theory of self-transcendent consistency combines both the 'how' and the 'what', the structure of the self and its content. However, the 'what' is assessed as predictor of vocational events like entrance, dropping out etc., only in function of the 'how'; thus, the theory adopts a structural model.

The vocational consistencies or inconsistencies of the theory tell us *what* the vocationer feels about, whether he is preoccupied or not with aggression or sex or domination and so forth. They also tell us *how* he feels, whether he is motivated consistently or inconsistently concerning aggression or sex or domination as they relate to the five fundamental values of vocation. However, the *what* is assessed as predictor, for instance, of dropping out, only in function of the 'how', i.e., of whether they motivate a person consistently or inconsistently with regard to his vocational attitudes and/or values. To put it in terms of the structures of the self: aggression or sex are assessed as predictors of dropping out or not, only if there is a significant inconsistency or consistency between the actual-self and the ideal-self of the individual (measured at the conscious level by the modified activities index, and at the subconscious level by projective tests; see Chapter 3). Proposition 4 of the theory spells out more precisely this *how*, i.e., the specific patterns of relationship between the actual-self and the ideal-self which influence perseverance and effectiveness.

Thus, the structural approach considers man as a composite of a definite number of structures, of subsystems of the self: the actual-self, the ideal-self, and their components. These subsystems are distinct, but dynamically related among themselves by some qualitative patterns (consistency, inconsistency). These patterns are specific for each vocational event they influence. Therefore, these events are predicted according to specific *qualitative* structural patterns of the self which are not subject to the quantitative variations of cultural or situational influences and, therefore, are more enduring dispositions.

The structural approach to the study of vocation sorts out trends and dispositions which may be considered as transcultural and transsituational. Of course, these dispositions are more or less influenced by different environments, but the environments always act through these structural dispositions, regardless of the different contents which characterize them. For example, an historical period of rapid, sometimes radical changes of sociocultural elements may lead to confusion about vocational values and attitudes, i.e., about the self-ideal-in-situation. These social changes would increase the *number* of structural vocational inconsistencies and thus would increase the dropping out. However, they would not change the basic psychodynamic *mechanism* which *explains* the dropping out. The research findings presented in this book have convinced us that these mechanisms are the

44

relevant dispositions for dropping out of males or females, of seminarians or religious, of people who belong to different religious orders, to different countries etc., either in the same historical period or in different ones. In this sense, the structural approach followed in this research project is, perhaps, a qualitatively new contribution to the research done up to now in the field of religious vocation. The crisis period in which we have collected our information has also been helpful for emphasizing this contribution.

Now each of the two ways of looking at the study of personality (that is, as content or as structure) can follow either a multidimensional or a typological model.

Typological model. In the typological model, what is observed is classified into *types*. These types which had been abstracted are then validated empirically. For example: a number of violent actions can be understood by differentiating different types of violence, such as violence related to a situation, pathological violence or accidental violence. So, someone can be moved toward violence by provocation (violence related to a situation), by illness (pathological violence), or simply by chance. One should then, examine empirically the different types of violence.

Multidimensional model. In the multidimensional model, qualitative variations are explained as depending on quantitative variations in a whole number of underlying dimensions. Statistical analyses of these underlying quantitative dimensions then allows the discovery of correlations between the qualitative differences which have been found; some of these intercorrelations then in turn present recurring configurations. For example: a number of violent actions could be analyzed as a function of quantitative differences regarding qualitative aspects such as 'aggression', and 'trust-mistrust'. Statistical analysis of the relation between the variables 'aggression' and 'trust-mistrust' could then lead on to a delineation of the steady correlations in the interplay of the variables. These intercorrelations correspond to qualitatively different violent actions, such as verbal violence (insulting someone), physical violence (hitting someone), and homicidal violence (killing someone).

Both models, typological and multidimensional, have their own advantages and disadvantages. For example, the typological model allows the exclusion of unimportant variables. Thus, in the purely accidental type of violence, the dimensions of 'aggression' and 'trust-mistrust' would not explain anything. On the other hand, however, the multidimensional approach allows the measuring of the strength of the aggression, of the mistrust, or of other variables. This quantitative assessment may, perhaps, allow the researcher to find lawful relationship between the dimensions studied, as for example between provocations and aggressive acts along the lines of the frustration-aggression formulation done by the Yale group.[6]

---

6 Dollard et al., 1939.

3. *The structural model and the multidimensional model in our research*

What is the position of our structural model in relation to these two research methods? In fact, both are used, as will gradually become more clear in our presentation of the problems involved in vocation.

Chapters 5 and 6 apply the structural approach according to the multidimensional strategy. Dimensions such as trust, affiliation, domination etc., were measured; the interplay of correlations between these variables was then observed, in order to determine the stable configurations of the subsystems of the self (e.g. ideal-self and its components etc.). These are the configurations which influence entrance into vocation.

Chapters 7, 8 and 9 will present results which, at least in part are based on the structural approach according to a typological strategy; first of all, types of vocational consistencies or inconsistencies are classified according to the structural conceptualization of the theory. As in the multidimensional strategy, stable clusters are found which connect the subsystems of the self. One difference with this strategy, as compared with the previous one, lies in the fact that here it is the patterning of consistencies and inconsistencies which *determines* the relative importance of variables such as trust, affiliation, domination etc.

Finally, note the different use we make of the two strategies. The multidimensional strategy will be used for analysis of groups of individuals, whereas the typological strategy will be used to evaluate each individual separately. First, we find out the needs, attitudes and values of each individual, and then we evaluate the consistencies and inconsistencies present in the individual. The evaluation thus prescinds from the particular or historically conditioned norms of a particular group of candidates set in a particular socio-cultural context. This is certainly not true of the multidimensional strategy, where the measurements of all the individuals in the group are considered and analyzed together. So then, it can be seen that the structural model, both typological and multidimensional, can lead to a more universally valid understanding of the dynamic of the individual, almost independent of those temporal and cultural factors typical of a given situation.

This comes out even more clearly in the light of the fact that this research includes certain concepts which are both trans-situational and transcultural: above all, the five basic vocational values which were presented in the previous Chapter as essential to the object of the research.

4. *Centrality*

By now the reader will understand that the structural method requires the correct evaluation of consistencies and inconsistencies. It is also important, however, to evaluate their importance in the individual's total dynamics. This is the question of their *centrality*.

The crucial factors which determine the centrality of a consistency or inconsistency have often been presented in the literature of psychology, but as separate units and without due regard for their dependence and their convergence so as to form a single dynamic process.

In so far as concerns our own research, it would be too simple a solution just to use the data of the questionnaires and the tests and then evaluate the degree of divergence between the subsystems of the personality for each of the *fourteen* variables used for this type of analysis (aggression, domination, etc.; cf. the N.B. in Appendix A-I). A notable gap between the scores of the actual-self and the ideal-self would show a considerable degree of inconsistency. Such an evaluation, even if necessary, would be insufficient. In fact, as has been shown by numerous writers, the inconsistency is tolerated, and in some cases even sought after.[7]

So, it is a question of not only ascertaining the presence of consistencies and inconsistencies, but also of evaluating their degree of importance for perseverance and growth in the religious life. In other words, for each consistency and inconsistency, it would be necessary to discover if it is central in the individual's psychodynamics, i.e., if it is functionally significant for the vocation of the individual.

Thus we will make a resumé of the concepts (presented in detail elsewhere[8]) which allow this integration of the various factors into one dynamic whole:

    1) An attribute of the self can determine a *functionally*

---

7   McClelland, 1961; Holland, 1960; Sears, 1968; Maddi, 1968; etc.
8   Rulla, 1971.

significant consistency or inconsistency if it is important for achieving the goals the person selects for himself.

2) The same attribute would have to be of *central importance* for the self-esteem;[9] this central importance (or centrality) can be present at the conscious or subconscious level. So, for example, there is a central vocational inconsistency when an individual has a positive affect for a variable like aggression which the person does not consider (consciously or subconsciously) instrumental in achieving the ideals of religious vocation. What is attractive (the importance of aggression for self-esteem) is considered unacceptable to the person for his own ideal of religious vocation (aggression as unacceptable as a vocational goal). In other words, his emotional wanting is incompatible with his rational wanting. The aggression, which for this individual is one of the contents attractive for self-esteem, is measured on the conscious level by the subject's answers to Stern's questionnaire,[10] the index of activities, modified for our purposes (MAI, see Chapter 3); on the subconscious level it is measured by the productions of the subject on the projective tests (TAT and Rotter ISB: see Chapter 3).

The unacceptability of aggression as an ideal of the religious life for the individual is deduced from a low-score answer given to the questionnaire (activities index, modified version) on those aspects which concern the ideal-self (SI) and the institutional ideal (II).

3) However, for a consistency or an inconsistency to be functionally significant, a third factor, mentioned by Arnold[11] and by Kelman and Baron,[12] is necessary. This third factor is the adequacy or inadequacy of the individual's coping mechanisms employed in attempting to achieve his goals. Thus, in the case of an inconsistency, the unacceptable attraction, which is the result of the other two factors, becomes really functionally significant in the life of a person if it is *kept* at the centre of his attention. But this is possible only if there is a relevant inadequacy of the person's coping mechanisms toward this unacceptable attraction. For instance, referring to the previous example about aggression, when the coping mechanisms of the individual do not

---

9 French and Sherwood, 1965; Smith, 1968.
10 Stern, 1958, 1970.
11 Arnold, 1960.
12 Kelman and Baron, 1968.

succeed in preventing aggression from remaining at the centre of attention of his emotional wanting, which is dissonant with his rational wanting.[13]

Use of the concept of centrality is obviously limited in the research to the cases where subjects have answered the activities index, modified version (MAI), on the three dimensions: ideal-self (SI), the institutional ideal (II), and the present behavior (PB), and when the results of these can be compared with what the subject reveals about himself on the projective tests (TAT and Rotter ISB). Only by making this comparison is it possible to determine the presence of central consistencies or inconsistencies. Thus, centrality is not used in interviews with the subjects when assessing their degree of *developmental* maturity (the latter will be discussed in Chapter 7).

By way of conclusion, we maintain that a variable which describes an attribute of the self takes on a functional significance for religious vocation when it is important both for the achievement of vocational ideals *and* for self-esteem. It is of course necessary to check whether the coping mechanisms used to control these variables are adequate or not. Considered from this point of view, the functionally significant inconsistencies can be seen as conflictual situations, at least in so far as *there is an unacceptable attraction at the centre of attention.*

5. *Recall of a fundamental presupposition*

Now that the reader is aware of the concepts used in our research and in the theoretical model used as their framework, he will doubtlessly comprehend more fully the basic assumption underlying our endeavour to understand the complex nature of the psychology of vocation. Thus, while a set of distinct average scores on personality tests is valuable, it is far from being a complete picture of a vocationer's personality. *Man is not only, nor especially, a composite of an indefinite number of separate psychological tendencies,* nor is vocation sufficiently explained in terms of role, professional career or other concepts related to

---

13 Evaluation of points 2 & 3 here were made by means of a series of statistical analyses through a computer. Details of this can be found in Chapter III of the original English version (1976).

cross-sectional aspects of personality. This is particularly true if the focus of inquiry is the significance of the basic vocational motivations for entrance, perseverance and effectiveness in vocation. The various individual motivational characteristics should be estimated in terms of the dynamic relationships among the major parts of the personality needs, attitudes, values. It is the dynamic balance or imbalance among such parts which determines the predominant motivation of a person.

The study of religious vocation, in this sense, cannot be separated from a broader understanding which gives due regard to the meaning of human existence, and also includes (whether we like it or not) a philosophy of life, an anthropology, and also in the subject of inquiry here), a theology. Even though these broader horizons are only rarely mentioned in this technical and introductory part, the reader should nevertheless realize that all our research is undertaken with them always in mind. Perhaps it is exactly from this understanding that our own psychometric *and* structural approach has brought advances to the field.

CHAPTER 3

EXPERIMENTAL PROCEDURES AND DESIGN

In the first two Chapters we presented the main concepts of the theoretical model used in this book. We attempted to connect them to the instruments (questionnaires, projective tests) which measure them, and to give examples explaining them concretely.

In this Chapter we present a more detailed description of the instruments used, and also add details of the interview on the family and the depth interview.

For the reader who does not want to venture into this more detailed description, the following Chapters will still be understood *if* he takes care to read section A on 'Subjects' and section D on 'Procedure for giving the tests'.

A. THE SUBJECTS

The subjects taking part in this research were religious of both sexes and seminarians, while Catholic students of both sexes, who were at various Catholic institutions (American colleges), were used as a control group. Table I (Appendix B) shows the sources for the observations which are analyzed in this book: institutions, formation centers and the corresponding groups, year of entry, age span, together with the experimental procedure (i.e. questionnaires, projective tests, interviews cf. Note Appendix B.) Notice that in the case of the religious male subjects, there are two training centers or settings which belong to the same religious institution (institution I) and one training center for seminarians (institution II). Similarly, in the case of the female subjects, training center I and II belong to the same religious institution (institution I) while training center III belongs to another

51

(institution II). The lay control students came from four different centers: two for males and two for females.

The subjects of the experimental group came from the Midwest, East, and West of the United States; the ones of the control group, prevailingly from the Midwest. However, it was assured that the representative samples for the control group would match with the religious population in age, high school grades, Catholic and rural-urban background. Also an appropriate matching in socio-economic class was obtained by considering the father's occupation and education. The foregoing data were abstracted especially from the biographical inventory. The subjects of the experimental group entered their communities as shown in Table I. The checking on the status of their dropping out was done during the summer of 1973. The majority of the subjects, especially of the religious, had gone through psychological testing, (usually questionnaires completed by the candidates and by those who observed them) before their entrance into the formation centers. Consequently, we were dealing with people who were neither 'neurotic' nor 'psychotic' etc., i.e., who did not show symptoms of mental illness. Nevertheless, as we shall see in the following Chapters, it is possible to discover in them subconscious inconsistencies which can influence their perseverance and vocational growth.

To conclude, since practically all the religious (both male and female) and the seminarians invited did in fact take part in the research, it is important to note that we are dealing with complete groups.

B. THE PSYCHOLOGICAL INSTRUMENTS

1. *The modified activities index*

A modification of the activities index[1] was devised in order to measure the self-concept, self-ideal, and institutional ideal of the subjects.

The activities index (AI) in its standard form yields information about 30 needs corresponding to the list developed by Murray[2], through answers given by the subjects to 300 items pre-

---

1   Stern, 1958, 1970.
2   Murray, 1938.

sented in a like-dislike format. In the modification (MAI) devised for this study, each item is responded to three times by the subject with different instructional sets: the first way is to determine 'whether the statement is *True* or *False* in regard to your present behavior, that is, if this goal is usually operative at this point in your life; the second way is 'to address yourself to the statement to whether it is *consistent with, inconsistent with,* or *irrelevant* to the ideals you hold for yourself'; the third way is 'to address yourself to the statement to determine whether it is *consistent with, inconsistent with,* or *irrelevant* to the ideals of the educational institution in which you are functioning at present'.

Each of the items is responded to three times with each of these different instructional sets, so that for each of the variables, information is obtained about the present behavior (MAI-PB) of the respondent, his self-ideal (MAI-SI), and his perception of the institution's ideal (MAI-II). This modification allows the determination of how each subject sees himself, how he would like to be, and how he perceives the demands of the institution. In this way, information about both the self-concept and the self-ideal of the subjects is made available.

For the special purposes of this research and because of their special relevance to religious life, seven other scales were added to the list of those used by Stern in the activities index (AI). For these new scales, some of the items present in Stern's index were used and 32 items were added. Appendix A-1 lists all the thirty scales of the AI, plus the six special scales (piety, mortification, obedience, etc.) which were used in this study.

2. *The modified general goals of life inventory (MGGLI)*

In order to obtain information about values, the general goals of life inventory (GGLI) of the Educational Testing Service[3] was given to each subject. The format of the test is a twenty items forced choice, yielding a rank ordering of ideals pertaining to biological, social and religious concerns. An additional item was added concerning intellectual endeavor. A modified form of this test was also given following the same patterns as already explained for the MAI. In Appendix A-2,

---

[3] Educational Testing Service, 1950.

53

the reader will find the list of the 21 variables as well as this modified form where each of the 21 items was responded to three times by the subject to obtain information about his present behavior (MGGLI-PB), his self-ideal (MGGLI-SI), and his perception of the institution's ideals (MGGLI-II) for the particular value corresponding to each of the 21 items.

3. The projective techniques

a) The thematic apperception test (TAT). Two projective techniques were administered in the study to obtain information at a less conscious level of the self. The first consisted of the administration of six cards of the thematic apperception test (TAT) prepared by Morgan and Murray[4] (cards 1, 2, 6GF, 12M, 14, 19 for males, and cards 1, 2, 6GF, 8GF, 12F, 19 for females) and a group picture from Henry and Guetzkow.[5] For details in the administration procedure, see the following section 'Procedure of Testing' on page 57.

The stories given by the subject on each card were analyzed separately according to a scoring system for the presence (1) or absence (0) of a list of needs, emotional styles, defenses, and conflicts. The list of needs follows Murray's[6] classification and his definitions were used for scoring. Emotional styles and defenses are found in the psychoanalytic literature, and Erikson's[7] conceptualization was used for the list of conflicts. In Appendix A-3 the reader will find a sample of the scoring sheet for the TAT with the list of needs, emotional styles, and conflicts. The analysis of each protocol, requiring approximately one and a half hours, was made separately by Rulla and Maddi without knowledge of the group to which the subject belonged. A comparison of their results was subsequently made to resolve scoring disagreements or confirm independent agreements. Periodic controls were instituted to check interscorer agreement. Such agreement was established analyzing the interscorers' consistency over 30 protocols. All these levels of agreement were found to be statistically highly significant.

---

4 Morgan and Murray, 1935.
5 Henry and Guetzkow, 1951.
6 Murray, 1938, 1953.
7 Erikson, 1950.

b) The Rotter incomplete sentences blank (ISB). The second projective technique used was the incomplete sentences blank (ISB) of Rotter[8] (see Appendix A-3). The scoring of this test was made according to the same list of variables as for the TAT by the same persons, Rulla and Maddi, using the completed sentence as a unit of analysis instead of the story given on a card. Such scoring was made for each subject immediately after the scoring of the TAT. Again, the scoring was made independently at first without knowledge of the group to which a protocol belonged, and then notes were compared to resolve disagreements. To establish interscorer agreement while working independently, 25 protocols were selected at different times during scoring. All the levels of agreement were statistically highly significant.

4. *The biographical inventory*

The biographical inventory was given to obtain information on basic biographical data concerning the individual and his family, religion and the religiosity of parents, the nature and amount of schooling, ethnic origin, socio-economic status, and geographical location etc. This inventory also provides other information about the subject's perceptions of some basic intrafamilial relationships, i.e., father-mother-siblings, about the influence of significant persons in his environment (see Appendix A-4).

C. TYPES OF CONSISTENCIES, CONFLICTS AND INCONSISTENCIES USED IN THIS STUDY AND MEASUREMENTS RELATED TO THEM

The following types of central inconsistencies, conflicts and central consistencies are analyzed in our research:

---

8   Rotter's sentence completion, 1950.

The Combination of A and B yields:	A. Relationship of PB—SI-II (present — self-ideal-behavior in situation)		B. Relationship of LS—SI-II (latent — self-ideal-self in situation)
1. Inconsistency:	Consistency		Inconsistency
2. Inconsistency:	Neutrality		Inconsistency
3. Conflict:	Inconsistency		Inconsistency
4. Conflict:	Inconsistency		Neutrality
5. Conflict:	Inconsistency		Consistency
6. Consistency:	Consistency		Neutrality
7. Consistency:	Neutrality		Consistency
8. Consistency:	Consistency		Consistency

Adapted from Rulla, 1971, p.88

In view of the theoretical frame of reference presented in Chapter 1, combinations 1 and 2 of the foregoing classifications are considered *central vocational inconsistencies*. Combinations 3, 4 and 5 can be called *conflicts* because the subconscious self is not in disagreement with the conscious self (3, 4) or with the vocational ideal (5); but since there is an inconsistency of the conscious self with the vocational ideal (SI-II), one can speak of a conflict. Combinations 6, 7 and 8 are functionally significant *vocational consistencies*. It will be noted that the foregoing ranking of combinations constitutes a continuum from most severe inconsistency (1) to greater consistency (8).

The sum of all the scores for inconsistencies, conflicts, and consistencies produced a final comprehensive measurement of each individual's psychodynamics. This total sum was used in calculating the various percentages.

For reasons that will be explained in Chapter 7, we computed and labeled: the *degree of compliance* as the percentage of all the inconsistencies and the defensive consistencies[9] over the total sum of the final comprehensive measurement; 2) the *degree of*

---

9 A defensive consistency is a central consistency between the actual-self and the ideal-self which, because of a central inconsistency of a vocationally dissonant variable, fulfils a defensive function. For example, a central consistency for 'nurturance' which coexists with a central inconsistency for 'affective dependence', i.e. to give in order to get. Because of their defensive nature these consistencies are considered liabilities and are added to the inconsistencies in the final calculation. In the example given, the score of the consistency for nurturance and that for affective dependence are added together.

identification as the percentage of all the conflicts over the total sum; 3) the *degree of internalization* as the percentage of all the non-defensive consistencies over the total sum.

Using these three percentages, three indexes were developed: an *index of adaptation* was calculated by applying the formula $\dfrac{A - C}{A + C}$, where A was the degree of compliance, and C was the degree of internalization. Such an index expresses the relative weight, therefore, the prevalence of the tendency toward internalization over the tendency toward compliance and vice versa. The concept of need motivation versus value motivation come to mind in connection with the concept of prevalence of compliance over internalization and vice versa. We will speak of this again in Chapter 7.

The *index of possible growth* is the result of the division of the degree of identification by two and then by a hundred. A more detailed explanation of the reasons for this division is given in Chapter VII of the original English version (1975). Here, we simply mention that the degree of identification is a composite measure of two processes: internalizing identification and non-internalizing identification.

The *index of vocational maturity* was obtained by means of an algebraic sum of the index of adaptation and the index of possible growth. This index of vocational maturity is a partial expression of the total psychodynamics of the individual. Appendix C gives the content-variables used in measuring each individual's inconsistencies, defensive consistencies, conflicts and the indices.

D. PROCEDURE OF TESTING

The *testing procedure* itself was so arranged to minimize the effects of 'setting', namely, the general context in which the subject takes the test.

The testing was offered to the lay students on their college campuses, and to the religious in their formation centers at the beginning of their training. Their participation in the study, free and optional, was asked as a natural and valuable part of their academic experience, emphasis being placed on how it would 'contribute to a greater understanding of educational practices', as well as to their personal growth. It was also made clear that those who participated would obtain results concerning their own performance at the end of the study. The educational institutions themselves supported this rationale since they, too, would profit from the general conclusions of the study.

Religious groups were approached as a whole, whereas the entering classes at the lay colleges were too large for such a procedure. Therefore, random sampling of entering lay college students was made, with care being taken to assure a representative sample of the entire class in age, high school grades, socioeconomic class, Catholic and rural-urban background. Virtually all religious subjects and 70-74% lay college students approached agreed to participate.

So as to facilitate frank and 'involved' cooperation, prospective subjects were guaranteed anonymity. Furthermore, it was made clear to them that the personal information they offered would not be communicated to their peers, superiors or the scientific community in any manner whereby they might be identified.

The religious groups then participated in three testing sessions at different intervals of their four year formation or training. Each session lasted about three days, the between-test time intervals being so arranged as to minimize fatigue and boredom. The three sessions occurred at the following times:

1) about 10 days after arrival into the religious training center (at entrance);
2) almost 2 years later;
3) almost four years following entrance.

Thus, the same tests were given three times to each group of religious.

For lay college groups, 2 sessions, each about 3 days' duration were used: the first, at the end of the first week on *campus;* the second, at the beginning of the *senior year.*

The observations presented in this book are limited to results of the *first* testing. The rare exceptions will be indicated in the corresponding chapters (cf. Chapters 8 and 9).

The test *content* has been presented above. Suffice it here to say that all the directions were clearly and carefully explained in an identical manner. The TAT was group administered.

In almost all cases, Father Rulla was the examiner; this was so that the effects of 'setting' would be minimized. He collected the data and was introduced to the groups as a priest and religious and a psychologist, who was not in any way a part of any of the institutions involved in the inquiry. The aim of the research was given, and, as previously stated, emphasis was placed on the scientific interest and then also on the personal knowledge given to those taking part.

E. FAMILY DYNAMICS AND DEPTH INTERVIEWS

Two types of interviews were used for some of the analyses presented in Chapters 7 and 8: the family dynamics interview (FI) and a depth interview (DI). Both of them were given by the first author. There were two sessions for religious and one for lay students.

The interviewer prepared the *family dynamics interview* by privately reviewing the information given by the individual in the biographical inventory, administered at entrance into the vocational setting. The interview would take place about four months after the biographical inventory had been filled out. Thus, it was assumed that the person, at least in part, had forgotten the more detailed information concerning the family interaction presented by him in the biographical inventory.

Each interview took about half an hour. It followed a relatively structured guide as to specific content, as can be seen in Appendix A-5. This interview focused upon incongruencies in the information obtained in the biographical inventory, with the goal of clarifying major family conflicts, major familial influences on the subject, and the degree of insight the subject had concerning family dynamics.

The *depth interview* (DI), the second for religious groups and the first for lay college students, took place for all subjects after about four years of training. In preparing for the depth interviews the interviewer would skim through the results of the completed FI and the aspects of the biographical inventory most relevant to early life. In addition, he would familiarize himself with the major findings from some of the tests given to the subjects in the three testing periods: at entrance, after two and after about four years of training in the religious settings or lay colleges.

Since the aim of the depth interview was to evaluate the developmental maturity of each subject, i.e. to establish the index of developmental maturity (the results of which are given in Chapters 6 and 7), it was important to obtain information which would bring out various aspects of the personality.

The following questionnaires were used: the Minnesota multi-phasic inventory (MMPI),[10] using the variables described by Harris and Lingoes,[11] and also those devised by Finney.[12] Other tests were Cattell's 16 Personality Factors,[13] the 36 scales of the present behavior (PB) of the MAI, and also Vassar's attitude inventory.[14] The total of variables assessed by all the foregoing tests was 162 at each of the three testing periods.

This perusal of the more objective findings provided *hypotheses* as to the major conflicts, defenses, attitudes or values, traits, and specific needs, plus the bases of these in early experience as revealed by the data of the interview on the family.

Once all this information had been assimilated by the interviewer the depth interview would begin.

The first part of the interview was rather *structured* and consisted of ascertaining certain features of the individual's interaction. As can be seen in the supplement for the depth interview (Appendix A-7), it was necessary first of all to determine certain aspects of interaction between the subject and his novice master or superiors and his peers. The subject's answers to questions permitted decisions as to the amount of interaction that took place, and how the subject evaluated the superiors or peers in these interactions. Note that the majority of these interactions (e.g. communication, affection, interactional conflict) is the same which had been evaluated in the biographical inventory and the family dynamics interview. By keeping in mind the information about the subject's relationship with parents and siblings available in the biographical inventory and the family interview, the interviewer attempted to determine whether the relationships with the superiors and/or peers were of the transference type, and if so, what the content of the transference could be. At the end of this part of the interview, the interviewer questioned and made judgements concerning the range of person-

---

10   Hathaway and McKinley, 1951.
11   Harris and Lingoes, 1955.
12   Finney, 1965, 1966 a,b.
13   Cattel, 1957.
14   Webster, Sanford and Freedman, 1957.

ality variables and patterns mentioned at the bottom of the depth interview supplement (see Appendix A-7).

The next part of the depth interview was a more *unstructured* exploration concerning the nature and content of conflicts in order to determine the degree of awareness of the problems and characteristics that existed in the subject. If the subject was found to be conscious of his conflicts, this part of the interview was brief. If he did not show awareness, he was gradually confronted with the substance of his conflicts. In 'borderline' cases, care was taken not to reveal underlying unconscious material in any manner that could provoke a traumatic decompensation.

The final part of the interview explored the sex life of the individual, and dealt with his fantasies and actions prior to and during religious formation. More specifically, questions were asked about dating, fears of the other sex, self-image as a man or woman, masturbatory practices, and latent or overt homosexuality. In general, questions began with indirect phraseology, proceding to a more direct format according to the appropriateness of the situation.

The time required for each interview was about two hours.

Immediately following the interview, the interviewer completed a form requiring him to judge the intensity in the subject of the emotional styles, specific needs and defenses used in analysing TAT protocols. The examiner also calculated the degree of intensity of conflict for psychosocial development in each individual.[15] In addition to this the interviewer ranked Erikson's 8 developmental stages or conflicts as detected in the interview in the order of their intensity.

The final step was the writing of a clinical summary concerning psychopathological, psychogenetic, and especially psychodynamic considerations. An outline for the depth interview appears in Appendix A-6.

As we have already seen, the aim of this depth interview was to evaluate the *developmental* maturiy to each subject (index of developmental maturity). This index should be distinguished from the index of *vocational* maturity both by its nature and method. The characteristics of this difference will be seen better in Chapter 7.

---

[15] Erikson, 1950, 1959.

F. STATISTICAL SIGNIFICANCE OF THE ANALYSES

In this book we will often use the concept of statistical significance, This concept indicates that the results are attributable to some *real* factor rather than to chance.

For example, chart 9 in Chapter 9 shows that non-persevering male religious have less predictible internalizing capacity for vocational values and attitudes when compared with those who persevered. This difference seems to be a *real* difference; in fact such a difference could have occurred by chance only five out of a hundred times (.05).

Similarly, .01 significance for the female religious in the same chart shows that the difference obtained between non-persevering and persevering subjects for the internalizing capacity for values and attitudes could have occurred by chance only one time out of a hundred.

Statistics used include: multivariate analysis of variance, the chi-square, the sign test, the Wilcoxon signed-rank test, the test for a significance of a proportion, the test for the significance of the difference between proportions and the test for the significance of a correlation.

In some analyses, the discriminant function analysis was used.[16] This method allows one to establish not only the level of statistical significance, but also the magnitude of that variable's unique contribution towards discriminating between the two groups.

Finally a cautionary word should be included here. Despite all efforts to the contrary, our specific values, preferences, insights, biases and prejudices naturally urged us to underscore some results while glossing over others, particularly those of a less pronounced psychodynamic orientation.

---

[16] Bock, 1963.

PART TWO

ISSUES

CHAPTER 4

GENERAL PREMISES

First, let us state once and for all that the present investigation always assumes the good faith, the sincerity of the people who volunteered to participate as subjects for the project. The whole theoretical approach of this study stresses the relevance of depth, i.e. subconscious psychology. Therefore, there can be no question here of sin, of malice, etc.

We formulated the hypothesis[1] that an individual enters religious vocation because he wants to realize his self-ideal in the sphere of a particular religious institution. In this sense it can be said that religious vocation is the implementation of the self-ideal in a given situation. This self-ideal-in-situation is the result of two elements: 1) what the individual wants for himself, his self-ideal (SI), and 2) the ideals proposed by the institution *as he perceives them* (II). This self-ideal-in-situation, of central importance for *entering* the novitiate or seminary, can only be psychologically at the centre of his future life and vocation if it is both *objective and freely chosen.*

It is objective when for each individual, the content predominant in its two components (SI-II) corresponds to the essential ideals proposed by the vocational institution; concretely, such content corresponds at least to the two terminal values of imitation of Christ and union with God as well as to the three instrumental values of poverty, chastity (as distinct from celibacy) and obedience; the latter in religious vocation become vows, while — in the words of Vatican II — for priestly vocation they are the three 'most necessary vitues of the priestly ministry'.[2]

The self-ideal-in-situation is not free when its content is the consequence of some underlying subconscious conflicts or inconsistencies of the person which 'drive', force him in his motivation;

---

[1] Rulla, 1967, 1971.
[2] Decree *Presbyterorum Ordinis,* Nos. 15-17.

in such a case, the person's ideal is consciously conceived but unconsciously held.

The objectivity and freedom of this self-ideal-in-situation may be impaired by interference coming from the following four sources:[3]

1. *Lack of knowledge* concerning the ideals of the institution. It would seem that this could occur more frequently at a time when institutions are changing rapidly.

2. *Identification* with the vocational institution. Because of his desires to identify with the chosen vocational setting, the individual projects these desires on the institution; thus he perceives the institutional ideals as quite similar to his own ideals. Research findings support this view.[4] It should be noted that this similarity and attraction relationship between the individual and his reference groups is a two-way process. Not only does real similarity produce liking, but liking also produces the perceived similarity of the reference group which is an exaggeration of the real similarity to the extent that the subject likes his group of reference.[5]

3. Influence of *intrapsychic conflicts or inconsistencies*. A person may enter religious life in part to defend himself against or to gratify underlying subconscious needs, which are less acceptable for a vocational commitment. In such a case, an inconsistency or conflict would be present between the self-ideal-in-situation proclaimed by the individual and his actual-self, either as manifest self or as latent-self. However, the inconsistency between self-ideal and *latent* actual-self produces greater anxiety and defensiveness than the inconsistency between self-ideal and conscious (manifest) actual-self. Wylie's findings, though they use a different terminology, arrive at the same conclusion.[6] Similarly, according to depth psychology thinking—especially psychoanalytic — subconscious conflicts determine greater fear, anxiety, guilt, shame, and defensiveness than conscious conflicts. In turn, higher degrees of the foregoing emotional threats lead to greater maladjustment.[7] In the case of religious vocation, dropping out may

---

3   Rulla, 1971, pp 57-58; 272-293.
4   For groups in general, cf. Vroom, 1960, 1966; for religious groups Rulla 1967, Maddi and Rulla 1972, Rulla and Maddi 1972.
5   Byrne and Blaylock, 1963; Campbell, Converse, Miller and Stokes, 1960; Sampson and Insko, 1964.
6   Wylie, 1957.
7   Janis, 1969; Levitt, 1967; Beier, 1951; Osler, 1954; Easterbrook, 1959; Berkun, Bialek, Kern and Yagi, 1962.

follow.[8]

4. *Pressure from the group,* the styles of *leadership* and the *institutional structure.* This fourth source of interference with the objectivity and freedom of the self-ideal-in-situation may be influenced by the previously described third source. In fact, subconscious conflicts may affect not only the self-ideal-in-situation but also the way in which the group is structured or perceived. An example in point may be the type of leaders who are chosen by the members of the group, where the underlying subconscious conflicts or inconsistencies may influence such a choice. Thus, a prevalence of subjects with an inconsistency for affective dependence (i.e. a strong need for affective support) can lead to the choice of a leader who will strongly favor ideals centred around the subconscious tendency of 'giving in order to get'.

Let us now look at the relative importance of the four sources of influence on the objectivity and freedom of the self-ideal-in-situation.

In the case of lack of knowledge of the institution and of the non-defensive identification with the institution, one can expect that the religious formation environment will contribute toward a reappraisal by the individual of his self-ideal-in-situation. During the first phase of religious life, he is helped toward this reappraisal via persuasive communications, interpersonal interaction with leaders, peers, further study of the nature of the priesthood and religious life; all of these should make both the personal and the institutional ideals more objective, and eventually lead to a free decision to remain or to drop out.

But if the third source of interference is also present, (i.e., if there are conflicts or inconsistencies between the self-ideal and the actual-self), then a free, objective reappraisal of the self-ideal-in-situation, and a free decision in the light of this ideal become more difficult. This is particularly true when the subconscious inconsistencies or conflicts influence not only the SI-II of each individual, but the group elements of the fourth source as well. In such a case, the individual is in a conflictual state with regard to his vocational commitment, and this latter is therefore threatened. He loses the capacity to be objective; but rather than change the source of his conflict, which he ignores, he distorts reality. When confronted with experiences in which the subject could choose between changing his own attitude or distorting the per-

---

[8] Ridick, 1972.

ception of the reference group, he would tend in the direction of the second solution.[9]

From the foregoing considerations, it would seem that in the final analysis, it is the third source of interference, especially in the form of *subconscious* vocational inconsistencies, which would constitute the most important obstacle to the creation of an objective SI-II or to its objective reappraisal. Consequently, such inconsistency lessens the individual's degree of freedom in his vocational choice. Furthermore, the inconsistency can push the individual to the point of dropping out.

On the basis of the considerations made in the theoretical model above, we can now confront the following questions:

1) Do people enter because of what they consciously think and feel themselves to be or because of what they would consciously like to be?

2) Should one take at face value the proclaimed motivation to enter or, in addition, should possible subconscious elements be considered?

3) If the conscious motivation to enter is not the *entire* motivation, i.e., if a subconscious psychodynamics is also present, to what degree does it affect the entering people? And what are the contents which characterize this psychodynamics?

4) Does the entering intrapsychic dynamics tend to persist in the individuals who remain in vocation?

5) Does the same psychodynamics tend to influence leaving the vocation as well as vocational effectiveness?

---

9 See a series of studies by Brock on theories of social comparison and Festinger's cognitive dissonance, Stotland's identification and Kelman's identification formulations (Brock, 1965; Brock and Blackwood, 1962).

CHAPTER 5

THE CONSCIOUS MOTIVATION TO ENTER: THE GERMINATIVE SELF-IDEAL-IN-SITUATION (SI-II)

A. INTRODUCTION

In this Chapter, which will confine itself to the conscious motivation, we will try to answer the question: In the realm of conscious motivation to enter a vocational setting, do people enter because of what they think they are or because of what they would like to be? Let us make it quite clear here that from the point of view of our research, just as do the subjects under study in the seminaries and novitiates, we consider vocation as a call from God; to be attentive to the call and to respond to it are a grace from God. In this Chapter and in those which follow, we will consider only the psychosocial aspects of vocation.

We will not deal with the problem of whether or not content characteristics of personality exist which distinguish people entering the religious vocation from the rest of the general population. In this regard, some authors[1] are inclined to give a rather positive answer. However, the majority of the reviewers of the pertinent literature[2] think that up until now the findings are rather inconsistent and ambiguous.

In terms of the theory of self-transcendent consistency, we have tried to ascertain whether those entering religious life or the priesthood are motivated by what they *believe* themselves to be or by what they would *like* to be.

Following the tenets commonly accepted by the experts, attitudes and values are thought to express a response predisposition. For the reasons discussed in presenting the theory,[3] two components of such predispositions are distinguished: 1) a rather

---

[1] For example, Darmanin, 1973.
[2] For example, D'Arcy, 1968; Potvin and Suziedelis, 1969; Rooney, 1968; 1972; Dittes, 1971; Godin, 1975.
[3] Rulla, 1971, p. 39.

cognitive component which refers to how an object is *perceived by a person*; this cognitive component is operationalized as 'institutional ideal' or II; it expresses, at least in part, the influence the vocational institution exerts upon the person; 2) a rather affective-conative component in the context of a vocational commitment; this component expresses the positive or negative *attraction* the person has toward that object (affective part) and the tendency to act according to such an attraction (conative part). In our theory, the self-ideal or SI operationalizes this conative-affective component. These cognitive, affective and conative parts are distinct, albeit interrelated facets of a person's response tendency.[4]

Whereas attitudes and values mean only the *predisposition* to act, *traits*[5] indicate the *capability* to act; that is, they are a sign that the predisposition may be translated into action. In the theory, traits are operationalized as 'present behavior' (PB), i.e., as manifest self-concepts, or a subject's cognitions about his own present behavior: what a person thinks he is or usually does.

The combination of the SI-II is the self-ideal-in-situation which expresses the predisposition of attitudes and of values, i.e., what people *would like to be* in a given situation. The combination of self-concepts about one's present behavior (PB) with a perception of the institutional ideals (II) is the self-concept-in-situation (PB-II), which means what the individual thinks he is or does in a given situation.

Why should people choose religious vocation because of their SI-II rather than because of the PB-II? Many considerations seem pertinent in answering this question.

Feldman and Newcomb[6] summarize the results of seven studies.[7] These studies asked the entering freshmen of lay colleges what they thought were the expected demands, characteristics and opportunities of their college environment. These 'expected' environments were compared with the 'actual' environments as revealed by the students already acquainted with their colleges. Both the expected and the actual college environments were assessed by means of the college characteristics index,[8] which measures the conception students have of their environmental pressures according

---

4   Kernan and Trebbi, 1973, Ostrom, 1969.
5   Wallace, 1966, 1967.
6   Feldman and Newcomb, 1969.
7   Stern, 1961; Weiss, 1964; Becker and Mittman, 1962; Webb, 1963; Pervin, 1966; Standing, 1962; Chickering, mimeo.
8   College Characteristics index in Stern, 1970.

to thirty scales.   These scales are parallel with the first thirty scales used
in the present research in the modified activities index (MAI).   Therefore,
the structure of the self measured by the college characteristics index is
quite similar to the one evaluated by the 'institutional ideal' or II in the
present book.   Both the college characteristics index and the II stress the
role concept, i.e., the perception the individuals have of their role.

The seven studies conclude that the entering students expected more
from the institutions than those who had been studying there already.
Generalizing from these studies as well as from other research findings,[9]
Feldman and Newcomb conclude that entering freshmen of lay colleges
describe their environment both realistically and unrealistically.   Their
view of the college environment is based on a general, stereotyped, and
somewhat idealized image of college life.   Similar results were obtained
by Stern[10] and other investigators in studies using different Catholic and
also non-Catholic colleges.

There seem to be several good reasons for predicting that
people who enter a religious vocational setting also have a rather
idealized image of religious life.   First of all, because the mission
to which they are called 'transcends all human energies and human
wisdoms'[11] their view of vocation may easily be both unrealistic
and idealized, at least in part.

In this sense, entering vocationers and entering lay college
students may be expected to be similar.   In addition to this,
further similarities between the two groups can be seen: 'In
general terms, the freshman in college is a novice in an unfamiliar
social organization, and is, therefore, confronted with the values,
norms and role structures of a new social system and various
new subsystems'.[12]   Both lay and religious undergo an experience
which usually involves desocialization (pressures to unlearn *some*
past values, attitudes and patterns of behavior) as well as
socialization (pressure to learn and participate in the new social
structure).   A number of investigators[13] have noted that young
persons entering lay colleges both expect and want to change and
develop.   They conceive of college as a vocational *preparation,*
as a specific instrumental scheme for job initiation, but not yet
as an occupational commitment.   Actually, the choice of the
school is frequently based upon inappropriate or transitory needs

---

9   Stern, 1966 a, b; Webb, 1963; Pace, 1965-6.
10   Stern 1970; Wood, 1963; Fisher, 1961; Scoresby, 1962; Standing
       and Parker, 1964.
11   Decree *Presbyterorum Ordinis,* No. 15.
12   Feldman and Newcomb, 1969, p.89.
13   Silber, Hamburg, et al., 1961; Freedman 1965; Douvan and Kaye,
       1962; Wallace, 1963.

and attitudes. The same may be said for people entering religious centers. Both lay and religious, especially in the first months, are people in training, in search, in preparation; they are not real 'vocationers', at least in the sense of being already vocationally or occupationally committed.

On the basis of the foregoing findings and considerations, one would expect that both lay and religious young people who enter their educational institution would present a rather idealized II or 'Institutional Ideal'. Furthermore, if the II is somewhat idealized, it seems reasonable to hypothesize that the attractive force to the institution resides more in the ideals the individuals have (SI) than in how these individuals see themselves to be (PB). In fact, if the institution is idealized, there is already a difference between what the person thinks himself to be and what he thinks the institution wants him to be. Therefore, because the person is choosing an idealized institution, he is reaching for something beyond his self-concept or PB. However, if a person sees himself as poor (PB) and does not desire to become better (SI), it is highly improbable that he would choose an institution which he perceives as expecting his improvement (II). Therefore, if this person chooses that institution, he does so because the institution matches with his ideals rather than because it does not fit with his behavior. Thus, in the final analysis, people would be consciously attracted to their own institution by what they ideally *would like to be,* more than by what they *think themselves to be.* If these assumptions are true, then for these individuals the correlation between SI and II should be more frequently significant than the correlation between PB and II. Consequently, the following hypotheses for the *conscious* motivation of religious or seminarians entering a vocation can be stated:

1) For entering religious vocationers, the correlations SI-II are more frequently significant than the correlations PB-II.

2) The first hypothesis is valid for the SI-II of both the values and the attitudes of the entering subjects.

3) The foregoing two hypotheses hold also for students entering lay colleges.

B. POPULATION STUDIED. TESTS RESULTS AND DISCUSSION

The groups of subjects came from the Mid-West, West and

East of the United States of America: there were 680 subjects, of both sexes (433 were female, of which 297 were religious; while 247 were male, of which 140 were religious). The lay students were in four different American Catholic colleges, while the religious were in six different centers of formation.

The observations analyzed came from *two questionnaires:* one for measuring values (the general goals of life inventory, modified version) and another for the attitudes (a modification of the activities index, i.e. the MAI). The former questionnaire has 21 variables, the latter has 36. Both can be seen in Appendices A-1 and A-2.

These two questionnaires measure the three key concepts of the present analysis; the present behavior (PB), the self-ideal (SI) and the institutional ideal (II). The method is as follows: the present behavior is measured by the subject's replies to a statement on a true or false basis with regard to his present behavior and activity, i.e., what is happening at the present moment of his life. The self-ideal (SI) is measured by the subject's addressing himself to the same statement and determining whether it is consistent with, inconsistent with, or irrelevant to the ideals he holds for himself.

The institutional ideal (II) is measured by the subject's addressing himself to the same statement a third time to determine whether it is *consistent with, inconsistent with,* or *irrelevant to* the ideals of the institution in which he now finds himself.

The results confirm the three hypotheses: both religious and lay students show a tendency to idealize, i.e. to choose the institution on the basis of personal *ideals*, self-ideal (SI) and institutional ideal (II), rather than on the basis of the conscious perceptions of their *actual*-self, i.e. correlation between present behavior (PB) and institutional ideal (II). It is precisely this contrast which indicates the tendency to idealize. This way of choosing leads to a considerably idealized view of the institution.

Some examples of the more idealized values and attitudes (correlation SI-II) are presented here.

For *values,* female religious want above all 'to have good relations with others', 'to control people and things', 'to courageously accept without recrimination whatever circumstances may bring'. The female lay students, on the other hand, want 'to get the best for themselves and their dear ones', 'to serve God and do his will', 'to survive, continue to exist'. For *attitudes,* the female religious emphasize 'being less superstitious', 'succeeding in life', 'being socially involved', and lay students (females) also emphasize 'being less superstitious', 'being poor', and 'succeeding in life'.

For *values,* male religious emphasize 'self-denial so as to achieve a better world', 'survival, continued existence', 'doing the best for myself and my nearest and dearest'. The lay students emphasize as values 'doing the best for myself and my own', 'intellectual endeavour', and 'living for the pleasure of the moment'.

As regards *attitudes,* the religious males emphasize their wanting to be 'less superstitious', 'obedient' and 'succeeding in life'; the lay students emphasize 'reflectiveness', 'not being superstitious' and 'obedience'.

As can be seen, these results taken together deal with content and are rather ambiguous. Vice versa, the structural approach, used in the formulation of the three hypotheses of this Chapter leads to results which all tend in the same direction. The results prompt some considerations, which are more general and other considerations more specifically related to religious vocation. The subjects studied here are people of college age who, at least in part, were unfamiliar with the social organization or institution which they chose to enter. Therefore, first of all, these people were confronted with a new experience of de-socialization and of socialization. Secondly, they were not real 'vocationers', i.e., not yet individuals totally or, at least, realistically committed to the vocation or occupation offered by the chosen organization.

It would seem that people with the foregoing characteristics tend, first of all, to choose the institution on the basis of ideals rather than of personal conscious charactistics. In fact, at least on the conscious level, they seem to choose the institution because of what they would like to be, rather than because of what they are, i.e. because of the ideal-self (SI-II) rather than because of the conscious actual-self-in-situation (PB-II).

Furthermore, since the ideals (SI) of these individuals correlated with the ideals of the institution (II) more frequently than did their present behavior or capabilities (PB), it would seem that the view of the chosen institution is somewhat idealized by these subjects. This interpretation of a somehow idealized view of the chosen institution is in agreement with that already seen in Chapter 4, i.e. that the similarity and attraction relationship between the subject and his reference group is a two-way street, the two elements form a reverberating circuit in which they mutually enhance one another. In other words, and in the context of our discussion, the attraction for a reference group or for an institution enhances the perceived similarity between the individual and the group or the institution. That is, this similarity is an exaggeration of the real one; now, here the perceived ideals of the institution are especially similar to the ideals the person has for himself rather than to his consciously perceived real capabilities.

Choice of institution is based on personal ideals, and the institution is perceived in an ideal way. These two interpretations seem valid for our sample. And since the results were obtained using a structural approach for personality (i.e. the structures of the self: PB, SI, II) they can therefore be generalized beyond the temporal and socio-cultural situation of the subjects. Furthermore, the results suggest the possibility of our conclusions being extended to non-Catholics, a possibility which is certainly suggested by the previously mentioned studies reviewed by Feldman and Newcomb,[14] and also by Stern.[15]

More specifically, with regard to religious vocation, it seems true that the SI-II is the basic conscious disposition for entering a vocational setting: according to the operational definitions followed in the present study, the ideal-self was more relevant than the self-concept-in-situation. This is in line with the first general proposition of our vocational theory according to which 'religious vocation is an implementation of the ideal-self-in-situation rather than of the self-concept-in-situation.' Of course, as was stated in the original formulation 'such a proposition is meant to be more assertive than exclusive.'[16] Whether this tends to become a fact prevalent for religious vocation in comparison to non-religious vocation, cannot be asserted on the basis of the data available here because, as we have seen, the subjects studied here are not yet real 'vocationers'.

This prevalence of the self-ideals over the self-concepts coincides with the call to self-transcendence which is appropriate (even though not exclusive) for the religious mission. In this

---

14 Feldman and Newcomb, 1969.
15 Stern, 1970.
16 Rulla, 1971, p.51.

sense, the SI-II is the germinative, conscious motivation to enter religious vocation: it has great potentials for growth toward self-transcendence and, as a *side effect* of it, toward self-fulfillment, self-actualization.

However, precisely because it is based on *ideals,* such a motivation may be, in part at least, non-realistic. Man is not motivated only by ideals, but also by needs, i.e. by action tendencies resulting from a deficit of the organism or from natural inherent potentialities which seek exercise or actuality: e.g. sex, affiliation, etc.[17] These tendencies, at least in part innate and universal to man[18] are inextricably mingled within every act of man. The attitudes and values of a person's SI-II may be influenced by needs, because human motivation is inextricably the result of three levels of psychic life. Man is a differentiated existing unity.[19] Therefore, a realistic view of the motivation to enter a vocational setting prompts the second question outlined in the general premises: Should one take at face value the proclaimed ideals to enter or, in addititon, should other factors be considered? We will look into this problem in the next Chapter.

---

[17] Cf. Appendix A-3.
[18] Allport, 1935, 1961; Murray, 1938; Etzioni, 1968.
[19] Nuttin, 1962.

CHAPTER 6

THE SUBCONSCIOUS MOTIVATION TO ENTER: THE VULNERABLE SI-II

A. INTRODUCTION

The previous Chapter has shown that individuals enter religious vocation with a conscious motivation which tends to idealize both themselves and the institution. Entrance is motivated more by personal ideals (SI) than by conscious personal attributes (PB); furthermore, role concepts (II) tend to correlate highly with the personal ideals (SI). Because the reality of the individual's capabilities (PB) is somehow overridden by the SI and II, the motivation to enter is — at least in part — not objective. In the light of the discussion of Chapter 5 it is understandable that at this moment in time it could not be so.

This partial 'idealization' and lack of objectivity of the entering vocationers may be either the consequence of their lack of knowledge concerning the institution or the expression of their germinative desire to identify themselves with the ideals of the institution in order to better themselves and to modify their present way of life for a more valued future. The first reason is readily understandable. The second one, too, is quite probably present; this is suggested by the fact that the choice is made more on the basis of what the individuals would like to be than on what they are. It is precisely this difference which urges us to pursue underlying reasons. If, in fact, the decision to enter the seminary or novitiate depends above all else on the ideals (that is, on values and attitudes), then it is necessary to examine more closely the *functions* these values and attitudes can have in the individual's dynamics. The instrumental values and attitudes generally serve four functions: *utilitarian, ego-defensive, value-expressive,* and *knowledge.*[1]

A brief discussion of these functions is now in order. A value or attitude is *utilitarian* if it is adopted so as to maximise the rewards or to minimize the punishments in one's external environment. A value or attitude is *defensive* if it is held to protect oneself from acknowledging unacceptable truths about oneself or the hard realities of one's external world. An example in point may be defensive nurturance, where the unacceptable truths about having an exaggerated need to get affection and attention is covered over by a proclaimed attitude or value of giving; the giving, however, is only a means to cover up the getting, to make it more acceptable for one's self-image. In the *value-expressive* function, the attitudes or instrumental values have the function of giving expression to the person's terminal, central values. Finally, the *knowledge* function serves man's aspiration to understand his universe and to give adequate structure to it.

While some attitudes or instrumental values serve a single type of the functions just described, others may serve more than one purpose for the individual; actually, they may serve needs or terminal values which are not homonymous. For example, an attitude of submissiveness in one person may serve a need for affective dependency, or in another person it may be a defense against a personally unacceptable need for rebellious autonomy. Similarly, for yet another person, the need for achievement may incline that person either to a utilitarian competition or to a cooperation which is expressive of the value of charity.

In reference to choice of religious vocation, the question arises: Are ego-defensive or utilitarian functions at work together with value-expressive and knowledge functions? In other words: are the conscious attitudes or values partially at the service of needs which are unknown to the subject and inconsistent with the vocational commitment? It should be stressed that the entering vocationer may be completely in good faith, i.e. he can use ego-defensive or utilitarian attitudes without being aware of doing so, and therefore in a subconscious way. In other words, someone may be responsive to inconsistent elements of his self without being aware of it. One can distinguish two types of lack of

---

[1] Katz, 1960; Katz and Stotland, 1959. Smith, Bruner and White suggest a very similar classification (1956).

awareness: unawareness of the existence of the inconsistency and of its associated stress; unawareness of the activities, of the behavior the person uses to overcome, to resolve the inconsistency and the related stress.

The foregoing considerations and findings have been conceptualized in the theory of self-transcendent consistency by the following predictions: 1) the role concepts (II) and the self-ideals (SI) of the vocationers are very close in content. 2) For *some* or *many* of the entering vocationers, the ideals of the institution as perceived by the individual (role concepts or II) may become his means not only of implementing his self-ideals (SI) but also of gratifying or of defending himself against underlying subconscious needs, which are less acceptable for a religious vocational commitment. 3) In such a case, the conscious ideal-self (SI and II) of the person is inconsistent with the subconscious part (latent-self or LS) of the actual-self. Following the findings of Wylie[2] and others, as well as the tenets of depth psychology, these *subconscious* inconsistencies are considered as influencing the motivation of the individual in a considerably greater way than the conscious inconsistencies. 4) The behavior of the individual as perceived by him (PB) is in part understandable in the light of the existing subconscious inconsistencies between LS and SI-II. 5) The patterns of defenses used by the person (such as compensation, projection, etc., cf. glossary under 'defense') and his emotional styles (such as the degree of anxiety, depression, guilt) are a further help in understanding the subconscious motivation underlying the entrance into religious vocation.

Consequently, the following hypotheses can be formulated:

1) In general, there is a good consistency among the components of the ideal-self of the entering vocationers, that is, among the content of the values and the attitudes proclaimed by the individuals in their initial commitment to a religious vocation.

2) The vocational consistency within the ideal-self is undermined by *some* central, subconscious inconsistencies of its components with the latent part of the actual-self (LS).

3) These subconscious inconsistencies between the ideal-self (SI and II and the latent self (LS) explain *in part* the patterns

---

2 Wylie, 1957.

of behavior (PB), of defenses and of emotional styles present in entering people.

1. *Tests and measurements*

The values and attitudes of the ideal-self were assessed by means of the general goals of life inventory (GGLI) and of the modification of the activities index (MAI) respectively. These were explained in Chapter 3.

It should be noted that the MAI measures the rather affective-conative component of attitudes, or SI, separately from their rather cognitive component, or II. In contrast, for the values these two components of the ideal-self, i.e. the SI and the II, are measured together by the GGLI. This 'single index' of values is a reasonably robust index of a person's response disposition. In fact, as the results of the previous Chapter showed, there is a high and positive intercorrelation between the two components both for values and for attitudes. Several other empirical studies[3] confirm the validity of this 'single index' to assess the individual's response predisposition.

The actual-self as consciously perceived by the subjects was assessed by means of the 'present behavior' (PB) of the MAI; this was the third set of reponses given on the MAI. The latent part of the actual-self (LS) was measured by two instruments: the incomplete sentence blank (ISB) of Rotter[4] and the thematic apperception test (TAT) of Morgan and Murray (1935).[5] We recall here that both these instruments assess the same 'needs' described by Murray.[6] Their scoring definitions were the same as those which guided item selection on the MAI and therefore the comparison of variables across these tests is feasible. The incomplete sentence blank (ISB) and the thematic apperception test (TAT) were also used to assess the emotional styles and defenses as well

---

[3] Rosenberg, 1956; Fishbein, 1963, 1965: Ostrom, 1969; Kernan and Trebbi, 1973.
[4] ISB, 1950.
[5] Morgan and Murray, 1935.
[6] Murray, 1938.

as the eight developmental stages or conflicts described by Erikson.[7]

B. POPULATION STUDIED. RESULTS AND DISCUSSION[8]

The subjects studied in this Chapter are the same as those analyzed in Chapter 5; i.e. a) 283 female religious belonging to six groups which were in three centers of formation. They were the entire population of these groups and were compared with the 136 lay female students who were beginning their studies in two different Catholic colleges; b) 135 male religious, the total number belonging to seven groups in three different formation centers; they were compared with 105 lay students who had recently begun at two lay Catholic colleges.

This Chapter also looks at a complete group of 45 seminarians beginning their university education. They were matched with a group of 64 lay students who were beginning their studies in the same college.

For all the lay control groups, the individuals taking part in the research represented 70% or more of a population chosen at random and freely invited to participate.

1. *Confirmation of the hypotheses*

The hypotheses were confirmed for the three groups analyzed: seminarians, and the religious of both sexes. These results derive from the analysis of correlations between the variables in play, for the two questionnaires GGLI and MAI, and the two projective tests (Rotter and TAT).

1) The findings of hypothesis 1 support the data of Chapter 5, that the ideal of a person expressed by his ideal-in-

---

7 Erikson, 1950, 1959. For definition of the variables used in the Rotter (ISB) and in the TAT, see Appendix A-3.
8 The resumé of the results given here is based on a rather involved statistical analysis (multi-variate analysis of variance and discriminant function analysis). A complete presentation of the analyses takes up about 30 pages of the original work, *Entering and Leaving Vocation,* 1976.

81

situation (SI-II) are the basic *conscious* disposition to enter a religious or priestly vocation. This initial force, in turn, may foster the self-transcendence which characterizes the vocational commitment. It also disposes the individual to what he considers the action of grace and, as a side-effect, to self-actualization, to self-fulfillment. The foregoing considerations are well supported by the significantly higher ideals shown by the entering vocationers in comparison with their lay control groups. Let us present some examples.

Religious women wish more than do lay to serve their community and God, find their place in life and accept what circumstances bring, so as to achieve immortality. They are not as concerned as lay women about making a place for themselves, but rather are interested in greater self-discipline and less pleasure, peace of mind, power or control. They wish to sacrifice themselves more and are also higher than lay women in their wish to become a genuine person through self-development. Security and fine relations with others are less important as values for religious women when contrasted with lay women. They prefer to be dutiful and are less willing to simply accept the bad features of the world while doing the best for themselves and those dear to them; they are less interested in the development of their minds in intellectual pursuits.

These young female religious present a general picture characterizing the values of highly disciplined and selfless people committed to religious and altruistic concerns.

The male religious, compared with the male lay students, strive less to make a place for themselves and rather wish to serve God. To accomplish this they are willing to forego personal security, intellectual pursuits and concern with doing the best only for themselves and those dear to them. With their ultimate goal — immortality in heaven — they strive less than lay men to merely cope with life as it comes. Through self-sacrifice, self-discipline, duty and the renunciation of pleasure, they seem to reach for goals beyond merely their own survival, rather seeking to serve their community, but not to obtain power or control.

Of the foregoing 15 differentiating values of the GGLI for males 12 are the same which distinguish the entering religious females from their lay control group. Therefore, again, as for the religious females, entering religious males stress values of self-discipline, selflessness, of dedication to humble service to

82

mankind and to God. The attitudes of the male religious seem very consistent with the values.

As we shall see in the next Chapter, none of these results up to now suggest that the religious subjects also present greater intrapsychic inconsistencies.

2) However, the results of hypothesis 2 indicate that the entering vocationers present an 'idealization' both of their real personalities and of the institution they choose to enter.

In fact, there are *many statistically significant inconsistencies* between the latent part (LS) of the actual-self of vocationers on the one hand, and their self-ideal (SI) and institutional ideals (II) on the other.

For example, the male religious entering the novitiate gave values and attitudes which emphasized in a consistent way those of deferent service, obedience, shunning of competitive power and control. In contrast, in the latent-self, they present a picture which stresses less deference and greater aggression, dominance, autonomy, emotionality, and — in this context — greater counteraction. Furthermore, in the ideal-self, religious stated ideals of less concern for personal safety and of greater adaptability or humility. In contrast, in the TAT they show greater concern for avoidance of censure and failure. Similarly, they proclaimed readiness to self-sacrifice for a better world, to self-discipline, to less narcissistic concerns, but they have greater needs for aggression, emotionality, dominance, autonomy, avoidance of censure and failure.

We have already shown how the individual's perceived similarity between his ideal-self and the institution has the effect of increasing the attraction felt for the institution. This attraction, in turn, influences the perception of the similarity, to the point where the perception is no longer conformed to the objective reality of the institution. Thus the choice of the institution is not wholly realistic.

This lack of realism seems to stem, at least in part, from the subconscious realities of some needs present in the latent-self, which are significantly inconsistent with the conscious realities of the vocational ideals. In fact, there are strong indications from the data that the consciously proclaimed ideals serve the two functions of attitudes described in the beginning of this Chapter[9] as value-expressive function and as knowledge function

---

[9] See the beginning of the Chapter for a description of the four functions of attitudes.

only in part. The data strongly suggest that part of the ideals consciously expressed may serve the other two possible functions of attitudes: utilitarian and ego-defensive. In other words, the choice and the decision to enter are made *also* as a consequence of subconscious needs, so that people may subconsciously direct themselves to the life in religious vocation as an attempt to gratify themselves (*utilitarian* function) or as a *defensive* effort to cope with underlying conflicts or inconsistencies (ego-defensive function).

3) The findings for the three groups discussed in hypothesis 3 suggest that, as it seemed to be true for the proclaimed self-ideal, so also the self-concept concerning the manifest behavior (PB) may be expressive of any one of the four functions of attitudes. Again, this fact is in part the consequence of the existing subconscious inconsistencies between the ideal-self (SI and II) and the latent-self (LS).

In the same line, it is interesting to notice a structural difference between the female religious group and the male groups of religious and seminarians. In the women, the PB is somewhat *intrinsically* inconsistent within itself and partially inconsistent with the ideal-self of values and attitudes, while in men the PB is quite consistent *within* itself and with the ideal-self. This does not change the fact that there are inconsistencies between the latent (LS) and the ideal-self (SI-II) for both sexes. In addition to this fact, and perhaps in relation to it, women use defenses which tend to change rather than to justify guilt-provoking behavior (PB) or thoughts (SI and II); men do the opposite. It is characteristic of conflicts, and of underlying subconscious inconsistencies to produce various different types of defenses; and this seems to be the case in the present study.

A conclusion is prompted by the findings and considerations discussed up to now in Chapters 5 and 6: in spite of the unquestioned sincerity and generosity of the individuals, the motivations and the manifest behavior *consciously* proclaimed by entering vocationers can not be taken at face value. Other elements should be considered, especially subconscious influences. In fact, people tend to idealize both themselves and the institutions.

People enter 'idealistically' and this 'idealism' may be realistic if it stems from ideals which are consistent with the actual-self, especially in its latent component; such consistencies dispose to self-transcendence and possibly to the action of supernatural grace. However, in more than a few people, it seems that entering idealism is quite unrealistic because of subconscious inconsistencies. Hence a germinative aspect of the SI-II frequently goes together with a vulnerable aspect of the SI-II, which is therefore neither fully objective nor free.[10] Ideals are consciously conceived, but unconsciously held.

2. Types of conflicts described by Erikson

Content-wise, the female religious of the present sample are characterized by the conflict described by Erikson as initiative vs. guilt.[11] Male vocationers (seminarians and religious) are concerned with the conflicts of autonomy vs. shame and doubt, of identity vs. role diffusion, of industry vs. inferiority, and, only for religious, of intimacy vs. isolation.

The structural approach to the study of vocation followed in this book underlines not so much this content aspect, but rather an interesting *structural* pattern which emerges in all the three groups studied. The content of the developmental conflicts described by Erikson[12] is often closely related to the content of the structural inconsistencies between the ideal-self and the latent-self. For instance, for the male religious, the conflict of autonomy vs. shame and doubt is in line with their inconsistencies between the proclaimed readiness for goals of humanitarian service, self-discipline and self-sacrifice, of deferent obedience, on the one hand, and their needs for competitive aggression and avoidance of censure and failure on the other. This relationship between the developmental conflicts described by Erikson and our measured structural patterns of inconsistencies between latent and actual-self seems to indicate that there exists some relationship between the developmental or affective maturity of vocationers and their maturity in making a vocational decision, i.e. between their affective maturity and what could be called their vocational maturity.

In Chapter 4 we formulated the hypothesis that four sources

---

10   Cf Chapter 4.
11   There is a description of Erikson's conflicts in Appendix A-3.
12   Erikson, 1950, 1959.

of influence could diminish the objectivity and freedom of the self-ideal-in-situation (SI-II): lack of knowledge, identification with the vocational institution, intrapsychic conflicts or inconsistencies, and pressures from the environment. The results considered in this Chapter indirectly confirm this hypothesis. Individuals who have conflicts or inconsistencies are particularly vulnerable; that is, they are more sensitive to the influence exerted by members of their family, of vocational institutions, teachers etc.

3. *Importance of values*

The foregoing results raise the complex question of the role which *values* play for the perseverance of people entering into vocation. It would seem that if vocational values are only *moderately* present, the rate of dropping out is significantly increased. The case in point is the group of seminarians when compared with the one of male religious: the two groups differ significantly in terms of values, the seminarians showing much lower values. At the end of four years of training, 47% of the male religious and 95% of the seminarians had dropped out. This is in line with the theoretical position presented in Chapter 1 with regard to values and vocational inconsistencies. Obviously, however, other factors such as the influence of vocational institutions, or pressure of the cultural milieu, may also have a considerable effect.

Do the values become a significant asset when they are *strongly* present? What is the mutual dynamic relationship between values and subconscious inconsistencies for the process of dropping out and for vocational effectiveness? The results of the research described in Chapter 9· offer some replies to these questions.

The policy of deferring the entrance of the applicants into religious houses has become frequent. The usefulness of this measure is evident, especially in the case in which developmental problems are at stake. But is it useful when unconscious or deeply preconscious vocational inconsistencies are present? Can they improve and to what extent, if they are approached merely by means of greater existential experience? It would seem that if the person is unconsciously inconsistent, he would continue to react to his central inconsistencies with ego-defensive or utilitarian attitudes, which in turn will sustain an unrealistic idealization of the self and the institution. And all these processes will take place without the person knowing it. Then, how can the existential experience made possible by the deferred entrance be of any real help if no means of becoming aware of the subconscious problems is offered in the meantime.

As the reader will readily understand, many of the hypotheses and questions touched upon in Chapters 5 and 6 need more data in order to be supported, confirmed with different populations. However, already with the groups available we will investigate if and how much the central consistencies/ inconsistencies influence the developmental-affective and the vocational maturities (Chapter 7), if they tend to persist (Chapter 8) and if they affect leaving vocation (Chapter 9).

These new analyses will point to a confirmation of the hypotheses already presented, and of the theory in general, both of which by now have become more familiar to the reader.

87

THE GERMINATIVE AND THE VULNERABLE SI-II: THEIR STRENGTH AND CONTENTS IN PEOPLE ENTERING

One of the conclusions suggested by the findings of Chapters 5 and 6 was that the ideals of an entering vocationer as expressed by his SI-II (self-ideal-in-a-given-situation) are frequently unrealistic and thus vulnerable because of *subconscious* forces. What individuals entering a vocational setting thought of their ideals was in part inconsistent with the latent components of their self.

How much of this SI-II is made vulnerable? What kind of variables undermine it more frequently: abasement, or aggression, or succorrance, etc.? The answer to the first question may be found by combining aspects of both the germinative and the vulnerable SI-II and by evaluating their corresponding strength. In terms of the theory and of the structural approach proposed in this book, this means to assess the degree of consistencies and/or inconsistencies present in *each* person. The second question will be answered by analyzing the content variables which most frequently appear as consistencies or inconsistencies: abasement, aggression, succorance etc.

Thus, the present Chapter will have two separate parts methodologically distinct, which will deal: 1) with a *quantitative assessment* of the strengths of the consistencies/inconsistencies underlying the SI-II; and 2) with a *qualitative evaluation* of their content. We will begin by recalling some of the basic concepts.

A. STRENGTH AND WEAKNESS OF THE SELF-IDEAL-IN-SITUATION

To measure quantitatively the extent of vulnerability of the
self-ideal, as well as its strength, we used indices which were
explained in Chapter 3; here we will now look at the theoretical
import of these, their application to the research, and also some
of their limitations.

In the previous Chapter the meaning of the four possible
functions of attitudes was discussed; e.g. when a person expresses
an attitude which can be qualified as of achievement, he may
do it to express vocational values (value-expressive function),
or to increase his knowledge (knowledge function), or to obtain
a reward (utilitarian function) or defend himself against some
underlying and unacceptable need or against some hard realities
in the external world (ego-defensive function). For some
examples of these, see the beginning of Chapter 6.

With regard to these four functions of attitudes, two sets
of hypotheses have been formulated elsewhere.[1] The first
hypothesis stated that the ultilitarian and ego-defensive functions
may prevail over the value-expressive and knowledge functions in
the case of *compliance* and *non-internalizing identification*, while
the knowledge and the value-expressive functions may prevail
over the other two in the case of *internalization* and of *internalizing identification*. The second hypothesis stated that compliance or non-internalizing identification may prevail in the
motivation of a person when he has central subconscious inconsistencies between his ideal-self and his latent-self, while
internalizing identification and internalization are fostered by
central consistencies between the same components of the self.

The foregoing two hypotheses need further explanation and
a more precise presentation. We shall follow at least in part,
the contribution of Kelman.[2] According to his theorizing and
observations, *compliance* can be said to occur when an individual
accepts influence from another person or group not because he
believes in the content of the proposed attitudes, but simply in
order to gain some external reward or to avoid some punishment
controlled by that person or group.

---

[1] Rulla, 1971, pp.150-151; 307-321.
[2] Kelman, 1958, 1960, 1961.

According to the theory proposed in this book, unconscious or deeply preconscious vocational inconsistencies lead to compliance.[3] In fact, when an individual has such inconsistencies, 'his sense of frustration will "drive" him to look for actual or potential sources of approval, of acceptance, of rewards and, conversely, to avoid sources of disapproval, of rejection, of punishment. To the extent to which he is "driven" by the foregoing central vocational inconsistencies, compliance will take place.'[4] Note that external pressure is not indispensible; relief of internal guilt is sufficient.[5]

Identification occurs when the individual adopts the behavior of another person or group because this behavior is associated with a satisfying relationship to this person or group. In contrast with compliance, the individual believes in the content of the induced behavior; however, he believes it only or especially because this content is associated with the satisfying relationships. Note that this gratifying relation to the other person may be established by the receiver either in actuality or within his own fantasy. In both instances, the relation is gratifying because it supports part of the image the individual has of himself.

Up to this point we have put forward Kelman's point of view. Are there personality structures which tend to favor this process of identification? As we have pointed out elsewhere:[6]

When an individual's psychodynamics is chiefly characterized by *not* deep preconscious vocational inconsistencies (psychological or social inconsistencies), and by *conscious* vocational conflicts (psychological consistency), his sense of mild frustration will 'incline' him to look for sources which will enhance his more or less shaky self-image, self-esteem, by means of gratifying self-defining relationships; thus identification will develop.[7]

In our conceptual model, identification can be *internalizing* or *non-internalizing*. A) In so far as *the part* of the self-image (or self-esteem) gratified by the relationship can be integrated with objective vocational values, to that extent the identifying relationship will lead toward internalization of vocational attitudes and values (internalizing identification). B) In so far as the

---

3 For the meaning of the terms 'preconscious', 'unconscious' see the glossary under 'subconscious'.
4 Rulla, 1971, p.317.
5 Freedman, Wallington and Bless, 1967.
6 Rulla, 1971, p.317.
7 Let us recall that in the theory, self-conception, self-esteem were defined in terms of PB-(SI-II) and/or of LS-(SI-II) congruence or discrepancy.

part of the self-image gratified by the identifying relationship
cannot be integrated with objective vocational values, to that
extent this relation will lead toward compliance or non-
internalizing identification or at least away from internalization.
As can be seen, identification is a powerful process of social
influence, but it is highly ambivalent as a means of affecting
internalization of vocational attitudes and values; it may enhance
it, but it may hinder it too.[8]

It can be hypothesized that vocationally dissonant variables
lead rather to non-internalizing identification, while vocationally
neutral variables lead to internalizing identification. The list of
these variables can be found in Appendix A-1.

Finally, Kelman states that *internalization* can be said to
occur when an individual accepts influence because the induced
behavior is congruent with his value system.'[9] Here the *content*
of the induced attitude or behavior is intrinsically rewarding since
it is consistent with the value system of the individual, it fits with
his psychodynamics (of values, attitudes, and needs). Thus the
induced attitude or behavior is 'internalized', because it is not
tied to an 'external' source and thus does not depend on social
support; the latter was the case for compliance or identification
where the induced attitude or behavior was not integrated in a
consistent way with the individual's value system, but rather
tended to be isolated from the rest of his values. Internalized
behavior gradually becomes independent of the external source;
in fact, 'it becomes part of a personal system, as distinguished
from a system of social-role expectation.'[10] Of course, the
intrinsic reward of internalization is obtained by the individual
also *by means of* his interaction with the environment (people,
work, etc.). This is not true for identification and even more
for compliance where the individual's gratification is attained
because of the interaction with the environment, under the form
either of a gratifying relationship (identification) or of reward-
punishment, approval-disapproval processes (compliance).

Are there structures of the personality which favor the
process of internalization?

When an individual's psychodynamics does not present preconscious
vocational inconsistencies and is characterized by conscious vocational

---

8   Rulla, 1971, p.317; Kelman, 1961; Schafer, 1968.
9   Kelman, 1961, p.65.
10 Kelman, 1961, p.66.

conflicts or consistencies (Psychological or Social Consistency), his sense of tension and his ego-strength will dispose him to look for value congruence of his behavior since this congruence is the intrinsically gratifying factor; thus, internalization of vocational attitudes and values is fostered.[11]

Kelman points out that the three processes just described are not mutually exclusive and seldom occur in pure form. However, in many situations a particular process predominates and determines their central characteristic.

The foregoing distinction may become clear if applied to vocational choice and commitment. This may be done by using the six motivational patterns for behavior in organizations proposed by Katz.[12] *Compliance* is present when a person enters a vocation or remains in it because of: 1) conformity to the norms of the system: people in the institution accept the fact that membership means 'complying' with its rules; 2) instrumental systems rewards: membership of the institution entails benefits to the individual; e.g., social and financial security, educational facilities: these benefits provide incentives for entering and remaining in the system; 3) instrumental individual rewards: while system rewards apply to all members, individual rewards of an instrumental character (e.g. a promotion) are obtained by some individuals because of their particular contributions or their privileged positions etc.

Identification is present when the individual enters or persists in religious life, 4) because of intrinsic satisfaction from specific role performance: the activity in a role is gratifying in itself because such activity gives the individual the chance to express his skills, his talents, to gratify his needs (e.g. for achievement, for dominance, etc.). This motivational pattern has to do with the opportunities which the institutional role, or professional roles within the institutions, provide for the expression of individual talents, abilities and the satisfactions of accomplishment.

There is *internalization* when the individual commits himself to a vocational institution, 5) because the individual has taken the values or goals of the institution as his own. Two examples will show the difference between internalization and identification as motivation patterns: a) the religious sister who derives her gratification from teaching (identification) could be equally happy in doing it in many different places — or, even, institutions (lay

---

[11]   Rulla, 1971, p.317-318.
[12]   Katz, 1964.

or religious) — but unhappy as a nurse in any one; b) on the
contrary, the sister who has internalized the values of her vocation, or even the goals of her own institution with its specific
problems and potentialities, is ready to stay on in her vocation
or institution and, furthermore, is willing to accept assign-
ments other than a teaching one. So what really matters, then,
is not the type of *role* exercised, but rather the type of *motivation*
(consistent or inconsistent) which lies at the basis of the choice
of this or that role.

In Katz's final group of motivations, the individual's
underlying motivation for the vocational commitment is especially
based on 6 gratifications derived from primary-group relationships. These are the social emotional satisfactions which
members of a small group obtain from interacting with one
another: mutual attraction, approval, support, stimulation, etc.
are among the many conscious or subconscious motivations
possible in this category. Strictly speaking, this affiliative
motivation is 'another form of instrumental reward-seeking, but
some of its qualitative aspects are sufficiently different from the
instrumental system and individual rewards previously described
to warrant separate discussion'.[13]

As we have already noted when discussing identification,
this process which is evident in groups can be favorable or
unfavorable to internalization. It will be favorable in so far as
the self-image gratified by the relation to the group can be
integrated with objective vocational values.

B. EVALUATION OF THE STRENGTHS AND WEAKNESSES OF THE SELF-IDEAL

A form of measurement constituted as an index will serve
to determine if, and to what extent, the internalizing forces of
the self of the person (internalization and internalizing identification) outweigh the non-internalizing forces (non-internalizing
identification and compliance) in the individual's psychodynamics.
This index will thus be taken as a measurement of the maturity of
the individual. What we intend to do here is to *understand* the

---

[13] Katz, 1964, p.143.

degree of maturity with which people enter religious life rather than to '*predict*' how this degree of maturity affects his perseverance or his effectiveness in vocation. It is an evaluation 'of', not an evaluation 'in view of'.[14]

Every reader familiar with the field knows the great complexity related to the task of conceptualizing and of measuring the *maturity of the self*. We will evaluate the degree of maturity in the context of our theory and operational definitions; that is, according to the degree of *compliance,* or *identification* (internalizing or not) and of *internalization*.

We have defined maturity as 'the knowledge and the acceptance of one's objective and free self-ideal-in-situation (SI-II) and the living of it.'[15] But what is this self-ideal-in-situation? What is the value-attitude system which characterizes it? In the case of vocation, this self-ideal-in-situation is evaluated in relation to two value-attitude systems: the one of vocation and the one of normal human development.

1) The first type of maturity emphasizes the vocational values, terminal and instrumental, and sees maturity especially in the light of them; hence, it was called 'vocational maturity'. A related *index of vocational maturity* (IVM) was developed and translated into measurement procedures. This index expresses the degree of compliance, identification and internalization which an individual has at the moment in which he actually enters a vocational setting.[16] Again, let us recall that this index *as such* has no predictive value concerning the future life in vocation. It only helps to understand the amount of consistency/inconsistency which motivates one's vocational choice and decision and thus the strength of this germinative and vulnerable SI-II considered together; i.e. how much the germinative SI-II outweighs the vulnerable SI-II or vice-versa. In a word, how mature, in psychological terms, has been one's decision to enter a religious vocation.

2) The second type of value-attitude system which was considered emphasizes the concept of *ego- or self-development*.

To evaluate the degree of maturity reached by our subjects, we took the common elements of normal developmental

---

14 Prelinger and Zimet, 1964; Wiggins, 1973.
15 Rulla, 1971, p.193.
16 Further information on this index can be found in Chapter 3, section C.

sequence: degree of impulse control, moral development, interpersonal relations, self-concept.[17] We created an *index of
developmental maturity* (IDM), which some writers would call
an index of 'affective maturity'. The index expresses the degrees
of compliance, identification, and internalization of an entering
vocationer as these can be inferred from his *capacity to handle*,
to control his major core conflicts. The handling capacity was
rated as I if the conflicts appeared to be strong enough to 'always'
have a debilitating influence on the person's functioning in any
one of the following areas: *academic performance, interpersonal
relationships*, and *moral-religious values in general*. The same
capacity to handle core conflicts was graded as II when any one
of these three foregoing areas of functioning was affected 'almost
always'; as III if affected 'frequently'; as IV if 'rarely' affected.

Degree I of developmental maturity would correspond to
prevailing compliance; degree II rather to non-internalizing identification, degree III rather to internalizing identification, and
degree IV to prevailing internalization. Judgement of the
capacity of handling core conflict(s) and the corresponding degree
of developmental maturity were based on concrete observations
deriving from an intuitive, *clinical synthesis* of test data collected
during all three testing sessions of this research and on the information which appeared during the *'depth interview'*. The
procedures followed in this assessment have been described in
sections D and E of Chapter 3.

We will now look at the similarities and differences between
the index of vocational maturity and the index of developmental
maturity.

Both indices intend to rate entering vocationers or lay
people of similar age according to a mile-stone sequence characterized by four stages or types of compliance, of non-internalizing
identification, or internalizing identification, and of internalization. Both indices are based on a typology of variables (e.g.
abasement, aggression, etc.) more than of persons, even though
for both of them the attention is focused particularly on the
variables which have greater influence on the person's functioning.
In fact, for the index of vocational maturity (IVM) the attention

---

17 Sullivan, Grant and Grant, 1957; Peck and Havighurst, 1960;
Kohlberg, 1964; Loevinger, 1966, a, b, 1970, 1976; Piaget, 1932;
Sullivan, 1953.

is on the central inconsistencies or consistencies (cf. Chapter 2) and for the index of developmental maturity (IDM) on the main core conflicts.

However, there are differences between the two indices, both conceptual and operational. Conceptually, both indices consider as important the system of moral-religious values and attitudes. Yet it is important to note that the index of *vocational* maturity is an expression of the central vocational consistencies and inconsistencies for the fourteen needs/attitudes defined by Murray,[18] and described at the end of Chapters 1 and 2. The index of *developmental* maturity, on the other hand, is an expression of the individual's capacity to control his conflicts in the three sectors of academic life, interpersonal relationships, and religious values in general.

On the operational level, the index of *vocational* maturity is calculated from the answers given by subjects, both from the modified activities index (MAI), that is from the present behavior (PB), self-ideal (SI) and institutional ideal (II), and also from the projective tests (TAT and Rotter ISB). These answers are in turn evaluated through a series of statistical analyses by computer. The index of *developmental* maturity, on the other hand, is worked out on the basis of answers given during the interviews and the clinician's evaluation of the interviews.

The two indices are conceptually and operationally distinct. However, distinctions do not necessarily imply complete divisions or separations. The distinctions discussed between the two indices do not in any way prejudice the question of correlations or of complex interaction or influence between the two of them. It is the task of empirical research to find some answer also to this question concerning the possible interdependence between the two aspects of maturity, developmental and vocational. This will be done to a limited extent in the present Chapter.

Before passing to the presentation of the research, it is proper to list briefly some limitations, among many possible, of the two adopted indices.

One limitation which we have already mentioned is the fact that our indices, while they may help in understanding the decision to become a priest or religious, and even allow an evaluation of the maturity of this decision (both from the point

---

[18]   Murray, 1938.

of view of vocation and development of the personality), yet
they cannot be used as such to predict perseverance in vocation
and apostolic effectiveness. A second limitation comes from
the fact that the index of vocational maturity used only fourteen
variables (needs and attitudes evaluated from their mutual
relationship of consistency or inconsistency).[19] It must be
stated, however, that these fourteen variables, taken over from
Murray's[20] theory of personality, are generally accepted to cover
broadly (even though not exhaustively) the spectrum of human
motivation.[21]

C. SUMMARY OF FINDINGS AND CONSIDERATIONS

1) 208 religious, males and females entering their religious
institutions, plus 39 seminarians entering their theological training
were assessed for the index of *developmental* maturity. 22
seminarians of another group were also studied; they entered
their college training on a lay college campus. In all, then, there
were 269 subjects.

333 subjects were studied for the index of *vocational*
maturity; they were a random part of the samples considered in
Chapters 5 and 6, divided as follows: 96 male religious from
two settings of the same institution; 95 female religious from two
settings of the same institution; 40 seminarians entering their
college training; 50 girls and 52 boys representing the freshmen
of lay Catholic colleges.

2) The findings for the groups studied for the index of
developmental maturity are shown in charts 2 and 3.

The 208 subjects in chart 2 are composed of all the
religious, male and female, with whom it was possible to have
an in-depth interview after four years in religious life. They
represent, respectively, 89% of the sample available among the
men, and 93% among the women. The last interviews took
place in 1972.

The 39 individuals evaluated in chart 3 represent a group
of seminarians who had just begun their theology. It is a group

---

[19] See Appendices A-3 and C.
[20] Murray, 1938.
[21] Jackson, 1970; Wiggins, 1973.

distinct from the group of 45 seminarians studied in Chapter 6. For these 39 individuals the interviews took place in 1973 and 1974.

CHART 2

DEGREE OF DEVELOPMENTAL MATURITY
PRESENT IN EACH INDIVIDUAL
AT ENTRANCE INTO THE RELIGIOUS INSTITUTION

| Group | Degree of Developmental Maturity | | | |
	I	II	III	IV
Religious Males (N = 80)	f 15% (12)	f 45% (36)	f 30% (24)	f 10% (8)
Religious Females (N = 128)	12% (16)	48% (61)	26% (33)	14% (18)
Totals (N = 208)	13.5% (28)	46.5% (97)	28% (57)	12% (26)

(Percentages; Number of subjects in parenthesis)

N.B. Degree I: always influenced by main conflict(s).
      Degree II: almost always influenced by main conflict(s).
      Degree III: frequently influenced by main conflict(s).
      Degree IV: rarely influenced by main conflict(s).

CHART 3

DEGREE OF DEVELOPMENTAL MATURITY
PRESENT IN EACH INDIVIDUAL
AT THE BEGINNING OF THEOLOGICAL TRAINING

| Group | Degree of Developmental Maturity | | | |
	I	II	III	IV
Beginning Theologians (N = 39)	f 31% (12)	f 48.5% (19)	f 18% (7)	f 2.5% (1)

(Percentages; Number of subjects in parenthesis)

N.B. Degree I: always influenced by main conflict(s).
      Degree II: almost always influenced by main conflict(s).
      Degree III: frequently influenced by main conflict(s).
      Degree IV: rarely influenced by main conflict(s).

An important difference between the groups in charts 2 and
3 is their geographical distribution. The subjects studied in
chart 2 come from five different settings or centers of formation;
settings 1 and 2 for men and settings 1, 2 and 3 for women (cf.
Appendix B).

The 39 subjects studied in chart 3 form 75% of a group of
invited subjects belonging to 45 dioceses, and geographically
representative of the whole of the United States.

The findings of charts 2 and 3 are clear: among those
deciding to undertake religious or priestly life, very few have
reached a degree of maturity (developmental degree IV) which
would allow them to control successfully their most important
conflicts. A second group, which oscillated between 18 and
30% of our samples, is often influenced negatively by their conflicts (degree III); and a substantial majority would be affected
negatively 'almost always' (degree II) or 'always' (degree I)
by one or several important conflicts.

In Chapter 6, the observations analyzed on a group of 45 seminarians
seem to indicate, on the basis of tests, that they had not yet really made
a serious decision with regard to their undertaking of the priestly vocation.
We have already expressed the opinion that the fact of living with lay
students on the campus of the same college might be one of the factors
which could explain their indecision. The in-depth interview was possible
with only 22 students after two years in formation; the others had in fact
already left the seminary. The index of developmental maturity of these
22 seminarians is as follows: degree I, 41% (9 subjects); degree II,
59% (13 subjects). Two years after the in-depth interview, which took
place in 1967, almost all had left the seminary.

The results we present in charts 2 and 3 are very similar
to the results obtained by other researchers at least as regards
percentages. While the different methodologies and criteria used
in the researches have to be taken into account, it might interest
the reader to know some of the results of other researchers.
According to Baars and Terruwe,[22] 10 to 15% of the priests
of North America and Western Europe are psychologically
mature, 60-70% are emotionally immature, and 20-25% have
serious psychiatric problems. From another angle, the data
obtained by Kennedy and Heckler[23] concerning 271 priests in
the USA indicate that 19 are 'developed', 50 are 'developing',
179 are 'under-developed', and 23 are 'mal-developed'. How-

---

[22] Baars and Terruwe, 1971.
[23] Kennedy and Heckler, 1971.

ever, this sample is not representative of the population studied, because only 31% of the religious priests and 24% of the diocesan priests initially chosen to participate in the project were eventually interviewed.

All the foregoing figures are quite close to the ones involving the general population both in Western Europe and in North America. Several of those studies have been published. Suffice it here to mention the best known among them: Srole et al., Leighton, and Essen Möller.[24]

Unfortunately, in the present research it was not possible nor advisable to compare the religious groups with their corresponding lay Catholic college groups of males and females for the index of developmental maturity (IDM). For one, the participation in the final depth interview of the lay college people at the end of the four years of college was too low: only 21% of the males and 59% of the females. Secondly, and more important, in the depth interview the fact of being lay or religious was, obviously, known and the criteria used in assessing the two groups, religious vs. lay, were different, at least with regard to the living of the three virtues of poverty, chastity and obedience. These two shortcomings were not present for the assessment of the index of vocational maturity (IVM) based on the data obtained at the beginning of the lay college training, (for differences see section B of this Chapter). Thus the percentage of the participants was 70% and 72% for the randomly selected males and females, respectively. Furthermore, while in the assessment of the index of developmental maturity (IDM) the interviewer knew if the subject was religious or lay, and thus was possibly influenced in his evaluation, the same was not true for the index of vocational maturity (IVM). The latter is based on a computer combination of data obtained from self-report questionnaires and from an evaluation of projective techniques in which the two persons scoring the protocols did so independently and without knowing whether the protocol belonged to a religious or lay person. Therefore, for the index of vocational maturity (IVM) a comparison between religious and lay persons is possible. Actually, this possibility is made even more acceptable because this index was conceived and operationalized according to a structural approach.[25]

---

[24] Srole et al., 1962; Leighton, 1963; Essen Möller, 1956.
[25] See Chapter 2.

3) There are three aims for the use of the IVM: 1) to obtain indirectly an evaluation of the strength of the germinative and the vulnerable self-ideal-in-situation SI-II of the entering vocationers, i.e. to express in one measurement the amount of consistencies/inconsistencies present in them; 2) to see if and to what extent there was a relationship between the two indices of vocational maturity and of developmental maturity; and 3) to compare among themselves the various groups of entering vocationers (religious, females and males, seminarians) and of freshmen of lay Catholic colleges.

4) When the foregoing results of the index of developmental maturity of *each person* are compared with the ones obtained for the same persons in the index of vocational maturity, one finds that the two sets of data have a significant correlation. This was true for the 91 subjects studied in this comparison. Furthermore, using the same two measures, when the individuals with a trend toward internalization, (i.e. the ones showing a prevalence of internalizing identification or of internalization) are compared with the ones with a trend not to internalize (because of their prevailing compliance or non-internalizing identification) a correspondence of 87% is found between these two sets of measurements.[26]

Thus, two procedures of measurement, which methodologically are completely independent, lead to similar results: at most, only 10-15% of the vocationers of our sample have made a decision to enter the vocational institution which was motivated by an internalized self-ideal-in-the-given-situation (SI-II). A substantial majority, oscillating between 60 and 80%, showed an entering motivation characterized by ego-defensive or utilitarian subconscious attitudes, i.e. for these people the choice of religious vocation was not only the means to implement their ideals, but also a *subconscious* attempt either to react defensively against underlying conflicts or to gratify conflictual needs. These attitudes expressed a prevailing compliance or non-internalizing identification related to subconscious forces. The relevance of the *subconscious motivation* underlying the decision to enter the religious institution seems to be quite great.

The frequency of central, unconscious inconsistencies found

---

[26] This statistical analysis followed the technique proposed by Wiggins (1973) which basically uses the chi-square.

in our sample confirms the relevance of this subconscious motivation. For variables like dominance, abasement, and defendance (i.e. pride-humility), such inconsistencies are present in about 70-75% of the vocationers studied; for aggression the proportion is 56%, etc. These findings support and quantify the results discussed in Chapter 6. They are convincing; the values proclaimed by the individuals when they enter religious life cannot simply be accepted at face value; the subconscious motivation must also be considered.

Also, it is interesting to note that the data confirm the observation made in Chapter 6 that among all the groups studied, the entering *seminarians* were the least differentiated from their lay controls. The results concerning the subconscious motivation confirm the ones of the conscious motivation.

5) The data of Chapter 6 suggested the possible relationship between the degree of *developmental maturity* reached by a person and his degree of *vocational maturity*. The present Chapter has shown that a correspondence between the two degrees of maturity is present in 87% of the individuals with regard to their prevailingly internalizing or non-internalizing personality. It would seem that the developmental maturity and vocational maturity represent two processes which are not dichotomous, but rather strictly interdependent, at least according to the conceptual and operational definitions followed in this research.

6) There are no significant differences between the groups of vocationers and groups of lay college students with regard to their index of *vocational* maturity. In contrast, the data of Chapter 6 had strongly suggested that such a difference existed with regard to their self-ideal-in-situation (SI-II). This contrast confirms the fact that the SI-II is the psychological force which disposes one to enter a vocation and which opens the person to the call of supernatural grace. However, for the SI-II the difference between vocationers and non-vocationers found in Chapter 6 concerned the *conscious* values and attitudes which, in the light of the findings of Chapters 6 and 7, appear to be somewhat unrealistically idealized. Thus, an important question remains: to what extent is the SI-II free and objective? How much is the SI-II conflict-free, i.e. how much is it the consequence of a genuine *value* motivation rather than of a motivation significantly influenced by *subconscious* and vocationally inconsistent *needs?*

7) Some light on this issue was given by the findings

102

discussed here in number 4) concerning the substantial strength
of subconscious motivation at entrance into religious vocation.
Further light comes from the results obtained in connection with
the problem of analyzing the *content* (e.g. self-confidence,
aggression) of the consistencies and inconsistencies, and they
confirm the weight of the subconscious motivation, adding at the
same time another significant insight. They point to the
vocationally *dissonant needs* as particularly relevant in the entering motivation, when one considers them in terms of the
substructures of the personality, like inconsistencies, consistencies,
etc. In fact, the vulnerable part of the SI-II is more important
than its germinative part in differentiating the various groups of
lay and religious people studied in this investigation at their
entrance into the institutions. Now, this vulnerable part of the
SI-II is expressed by the inconsistencies, defensive consistencies
and conflicts of vocationally *dissonant* variables, that is, by
forces which are prompted and sustained especially by vocationally dissonant needs.[27]

This relevance of both the vulnerable, conflictual part of
the SI-II and of the vocationally dissonant variables is confirmed
by our data and related statistical analyses. In fact, the data
analyses show that while the difference between the germinative
and the vulnerable part of the SI-II of the various groups for the
vocationally neutral variables is not significant, the same difference
is significant for the vocationally dissonant variables.

8) As a consequence of the results and considerations
discussed in the foregoing points 4) and 7), one would expect
that the unconscious inconsistencies between the attitudes and
the needs of vocationally dissonant variables, like aggression,
exhibition, etc. do play an important role in influencing the future
commitment of the vocationer in terms of his perseverance and
vocational effectiveness. In Chapter 9, when considering the
process of dropping out, we will see if these expectations are
confirmed by the empirical data.

9) At this point of our investigation, two general conclusions are prompted by the findings. First of all, at their entrance
into the vocational institution, the vocationers present many and
strong shortcomings of personality which, without being signs of
psychopathology, make their *vocational* motivation vulnerable.

---

[27] See Appendix A-1.

The important point here is that these vocational shortcomings are already there before the individuals start their training in the institutions; therefore they are not determined by the institutions. A second general conclusion is that the shortcomings considered here come from *subconscious* forces.

But do the institutions usually offer an appropriate help to handle these subconscious forces? It seems that, in general, this is not the case. And yet, these subconscious factors seem to be important for the future commitment to religious life. They are important because: 1) they tend to persist; 2) they tend to affect the future perseverance in the vocational commitment. The following two Chapters will consider these two trends of the entering motivation.

CHAPTER 8

THE INTRAPSYCHIC DYNAMICS OF ENTERING AND THEIR TENDENCY TO PERSIST

A. INTRODUCTION

On the basis of the data studied in Chapters 6 and 7, we are led to emphasize the unconscious motivation of entry into religious vocation. In fact, for many subjects the choice of vocation is *also* determined by an attempted self-defense against subconscious needs, or is a means of gratifying certain underlying needs.

More exactly, our data indicate that the substantial majority of our subjects seem influenced in their choice by a subconscious motivation.

Furthermore, our data clearly suggest that for numerous subjects the ideals expressed at the time they entered the centers of religious formation were significantly more vulnerable than germinative. In other words, these ideals seem to indicate a lack of freedom characteristic of compliance and non-internalizing identification, rather than the presence of growth factors characteristic of an active internalization. They seem to be a means of self-defense against conflictual needs rather than a means of free self-transcendence in affirming values, a forced retreat rather than a free advance. This passive, reactive way of dealing with internal subconscious needs may be tied to the family or educational background of our subjects. There is in fact an abundance of scientific literature available which deals with the probable effects of infantile residue from family influence on the choice of religious vocation.

It has been observed that the experiences of early infancy, such as the socialization processes in the family and school, are correlated with the methods of personal control and with the capacity to postpone gratifications and resist temptations.[1] At the same time, as Becker[2] suggested after reviewing numerous studies, the 'non-moral' type of expectations which the parents had with regard to aggression, dependence, etc. were transmitted to their offspring; here we are considering vocational attitudes as general and 'non-moral'. In the same line, we are reminded of the many researches showing that youngsters tend to adopt the values of their parents.[3] The reader might like to consult the interesting critical reviews of the existing literature dealing with this argument, in relation either to religious values in general[4] or, more specifically, to vocational motivation.[5] All these studies stress the enduring and tenacious influence of the past.

We have also noted the unconscious character of numerous aspects of motivation which lead to entry into religious life. 'He who does not know his past is condemned to repeat it.' This thought of Goethe is one of the basic convictions of depth psychology concerning unconscious conflicts.[6] We have indicated elsewhere[7] that there is a psychodynamic 'similarity' between unconscious conflicts in general and vocational inconsistencies as defined in Chapter 1. We are of the opinion that those individuals whose inconsistencies are unconscious or deeply preconscious are not changed much by new information; more exactly, the information they receive from the environment may influence them momentarily but not in the long run. These persons have defenses which prevent their becoming conscious of the true nature of their frustration, and which, as a result, make them incapable of modifying their behavior through a new evaluation or new learning. This inability to re-evaluate affects their vocation too; these individuals are unable to re-evaluate an unrealistic and unobjective self-ideal-in-situation (SI-II). From among the many types of defenses it is useful here to point out that 'transferences' especially can have a considerable negative

---

1 Bandura and Walters, 1963; Kohlberg, 1964; Hoffman, 1970; Brofenbrenner, 1961; Berkowitz, 1964, etc.
2 Becker, 1964.
3 Keniston, 1967; Adams, 1968; Sampson, 1967.
4 Fairchild, 1971; Milanesi and Aletti, 1973.
5 Godin, 1975.
6 Cf., for example, Mahl, 1969.
7 Rulla, 1971, pp. 129-142, 163-165.

influence on behavior; more will be said about them later in this Chapter.

These principles and observations of depth psychology have also been confirmed by the research of social psychology. It suffices to note here that a person who has made a difficult decision ideologically, tends to adopt attitudes which support or justify his choice thus helping him to avoid painful post decisional regret.[8] The researches of Brock[9] have shown that there is a tendency to distort perception of the reference group, such as the religious institution, rather than to change these personal attitudes. One would expect these subconscious defenses to be particularly active in those individuals who have central unconscious vocational inconsistencies.

These researches and reflections suggest that, in a similar way, the motivation of a young religious may persist after he has entered. We can verify this, at least with regard to the vulnerable side of motivation which, as we have seen, is the predominant side in our subjects. We shall do this in the present Chapter, utilizing the observations from our research.

This inquiry will proceed in three principal directions: 1) Using data obtained in depth interviews and expressed by means of the index of vocational maturity described in Chapter 7. 2) The relationships between the data regarding the family background of our subjects on the one hand, and the degree of developmental maturity as well as the degree of vocational maturity reached by them, on the other hand. 3) The transferences developed by the subjects during the first four years of formation in the religious life.

Chapter 9 will continue with the analysis of the same data, but with regard to perseverance or non-perseverance in vocational commitment.

B. RESULTS AND DISCUSSION

Let us remember that, according to the observations analyzed earlier, the vulnerable side of the SI-II is very important in the

---

8 Aronson, 1968; Brehm and Cohen, 1962; Festinger, 1957, 1964; McGuire, 1969; Secord and Backman, 1974.
9 Brock, 1965; Brock and Blackwood, 1962.

motivation for entering, since it prevails over the germinative side in 60-80% of the individuals studied.

The vulnerable side of the SI-II is defined by the following *subconscious* factors: central inconsistencies, defensive consistencies and conflicts with regard to the vocationally dissonant variables as defined in Chapter 3, at the beginning of section C and in the Appendix A-1. These inconsistencies, defensive consistencies and conflicts arise from the needs and attitudes of the individual and they undermine sub-consciously (and thereby render vulnerable) the vocational ideals to which he consciously aspires. The germinative side of the self-ideal-in-situation (SI-II) is expressed by the central consistencies and by the conflicts relating to vocationally neutral variables; this type of conflict and the consistencies, in so far as they favor or do not oppose the ideals, may sustain the germinative side of the SI-II.

According to our conceptual model, the vulnerable side of the SI-II tends to impede the internationalization of vocational values because the individual in this case is characterized by compliance and non-internalizing identification, whilst the germinative side tends more towards the internalization of values since the individual in whom it is present is characterized by internalizing identification and by internalization.

These data and considerations, as well as the observations, researches and tenets of depth psychology, social psychology and studies on religious or vocational development, have led to our formulating the hypothesis that the motivation at entrance tends to persist during the years of religious formation.

1) For the research concerned with the level of *developmental maturity,* we evaluated 208 religious of both sexes and 39 students of theology. These samples are the same as those in Chapter 7. For one part of the research we also used an additional sample of 22 seminarians who were beginning their studies in a Catholic college.

For the research concerned with the *vocational maturity,* we evaluated a sub-sample of 70 religious of both sexes chosen at random from the 208 subjects just mentioned.

2) The tendency for the entering motivation to persist was studied directly and indirectly.

Directly, we compared for 208 religious of both sexes the level of developmental maturity at the time of entry with that after four years of vocational formation. As indicated in chart 2[10] and in chart 4 below, at the end of four years of religious life no significant change had taken place either in the vulnerable side of the self-ideal (degree of developmental maturity I and II) or in the germinative side (degree of developmental maturity III and IV).

CHART 4

DEGREE OF DEVELOPMENTAL MATURITY
PRESENT IN EACH INDIVIDUAL
AFTER 4 YEARS OF VOCATIONAL FORMATION

Group	Degree of Developmental Maturity			
	I	II	III	IV
Religious Males (N = 80)	f 21% (17)	f 37% (30)	f 29% (23)	f 12% (10)
Religious Females (N = 128)	13% (17)	44% (56)	27% (35)	16% (20)
Totals (N = 208)	17% (34)	40.5% (86)	28% (58)	14% (30)

(Percentages; Number of subjects in parenthesis.)

N.B. Degree I: always influenced by main conflict(s).
   Degree II: almost always influenced by main conflict(s).
   Degree III: frequently influenced by main conflict(s).
   Degree IV: rarely influenced by main conflict(s).

---

10 P. 74

CHART 5

DEGREE OF DEVELOPMENT
PRESENT IN EACH INDIVIDUAL
OF TWO DIFFERENT GROUPS

Group	Degree of Developmental Maturity			
	I*	II	III	IV
Beginning Theologians (N = 39)	f 31.0% (12)	f 48.5% (19)	f 18.0% (7)	f 2.5% (1)
	Degree of Development			
	Mal-developed	Under-developed	Developing	Developed
Priests** (N = 271)	f 8.5% (23)	f 66.5% (179)	f 18.0% (50)	f 7.0% (19)

(Percentages; Number of subjects in parenthesis.)

*Degree I: always influenced by main conflict(s).
Degree II: almost always influenced by main conflict(s).
Degree III: frequently influenced by main conflict(s).
Degree IV: rarely influenced by main conflict(s).
**(Kennedy and Heckler, 1971)

Furthermore, 86% of the males and 87% of the females in this sample were partially or completely unaware of their major conflict(s) at the time of entry into the novitiate. After four years of formation, the vast majority (83% of the males and 82% of the females) were still unaware of this conflict.

Chart 5 gives us additional indirect information about the tendency of the psychodynamics to persist. Here we compared two researches whose subjects have in common the fact of being a random sample from people coming from different regions of the United States. Our group of 39 first year students of theology has been described earlier; the 271 *priests* are the sample studied by Kennedy and Heckler.[11]

A statistical analysis comparing the two groups of chart 5,

---

[11]   Kennedy and Heckler, 1971; cf. Chapter 7.

despite the difference in age and in data classification, reveals no significant difference.

3) The *indirect* study of the tendency of the entering motivation to persist consists of bringing together the two sides of the self-ideal-in-situation (SI-II), the vulnerable and the germinative, with the data relative to the family history on the one hand, and the evidence of transferences in the religious life on the other. We maintain that there is a transference whenever the subject, in his relationships with the authorities and with his peers, relives a relationship he has already had with the members of his family during his childhood and adolescence. An example of transference would be the case of a young religious who establishes an over-dependent affective relationship with one of his superiors as a result of an earlier similar relationship with, say, his father or mother. This regressive repetition of past experiences reinforces the vulnerable side of the SI-II and so leads to its persistence and self-perpetuation.

Our results indicate that approximately 69% of male religious and 67% of female religious seem to establish transferential relationships during formation. More importantly, however, the results obtained in our research indicate some interdependencies.

a) We find that the subjects who enter into vocation change their judgements about their own relationships with one or both of their parents. A comparison is made between the information they give at the time of entry in the biographical inventory (BI),[12] then after four months of religious life in a family interview (FI),[13] then after four years in a depth interview (DI).[14] As indicated in chart 6, whilst 74% of the subjects, at the time of entry, judged their relationships with their parents as positive, four years later only 10.1% expressed the same positive judgements.

It must be noted in this regard that it is the subjects themselves who changed their opinions after being helped by the interviewer to see their own family situation.

---

12 BI, cf. Chapter 3.
13 FI, cf. Chapter 3.
14 DI, cf. Chapter 3.

CHART 6

PARENTAL CONFLICTS IN MALE AND
FEMALE RELIGIOUS AND SEMINARIANS
AS INDICATED IN THE BIOGRAPHICAL INVENTORY,
FAMILY INTERVIEW, DEPTH INTERVIEW

Groups	Biographical Inventory		Family Interview		Depth Interview	
	Positive	Negative	Positive	Negative	Positive	Negative
	f	f	f	f	f	f
Males (N = 102)	78.4% (80)	21.6% (22)	56.2% (45)	43.8% (35)	8.8% (9)	91.2% (93)
			(sems excluded)			
Females (N = 125)	71.2% (89)	28.8% (36)	46.4% (58)	53.6% (67)	11.2% (14)	88.8% (111)
TOTALS (N = 227)	74.4% (169)	25.6% (58)	50.2% (103)	49.8% (102)	10.1% (23)	89.9% (204)
			(sems excluded)			

(Percentages; Number of subjects in parenthesis).

b) These family conflicts, expressed by the lack of correspondence between the declarations made on the biographical inventory (BI), in the family interview (FI) and in the depth interview (DI), are related both to the levels of developmental and vocational maturity of the religious on entrance and to the frequency with which these religious develop transferences during the first four years of formation.

So we can note the following relationships of interdependence: conflicts which persisted in the family may lie behind those persisting in the individual, which show up in the low level of vocational and developmental maturity of the religious at the beginning. The personal conflicts may be expressed in the defensive adoption of transferences, which in their turn represent the fact of reliving the original conflicts of the family.

These relationships of interdependence are presented schematically in chart 7.

CHART 7

**PERSONAL MATURITY,
DEVELOPMENTAL OR VOCATIONAL**

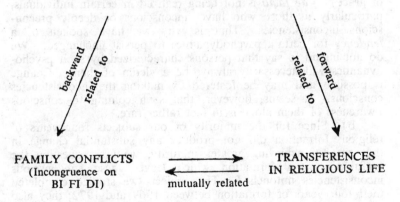

FAMILY CONFLICTS   TRANSFERENCES
(Incongruence on   IN RELIGIOUS LIFE
BI FI DI)   mutually related

Examining this chart one can easily understand why the intrapsychic dynamics discovered at entrance are such an enduring and tenacious process. It is interesting to note that this is especially true for those individuals who have only a low level of maturity (vocational or developmental), whilst it is not necessarily true for those who have a high level of developmental and vocational maturity.

Thus we obtain a convergence of numerous results which, directly and indirectly, strongly suggest that the vulnerable side of the self-ideal-in-situation, characteristic of immature persons, tends to persist. Furthermore, the data of this Chapter and the preceding one also indicate that at least 60-80% of those who enter religious life are less than mature.

4) These results suggest the following considerations:

a) The adaptability and the capacity for development of a human being, by his or her very nature, go beyond every quantifiable prediction or observation. Two extreme positions are untenable: there do not exist perfectly integrated people, but only people working towards such as integration; nor are there human beings totally incapable of any integration (excepting, of course, cases of extreme pathology which we are not considering here). Nevertheless, it appears that the intrinsic tendency towards change and perfection, which every man is capable of by his own efforts — also from the prospective of self-transcendence based on religious beliefs (collaboration with the work of grace) — de facto is not being realized in certain individuals, particularly in those who have unconscious or deeply preconscious inconsistencies. That is why we have spoken of a tendency for certain psychodynamics to persist unchanged. We do not intend to say that persons characterized by such psychodynamics will necessarily always be a victim of them. Change is possible and may be fostered by making the inconsistencies conscious. It seems, however, that such coming to conscious awareness of them alone is in fact rather rare.

b) Since for the majority of our subjects four years of religious formation did not produce any substantial change in the sense of achieving greater maturity, we must question the usefulness of a formation which leaves these subconscious inconsistencies untouched. The subjects we studied completed their four years of formation between 1969 and 1972; they also profited from the new methods of formation adopted after the Second Vatican Council. Over and above this, the fact that the psychodynamics of entrance tend to perpetuate themselves indefinitely in the majority of the subjects, brings us to question the effectiveness of the trend to delay the time of entrance into religious life, if that is seen as the *only* way to correct a *subconscious* dynamic. In most cases, merely postponing entrance helps the individual but little, if at all.

c) The results obtained in this Chapter suggest some further considerations less directly concerned with the argument of this Chapter, but interesting in so far as they touch on the problems of vocation in general.

Having reviewed the literature on the topic,/ Kohlberg[15] arrives at the conclusion that research results contradict any theory which pretends to affirm that good relationships with parents are necessary for a normal social development, especially in the moral and psychosexual areas; some data suggest, however, that bad relationships with parents retard or impede this development. The results of this Chapter, presented schematically in chart 7, seem to indicate that this conclusion may be extended to those who enter religious life, especially the point about maturity. The religious who had good relationships with their parents do not necessarily have a high level of developmental and vocational maturity.

d) A final interesting observation. There seems to be a difference between those who repress their poor relationships with their parents and those who do not. The former, that is those who show discrepancies between the biographical inventory, the family interview and the depth interview, tend to reach only a slightly elevated level of maturity in their development and in their vocation. Those who, on the contrary, do not show any discrepancy (i.e. who describe in a constant way, even though in negative terms, their relationships with their parents) tend less frequently to show a lower level of maturity. In simpler terms, the individuals with discrepancies in their statements, written or oral, are part of the low maturity groups more often than those who are openly and constantly negative in their statements.

All this may mean that the level of maturity is negatively influenced when a relationship with the parents is not only poor but is *also* repressed and kept out of consciousness; a poor relationship with parents does not necessarily lead to immaturity. The denial of a bad relationship with parents and the further conceiving of this relationship in optimistic and unreal terms

---

[15] Kohlberg, 1969, 1966.

115

have a much greater influence on development than the frank admission of a negative reality.

The following Chapter will continue the study of this tendency for the initial psychodynamics to persist after entrance into religious life. By studying the perseverance in or departure from religious life, one can see if the initial psychodynamics tend to persist or not.

CHAPTER 9

THE INTRAPSYCHIC DYNAMICS OF ENTERING AND THEIR TENDENCY TO INFLUENCE LEAVING

A. DIMENSIONS OF THE PROBLEM

In the last ten years, the number of priests and religious returning to the lay state has increased considerably.[1] A simple comment by the General of the Society of Jesus gives us a revealing picture of the situation now becoming widespread in the Church: every *week* in the Society of Jesus, 6 enter, 7 die and 20 leave.[2]

This striking phenomenon of mass departure must be put into a comprehensive framework of a 'vocational anthropology'. Elsewhere[3] we have presented some considerations in this regard. This complex problem can be seen from different perspectives and is the result of numerous diverse factors. Generally speaking, the process leading to departure from the priestly and/or religious vocation can be related to the following five aspects:

1) Changes in the way of looking at supernatural factors and at human co-operation with grace
2) Some characteristics of individual personalities
3) Group pressures and styles of community life
4) Factors tied to the norms, constitutions and structures of the vocational institutions
5) Pressures arising from the historical and sociocultural

---

[1] The interested reader may consult some disturbing statistics in Kaufman, 1970; Harvey, 1973; Fratellière, 1972; Pro Mundi Vita, 1971; Modde, 1974; Godin, 1975.
[2] Arrupe, 1972.
[3] Rulla, 1971, pp. 194-224 and, less directly, pp. 225-384.

environment in general and from the structural functioning of the Church.

Obviously our information does not allow us to study all of these five factors, but only one: the characteristics of the individual's personality.[4]

Godin[5] makes the fine point that a vocational crisis centered on a conflict between institutional structure and values will inevitably influence the opinions expressed by the individual in response to psychosocial questionnaires and the implicit meaning of the language they use. Hence there arises the difficulty of establishing objective criteria for success or failure in vocational commitment either through apostolic effectiveness or through perseverance. With regard to this difficulty, Godin analyzes three important studies by Rashke, Neal and Carroll.[6] We will look at this last one.

Carroll[7] has compared, for a certain number of subjects, a prediction of vocational success based on psychological tests (MMPI and sentence completion) done at the time of entrance, with an evaluation of vocational success expressed several years later by their professors of theology. He has also compared the same prediction based on these tests with another evaluation also made some years later, this time by the peers of the subjects studied. Carroll has shown that there is a statistically significant correspondence between the psychologist's prediction and the

---

[4] To deepen other aspects of the complex problem of leaving, the interested reader may consult first the sociological researches of Greeley (1973) and NORC (1971); then the inquiry conducted by Olabuenaga in the Spanish environment (1970 and Pro Mundi Vita, 1971); the research of Stryckman (1971) for the region of Quebec; the studies of Schallert and Kelley (1970) and of Modde and Koval (1974) for the United States; the publications of Schmidtchen in co-operation with the *Institut für Demoskopie in Allensbach* (1973) and of Mönikes (1973) for West Germany. In general, these studies highlight the following aspects: the individual leaves his vocation because of personal discontent which expresses itself in a feeling of isolation or solitude (Greeley, 1972) and which arises mainly from a lack of personal fulfilment in pastoral work or from conflictual tension between values and institutions (see e.g. NORC p. 262); the desire to marry is more a consequence of leaving than a factor determining it.

[5] Godin, 1975.

[6] Rashke, 1973; Neal, 1970; Carroll, in Bier, 1970 pp. 159-189.

[7] Carroll, 1970.

professors, evaluation, but he has not found a significant concordance between the prediction of the psychologist and the evaluation by the peers. Note, however, the pertinent objection to this research raised by William G. T. Douglas. The classification system used by Carroll runs the risk of consolidating the criteria established a long time ago by the ecclesiastic superiors: 'If we psychologists select people who are judged as good people by those already established, we are implicitly reinforcing present patterns' as well as 'getting a picture of what is valued by those who are ecclesiastically established.'[8]

Is it therefore impossible to predict perseverance and effectiveness in vocations? Note the difference between the judgements expressed by the peers and those expressed by the people responsible for formation. This goes to show how difficult it is to predict the outcome of a vocation, especially at a time when institutional structures and values are being questioned and evaluated differently by those responsible for formation and by peers. On the other hand, the researches we have quoted, the studies of Rooney, Weisgerber, the concepts and researches of Lee,[9] all show that, in fact, certain elements of personality do allow *some* predictions with regard to vocation.

Our efforts are not geared directly towards prediction as a means of selecting candidates for the religious life, but rather towards uncovering the fundamental psychodynamic mechanisms underlying the process of entrance into and of growth in religious vocation. The structural model of personality, presented in Chapters 1 and 2, ought to contain *within itself* criteria by which to predict perseverance and growth in vocation. One of the important aspects of this theory consists in introducing objective vocational values, both terminal and instrumental, which allow two types of contrasts to be made. The first is between these objective values, on the one hand, and on the other hand what *each* individual's *perceptions* are, whether of his own personal values and attitudes (SI) or of the values and attitudes proposed by the institution he has chosen (II).

In this way, the image each individual has of his own role, how he perceives it and wants it to be, is more important psycho-

---

8 Douglas, in Bier, 1970, p.182.
9 Rooney, 1966; Weisgerber, 1969 and in Bier, 1970 pp. 190-208; Lee, 1968, 1969, a,b, 1970 a,b,c, 1973.

dynamically than the actual exigencies of the role as perceived by the institution or by peers.

The second type of contrast derives from the fact that the evaluation of these personal perceptions of values, attitudes and roles is based not so much on their content as on their consistency or inconsistency with the major *needs* of that particular individual. Such a method of evaluation is therefore independent of the typical norms of a definite group or of a particular religious institution; it is equally independent of a specific sociocultural environment or a particular time in history. Furthermore, the evaluation is not intrinsically tied to the norms, valid or not, of any particular test. This method is therefore in some way transituational and trans-temporal. Therefore, the structural model proposed must contain within itself the elements which allow us to predict the individual capacity to *internalize* vocational attitudes and values. Now it is necessary to clarify and explain the nature of the predictions we can make.

B. RELATIONSHIPS BETWEEN MOTIVATION FOR ENTRANCE AND PERSEVERANCE: THEORETICAL PREMISES

Proclaiming values does not necessarily mean practising them.

In *The Brothers Karamazov*, Dostoyevski wrote that many people can love all men but find it almost impossible to love one man in particular. Harding[10] has shown that values accepted on a speculative level tend to vacillate when the individual has to face specific situations. What is important for candidates for the religious life is that they be capable of internalizing the instrumental values and attitudes in the service of the objective terminal values of religious life. Rokeach,[11] through theoretical efforts and researches of considerable importance, has shown that values exercise their own independent influence on human motivation. The same can be said for attitudes, which are the cornerstone of social psychology.[12] Concretely, attitudes may become values. Therefore, a religious may transform into an end in itself an attitude or observance which ought to be only a means of realizing a value: for example, the attitude of helping others could in his case be conditioned by the need to be helped or comforted by others (affective dependence).

---

10 Harding, 1944, 1948.
11 Rokeach, 1968, 1973.
12 Cf. the comprehensive presentation of McGuire, 1969 and Freedman, Carlsmith and Sears, 1974.

Or again, the letter of the law may prevail over the spirit and a certain observance of its letter may result in sacrificing its spirit. With regard to motivation, attitudes are, by their very nature, dynamically less important than values. On this point the researches of Homant, Hollen and Rokeach [13] may be consulted.

The data analyzed in Chapters 5, 6 and 7 have indicated that the self-ideal-in-situation (SI-II) constitutes the psychological force which disposes the individual to choose religious life. Nevertheless, the same data also indicated that the values and attitudes of the ideal-self (SI-II) are often undermined by needs which are unconsciously or preconsciously inconsistent with the values and attitudes. The results of Chapter 8 strongly suggest that the psychodynamics of entrance persist during the successive years of religious life; we have seen that this is due, above all, to the vulnerable side of the ideal-self. We have seen in particular that the data relative to this persistence suggest the existence of a strict relationship between needs and corresponding attitudes as evaluated by the index of vocational maturity.

Following these data and considerations, it seems that the attitudes of the self-ideal-in-situation can exercise their influence on the motivation of candidates for the religious life. This force is presented under three aspects. First of all, we have the influence of an attitude, domination for example, *in accordance with* the corresponding need, *or* again, *in accordance with* the corresponding value, for example the instrumental value of the general goals of life inventory, 'power, control over people and things'; we can also have the influence of an attitude which is in accord with *both* its corresponding need and value.

A second aspect consists of the influence exercised by an attitude *independently* of the corresponding need or value. For example, an attitude of 'personal success', instead of satisfying a need for 'success' or corresponding to the value of 'collaboration with others', could exist independently of this need and of this value and satisfy rather a need for competitive aggression[14] inconsistent with vocation. In this last case, the attitude of 'success' is found to be in some way tied to the inconsistent need for aggression and therefore is defensive and thus cannot easily be integrated with the need for success and/or the value of charitable co-operation.

---

[13] Homant, 1970; Hollen, 1972; Rokeach, 1973.
[14] Hollander, 1971.

A third aspect of the influence exercised by an attitude consists of its *resistance* to being integrated with values and needs when *two* conditions are present. First of all, an attitude must have acquired its own strength in time. The second condition consists of the centrality of the consistencies or inconsistencies tied to that attitude. An attitude becomes even more resistant to integration when there exists central consistencies/inconsistencies between the attitude and its corresponding need in the individual psychodynamics. Since these consistencies/inconsistencies are significantly important for the individual and for his self-concept, they will resist more or less consciously any force seeking to introduce some change.

The important theoretical efforts of Rokeach[15] should be quoted in particular. He maintains that self-conceptions, conscious and unconscious, are more central for a person than values and attitudes. By 'self-conceptions' Rokeach means all the particular bits of knowledge an individual has of himself. These self-conceptions include elements which are conscious and unconscious, positive and negative, together with their affective connotations. Any dissonance between these self-conceptions can influence behavior. Furthermore:

> paradoxically ... under certain conditions, values may be easier to change than attitudes. Values are less central than the self-conceptions but more central than attitudes. If a person's values are in fact standards employed to maintain and enhance self-conceptions, then a contradiction between values and self-conceptions can be most effortlessly resolved by changing the less central values.[16]

The first three Chapters of this volume have presented an operational description of these self-conceptions; they are the central inconsistencies, central consistencies and conflicts.[17] The major resistance to integration in the personal psychodynamic system comes normally from *central* motivations. We can propose that, for a religious, the classification of resistances can be ranked as follows: the strongest resistance comes from the central inconsistencies in the variables which are dissonant with vocation. In fact, these inconsistencies are central by definition (they are functionally significant), they are unconscious and their

---

15 Rokeach, 1973.
16 Rokeach, 1973 p. 217.
17 For the distinctions between inconsistencies, conflicts and consistencies, see the schema inserted in Chapter 3, at the beginning of section C.

content is objectively contrary to vocation.[18] In decreasing order
of resistance we find the central consistencies of the dissonant
variables, the central inconsistencies of neutral variables and
finally, the non-central conflicts of dissonant and neutral
variables.[19]

We make, therefore, the following general assumptions:

1) The vulnerable side of the self-ideal-in-situation will
prevail over the germinative side to a degree directly proportionate
to the strength of the central inconsistencies in vocationally
dissonant needs/attitudes.

2) As a result, the lack of realism of the self-ideal-in-
situation (for attitudes) will be directly proportionate to the
degree of imbalance between the vulnerable and the germinative
sides. In other words, the predominance of central inconsistencies for the dissonant and neutral variables, as well as the conflicts for the dissonant variables, will produce and maintain a self-
ideal-in-situation whose lack of objectivity and freedom will
result in the production of false expectations in the individual.

3) For reasons already given, we assume that the individuals are incapable of integrating (Kelman would say 'internalizing', cf. the beginning of Chapter 7) the false expectations created
at the level of their personal ideals (SI-II for attitudes) with the
consistencies or inconsistencies, or with the conflicts existing in
their individual psychodynamics. The discrepancies resulting
from this lack of integration will therefore constitute a liability
for the motivation of a vocationer.

In fact, a vicious circle is established which threatens to
gradually destroy the basis for religious commitment: a) The
balance or imbalance between the central consistencies and

---

18 Cf. Chapter 1.
19 Note that here we are not considering the influence that some values
may exercise independently on the personal dynamics. For example,
even if the central inconsistencies or consistencies of a religious
resist every attempt at change (as in the case of 'scrupulosity'), it
could be that the values would continue to have their own effect on
the total psychodynamics of the individual who would continue to
grow in his values, but without touching those aspects of his behavior influenced by his central inconsistencies or consistencies. We
have shown elsewhere (Rulla, 1971, p. 102 ff.) that central inconsistencies and consistencies may directly influence perseverance and
apostolic effectiveness, but that they do not necessarily have any
intrinsic effect on personal sanctification.

inconsistencies will produce or maintain in time in the individual, expectations (SI-II) which are more or less realistic with regard to his future vocational roles; b) In turn, these unrealistic role expectations will strongly resist *internalization* or personalization according to the objective system of vocational values chosen at the time of entrance; c) The unrealistic attitudes may negatively influence the existing balance between the central consistencies and inconsistencies, and this will gradually weaken the fundamental vocational values and attitudes.

The capacity of young religious to internalize the vocationally important values and attitudes is therefore expected to be inversely proportionate to the strength of their inconsistencies for the vocationally dissonant variables, and thus to the degree of vulnerability of their self-ideal-in-situation. The vocationers' psychodynamics at entrance thus have potential which allows one to predict their future capacity to internalize vocational attitudes and/or instrumental values. It is therefore possible to partially indicate the *dispositions* and the *tendencies* towards a successful vocational commitment. We do not imply that the bases of decisions to enter religious life themselves become predictors of vocational perseverance. Dittes[20] has insisted on the distinction between the two criteria. In Chapters 5, 6 and 7, we have sought to show how the decision to enter religious life is based on the self-ideal-in-situation (SI-II), more precisely on the vocational attitudes and values. In this Chapter we are formulating the hypothesis that perseverance and apostolic effectiveness are based, *in the final analysis,* on the type, degree and number of conscious or unconscious central consistencies and inconsistencies between the actual-self and the vocational attitudes and/or values (proposition 4 of the theory).

C. FORMULATION OF THE HYPOTHESES

To sum up, we consider three groups of elements, mutually distinct but dynamically inseparable:

1) The conscious force (motivation) which influences entry into religious life, represented by the vocational *values* and, to a lesser extent, by the *attitudes* of the self-ideal-in-situation.

---

20 Dittes, 1962, 1965.

2) Other forces, conscious and unconscious, which can
eventually act on the decision to enter; they arise from the *self-
conceptions* expressed by the consistencies, inconsistencies and/or
vocational conflicts between *attitudes* and *needs* (which may be
on the same or different content variables).

3) The *unrealistic expectations* the individual has on the
level of his ideals (SI-II) with regard to his future vocational
roles. This unrealistic SI-II is, in the final analysis, the result
of the imbalance produced by the *central consistencies and
inconsistencies* between needs and their corresponding attitudes.
This same unrealistic SI-II can influence perseverance and
apostolic effectiveness in so far as it influences the capacity to
internalize vocational values and attitudes. The elements considered in 1) and 2) allow an 'assessment of',[21] a study of the
psychodynamics of entrance which helps above all to 'understand'
the mechanism of the entering process. The elements in 3)
allow rather an 'assessment for' (according to the terminology of
these same authors), that is, a study of the psychodynamics of
entrance which seeks above all to 'predict' the influence of these
dynamics on perseverance and apostolic effectiveness. Chart 8
schematizes this idea.

CHART 8

**THREE SETS OF ELEMENTS WHICH INFLUENCE
ENTRANCE, PERSEVERANCE AND EFFECTIVENESS**

Assessment 'of' entrance	1) SI-II of conscious values and attitudes 2) SI-II of attitudes *with* homonymous and/or heteronymous needs (self-conceptions)
Assessment 'for' perseverance and effectiveness	3) SI-II versus central self-conceptions, i.e. in-consistencies and consistencies (pre-dictable internalizing capacity)

The results analyzed in Chapters 5,6,7 and 8 substantiate the
foregoing considerations.

We will now formulate six research hypotheses regarding

---

21 Prelinger and Zimet, 1964; Wiggins, 1973.

perseverance or non-perseverance in vocation, in relation to the psychodynamics of entrance.

1) The *values* and *attitudes* which are vocationally important predispose the individual to leave his vocation *when they are only moderately* present. When they are strongly present, they do not necessarily predispose him towards perseverance.

2) The predictable internalizing capacity (PIC) proper to each entering vocationer tends to be lower in the future 'dropouts' (DO) than in the future 'non drop-outs' (NDO).

3) This difference between the DO and NDO is found more in the vulnerable aspect than in the germinative aspect of the SI-II. This third hypothesis can be further confirmed by comparing the two aspects (germinative and vulnerable) as to frequencies of their elements (inconsistencies, consistencies, etc.), in differentiating the DO/NDO.

4) The predictable internalizing capacity (PIC) lower in the DO than the NDO, is attributable to certain *structural configurations of self-conceptions* which are, in order of decreasing importance: central inconsistencies of dissonant variables, central consistencies of dissonant variables, central inconsistencies of neutral variables, central consistencies of neutral variables, conflicts of dissonant variables and conflicts of neutral variables. This fourth hypothesis can be further confirmed when the frequencies of the dissonant variables are compared with the frequencies of the neutral variables.

5) For the process of entrance into religious life, motivation is based mainly on values and to a lesser degree on attitudes important for vocation; for the process of leaving, motivation is based mainly on the predictable internalizing capacity related to the structural self-conceptions.

6) The subjects who persevere for a shorter time in religious life show vocational values and attitudes lower than those who persevere longer. This hypothesis should be valid at least for vocational attitudes.

Before giving the results of our research a few further remarks are in order. Our hypotheses, in so far as they are based on the predictable capacity for internalizing vocational values and attitudes, can also be applied to perseverance and growth in vocation. Nevertheless, there is an important difference between perseverance and growth in vocation. A person may persevere in religious life despite a poor internalizing capacity. As we have seen in Chapters 6 and 7, entering and persevering in religious life can *also* be, for some people, a defence against conflictual needs or a gratification of other needs. Notwithstanding that, our hypotheses sustain the view that, in general, the dropouts have an internalizing capacity inferior to that of the non drop-outs.

Our data do not *directly* touch the area of freedom or of spiritual dynamism. We are speaking only of affective *tendencies* which, nevertheless, can have a considerable influence on a person's predisposition towards perseverance and apostolic effectiveness.

D. OBSERVATIONS, RESULTS AND DISCUSSION

With regard to predicting perseverance, the following are some results and observations which will confirm whether or not our structural method provides in itself factors for evaluating the predictable internalizing capacity of our subjects.

1. *Observations*

The subjects studied in this Chapter consist of 107 male religious, 136 female religious and 45 seminarians, (we studied the entire groups). Alongside this vocational group (total number of 288 subjects) we analyzed control groups composed of laity beginning college; 124 male and 126 female students who represented 70% of the individuals selected at random and invited to participate in the project.

We thus took into consideration a total population of 538 subjects from the Mid-West, the East and the West of the United States, and we administered to them a series of tests at the time of entrance into their respective institutions (1965-1966-1967).

To study *values* we used the general goals of life inventory (GGLI). Basing ourselves on the content of the values and on the results obtained in Chapter 6, and after making analyses of variance and/or of descriminant functions, we decided to consider seven values of the GGLI dissonant with regard to vocation; they are the values which correspond to the letters C, K, L, M, N, O and P of Appendix A-2. The other values of the inventory are considered as vocationally neutral, that is, as less useful in

127

differentiating those individuals who choose religious vocation from those who do not.[22]

The twelve *attitudes* we are studying in this Chapter are all taken from the modified activities index (MAI). We chose attitudes whose contents are particularly important for religious vocation. These attitudes are: abasement, adaptability (or defendence), aggression, chastity (as related to sexual needs), exhibition, harm avoidance, succorance, mortification, piety, obedience, poverty, responsibility. The first seven variables correspond to the seven homonymous variables, dissonant with regard to vocation, which we use for the evaluation of the predictable internalizing capacity (PIC). The other attitudes are taken from the 'religious scales' of the MAI.[23]

The fourteen *variables (needs-attitudes)* used to evaluate the predictable internalizing capacity (PIC) are described in Appendix A-1.[24] Their influence is particularly noticeable when the needs-attitudes act as central consistencies or inconsistencies.[25]

Because of the considerable time required to analyze the projective tests (TAT and Rotter), we had to select samples at random from our vocational and lay groups. These samples consisted of 96 male religious, 95 female religious and 40 seminarians. We had evaluated the index of vocational maturity of all these subjects (cf. Chapter 7). We also selected a sample of 102 laymen, 52 male and 50 female students. All these samples formed a total of 333 subjects.

Since 95% of the seminarians had already left the seminary after four years of formation, we divided them into 'drop-outs' (DO) and 'non-drop-outs' (NDO) according to their situation

---

[22] In calculating the statistical significance, we have used a Wilcoxon test, one-tailed for the dissonant variables and two-tailed for the neutral variables (Siegel, 1956; Wallis and Roberts, 1956).

[23] Cf. Appendix A-1.

[24] The reader can see for himself to what degree these 'needs', defined by Murray (1938) and subsequently used in most of the best available tests, may have a profound effect, positive or negative, on the 'fruits of the Spirit' of which St Paul speaks: 'love, joy, peace, patience, kindness, goodness, faithfulness, gentleness, self-control' (Gal 5:22,23).

[25] The different statistical procedures and the different techniques used in order to 'combine' these data (especially the needs and attitudes) with the aim of obtaining the index called the 'predictable internalizing capacity' are explained in detail in Chapters 3 and 9 of Rulla, Ridick, Imoda, 1976.

after *two* years of formation. At this stage, 21 (52.5%) of the 40 subjects had left. Among the religious, 47% of the males and 59% of the females had left after four years and 59% and 81% respectively had left after 6-8 years. We therefore evaluated 155 DO and 76 NDO who formed the sample, *chosen at random,* from 193 DO and 95 NDO. As we have already noted, all these individuals had entered the formation centers in the summers of 1965, 1966 and 1967. Verification with regard to their perseverance was made in the summer of 1973.

2. Results

The six hypotheses previously formulated were confirmed by the results:

1) First of all, the data already analyzed suggest that the values and, to a lesser extent, the attitudes which we had chosen for these analyses play an important role in the initial *conscious* decision to *enter* the seminary or novitiate. Furthermore, these values and attitudes differentiate reasonably well the religious and the seminarians from the laymen.[26]

The *values* and, to a lesser extent, the *attitudes* predispose the individual to leave his vocation when they are only moderately present. But when the values are strongly present, they do not necessarily predispose him to persevere; this is true, at least in part, for the attitudes too. The seminarians show how true is the first affirmation: 95% had left after four years. Now these seminarians presented, even on the level of conscious declarations, a level of vocational values and attitudes inferior to that of the religious.[27] The statistics referring to the religious, male and female, confirm the second affirmation: despite the very high vocational ideals, evaluated at the time of entrance, 59% and 81% of them respectively had left religious life after 6 or 8 years. Our data do not confirm the opinion that the drop-outs, *at the time of entrance,* had higher values; our data indicate rather the opposite tendency, at least for the male religious.

2) All these results suggest that factors, other than the

---

26 Cf. chart 10 and Chapter 6.
27 Cf. Chapter 6.

values and attitudes of the ideal-self (SI-II) consciously proclaimed at the time of entrance, may exercise an influence not
only on entrance but also on perseverance and growth in vocation. Chapters 5, 6 and 7 have already indicated the existence
of a large number of *subconscious forces* in our subjects, thus
showing that the values and attitudes of the SI-II often serve a
utilitarian or defensive function of the ego. Chapter 8 has
strongly suggested that these subconscious conflictual forces tend
to persist after entrance. When these subconscious forces are
taken into consideration in evaluating each individual through
their predictable internalizing capacity, the results obtained
confirm the persistence of these subconscious forces, by indicating
that they do have an influence on perseverance in vocation.

The most pertinent results in this regard are those which
refer to the second hypothesis. This hypothesis states that the
predictable internalizing capacity (PIC) existing in *every*
religious at the beginning, tends to be lower in the future drop-
outs (DO) than in the non-drop-outs (NDO).

The reader is referred to chart 9 and Table II, in Appendix

CHART 9

RESULTS RELEVANT TO THE PREDICTABLE INTERNALIZING
CAPACITY CHARACTERIZING FUTURE DO AND NDO
(WILCOXON TEST)

Institutions	DO% after 4 yrs.	6-8 yrs.	vs. Controls	DO vs. NDO	vs. Males DO vs. DO	NDO vs. NDO
Seminarians	95%	—	ns	ns	ns	.05 (Sems<)*
Female Religious	59%	81%	ns (.08)	.01 (DO < NDO)*	—	—
Male Religious	47%	59%	ns	.05 (DO < NDO)*	—	—

* < = lower in predictable internalizing capacity.

B, where the data important for the second hypothesis are
presented.

Since the rate of leaving varies according to the vocational
groups, a variation is also to be expected in the difference
between the predictable internalizing capacity of the DO and
NDO. More exactly, one does not expect a significant difference
between seminarian DO and NDO, since 95% left during a
period of four years, but one does expect to find a significant
difference between DO and NDO among the male and female
religious where the rates of leaving were lower (59% and
81%). In fact, the tests for significance show no difference
between seminarian DO and NDO, but the male and female
religious DO have a PIC lower than that of the NDO (level
of significance: .01 for females, .05 for males).

These results receive further confirmation from a comparison of the DO and NDO in the seminarians, and the DO and
NDO in the male religious. Remember that 52.5% of the
seminarians had left after two years and 95% after four years,
whilst 59% of the male religious had left after 6-8 years of
formation. One would expect to find no difference between
seminarian DO and religious DO, but a significant difference
between the NDO of seminarians and male religious:
the seminarian NDO ought to have a lower PIC than the religious since those who were still NDO after 2 years of formation
had nearly all left after 4 years. This is what the results indicate:
no significant difference between the DO and a significant
difference between the NDO, the lowest mean being that of the
seminarians (Wilcoxon's two-tail test, p = .05).

Finally, would one expect a difference in the predictable
internalizing capacity (PIC) between the vocational groups and
the groups of laymen? It seems not, since these are not two
completely different callings nor 'privileged states'; all are equally
called to bear witness to the Kingdom through varied professions
and states of life. In fact, our results indicate no significant
difference between the vocational groups and the lay control
groups. Although the female religious showed a *tendency*
towards a lower capacity for internalization when compared with
female lay girls, a further analysis indicated, however, that this
trend is related to the DO religious. The NDO are not significantly different from the lay controls, whereas the DO have a
lower predictable internalizing capacity (PIC). Remember that

here we are not speaking of personal sanctity but only of a *disposition* towards growth in vocation as measured by limited instruments.

In summary, hypothesis 2 is confirmed, since the psychodynamics of the future DO always indicate a predictable internalizing capacity (PIC) lower than that of the future NDO.

3) The results confirm hypotheses 3 and 4. They indicate that the inconsistencies for the vocationally dissonant variables are the most important in predicting perseverance. In our samples, what are the contents of these inconsistencies which seem to be most important? Table II in Appendix B indicates that the male religious DO present the greatest inconsistencies, especially for exhibition, succorance and abasement compared with the NDO. The same table indicates that for the female religious the variables are exhibition, aggression and succorance.

Of particular interest are the results which refer to the frequencies and percentages of the inconsistencies, conflicts and consistencies which contribute to the differentiation of the DO from the NDO. They indicate how many subjects present consistencies, conflicts and inconsistencies for specific contents, such as abasement, achievement, etc. when the NDO are compared with the DO. The results show that for this differentiation (DO-NDO), the vulnerable aspect of the self-ideal-in-situation (SI-II) is more important than the germinative aspect. That is, the central inconsistencies are more important than the central consistencies. Furthermore, DO and NDO tend to be differentiated less by the vocationally neutral variables than by the vocationally dissonant ones.

4) Up to now we have progressively described *two groups of forces* which may influence both the entering into and the leaving of religious life. The first consists of *values* and, to a lesser degree, attitudes. The second consists of the *balance* or *imbalance* of the *consistencies* or *inconsistencies* which exist between needs and attitudes and/or values. Which of these two groups seems to predominate in the process of entering and leaving vocation?

An analysis of the individual psychodynamics *at the time of entrance* (the data of which were discussed in hypothesis 5), indicates that the first group is of greater importance *for entering*: the values and attitudes have a greater motivating force than the balance/imbalance between central consistencies and inconsistencies expressed through the index of vocational maturity. For

132

leaving, the opposite is true; the values and attitudes do not help
to differentiate the drop-out from the non-drop-outs. But, the
predictable internalizing capacity, calculated from the psychodynamics at the time of entrance and expressing the balance/
imbalance of the consistencies/inconsistencies, *is* useful in the
differentiation of the DO from the NDO. A juxtaposition of
charts 10 and 11 helps to visualize the difference between the
two processes; for entering (chart 10), the statistically significant

CHART 10

ENTRANCE INTO VOCATION:

Influence of Values (GGLI) and of Vocationally
Relevant Attitudes (MAI) vs.
Influence of Balance/Imbalance of Consistencies/Inconsistencies
as expressed by the index of vocational maturity (IVM)

Institutions	*Value* ANOVA* and Wilcoxon	*Attitudes* ANOVA	Wilcoxon	Balance/Imbalance of Consistencies/ Inconsistencies in the IVM
Seminarians vs. Lay	Sema > Lay**			
Female Religious vs. Lay	Rel. > Lay**	Rel. > Lay (4 vs. 2)***		
Male Religious vs. Lay	Rel. > Lay**	Rel. > Lay (7 vs. 2)		

N.B. Blank spaces indicate no statistically significant differences.
     > = greater than.
     * ANOVA = Analysis of Variance.
     ** Analysis of Variance for 21 values and Wilcoxon for 7 dissonant
     values of the GGLI.

differences are found mainly on the left of the chart, in the area
of values, whilst for leaving (chart 11), the statistically significant
differences are found mainly on the right of the chart, in the
area of consistencies-inconsistencies represented here by the
predictable internalizing capacity.

133

CHART 11

LEAVING VOCATION:

Influences of Values and Vocationally Relevant Attitudes vs.
Influence of Central Consistencies (CC) and Central Dissonant
Inconsistencies (CDI); and of the
predictable internalizing capacity (PIC)

Institutions	Values	Attitudes	PIC as related to: CC	CDI	PIC	% DO after 4 yrs.	% DO after 6-8 yrs.
Seminarians DO vs. NDO					.05 NDO Sems $<$ NDO Male Rel.*	95%	81%
Female Religious DO vs. NDO			.01 DO $<$ NDO	.04 DO $<$ NDO	.01 DO $<$ NDO	59%	
Male Religious DO vs. NDO	.01 DO $>$ NDO for dissonant BUT DO $<$ Controls (.05) NDO $<$ Controls (.04)	.02 DO $<$ NDO for consonant BUT DO $>$ Controls (.06) NDO $>$ Controls (.04)	.01 DO $<$ NDO	.04 DO $<$ NDO	.05 DO $<$ NDO	47%	59%

N.B. Blank spaces indicate no statistically significant differences.
$\vee$ = less than.
$\wedge$ = greater than.

These observations are further confirmed when the different
groups are compared with regard to the frequencies of the structural configurations of self-conceptions (inconsistencies, consistencies, etc.). More precisely, comparing the contribution of
these configurations to the process of entering with their contribution to the process of leaving, one can easily see that the
vocationally neutral variables of the germinative self-ideal-in-
situation (SI-II), expressed by the consistencies etc., are significantly more useful for differentiating groups at the time of
entrance than for differentiating DO-NDO (see the lower right
part of chart 12). On the contrary, the vocationally dissonant
variables of the vulnerable SI-II, expressed by the inconsistencies,
etc., exercise an influence psychodynamically more important
with regard to perseverance than with regard to entering (see the
upper left part of chart 12).

CHART 12

SUMMARY OF PERCENTAGES (AND FREQUENCIES)
OF DISSONANT AND NEUTRAL VARIABLES
DIFFERENTIATING GROUPS
AT ENTRANCE AND FOR DROPPING OUT

	Vulnerable SI-II		Germinative SI-II	
Dissonant Variables	At Entrance* 34%	(22)	At Entrance 12.5%	(8)
	Dropping out** 48%	(36)	Dropping Out 11%	(8)
Neutral Variables	At Entrance 28%	(18)	At Entrance 25%	(16)
	Dropping Out 29%	(22)	Dropping Out 12%	(9)

  * Total N of Variables = 64
** Total N of Variables = 75

5) At the time of entrance, the future DO had a predic-
able internalizing capacity (PIC) lower than that of the future
NDO. However, not all the DO left at the same time; some
left earlier, others later. At the outset, there was no difference

135

between them on the level of values and attitudes.

It is to be expected that the values and attitudes of those who leave first become progressively different from the values and attitudes of those who leave later. The results which concern hypothesis 8 and which compare the first testing with the second, done two years after entrance, do in fact indicate that the early drop-outs (those who left after 2 years of religious life) had vocational values and attitudes lower than those of the later drop-outs (those who left after 4 years). This is represented in chart 13. These results are more obvious with regard to attitudes, as was predictable, in so far as they constitute a weaker motivation — more easily modifiable — than values.

Chronologically, it seems therefore that at the time of entrance the DO and NDO may be differentiated solely by the predictable internalizing capacity (PIC), the most important factor of which consists of the *subconscious* inconsistencies of dissonant variables. But as time goes by, DO and NDO may *also* be distinguished by vocational *attitudes*; and finally, the values too become different. Values and attitudes are therefore important for leaving vocation too.

Obviously, these results need to be confirmed by further researches.

What are the vocational values and attitudes which, in the long run, are seen to be most threatened by an insufficient PIC? The reply to this question obviously turns to the *contents* rather than the *structure* of personality.

Values (GGLI, Appendix A-2). We found in our sample that for *male religious* those who left earlier, i.e. after two years, showed less 'self-discipline' and a greater tendency to 'live for the pleasure of the moment' than those who left later. For *female religious*, those who left earlier, i.e., after two years, showed less 'self-discipline' and a greater tendency 'to promote the most deep and lasting pleasures for the greatest number of people' than those who left later.

Attitudes (MAI, Appendix A-1). For *male religious,* those who left first declared a lower concern for 'obedience', 'chastity'

136

and 'poverty' than the others. For *female religious,* those who left first declared a lower concern for 'obedience', 'adaptability' and 'piety' than the others.

6) Perhaps the most interesting results of our inquiry are concerned with the establishment and the self-perpetuation of a vicious circle in the psychodynamics of numerous subjects. In fact, to the degree to which the vulnerable or conflictual aspect of the SI-II predominates over the germinative aspect, so the individual creates and maintains unrealistic expectations with regard to his future vocational roles. In turn, with a feedback effect these unrealistic ideals or role expectations influence the capacity to internalize values and attitudes, and so they further weaken the balance between the vulnerable and germinative aspects of the SI-II. In this way, the vicious circle gradually undermines the basis for future vocational commitment. It seems that this circle originates mainly from unconscious central inconsistencies with regard to vocationally dissonant variables such as aggression, exhibition, etc. These very important structural elements also contribute to the self-perpetuation of the

CHART 13

EARLY vs LATE DROPPING OUT:
THE DIRECTION AND SIGNIFICANCE OF THE DIFFERENCES IN
ATTITUDES AND VALUES OF MALE AND FEMALE
RELIGIOUS AS MEASURED BY THE FIRST
AND THE SECOND TESTINGS (Wilcoxon Test)

	Male (EDO* : N = 25) (LDO** : N = 9)			*Female* (EDO : N = 32) (LDO : N = 17)		
	Values	Attitudes	Dissonant Values Relevant Attitudes	Values	Attitudes	Dissonant Values Relevant Attitudes
First Testing	NS ***	NS	NS	NS	NS	NS
Second Testing	NS	EDO < LDO Z = 2.63 P < .004	EDO < LDO Z = 2.76 P < .003	NS	EDO < LDO Z = 1.69 P < .05	EDO < LDO Z = 1.97 P < .02

* EDO = Early Drop-outs.
** LDO = Late Drop-outs.
*** NS = No significant difference between early and late Drop-outs.

vicious circle within the individual. When the psychodynamic of a subject is characterized by unconscious inconsistencies, it seems he would continue to react to the central inconsistencies by adopting utilitarian and defensive attitudes which, in their turn, maintain the unrealistic hopes and ideas about vocational roles.[28]

Chart 8 and the comments which accompany it explain the nature of the vicious circle. Basically, the analysis of individual psychodynamics indicates that the future drop-outs have a predictable internalizing capacity (PIC) always lower than the non-drop-outs (see hypothesis 2). The results of the discussion of hypothesis 3 indicate that this difference between DO and NDO is found more in the vulnerable than in the germinative aspect of the SI-II. Furthermore, this difference is connected particularly to unconscious central inconsistencies in the vocationally dissonant variables (hypothesis 4).

3. Discussion and new problems

1) Why does a lower predictable capacity for internalizing vocational values and attitudes lead to departure from the religious life? First of all, this fact is obvious: the basis for vocational commitment is gradually undermined when values and attitudes cannot be internalized.

The analysis of our observations demonstrate more precisely that a lower PIC implies greater contradictions between the *ideals* or expectations an individual has with regard to his role, and his *self-conceptions*[29] (see chart 8). When an individual perceives in some way a discrepancy between his self-conceptions and his expectations about his role, he becomes discontented *with himself*. This dissatisfaction will be even greater when his self-conceptions are central, that is, particularly important for his

---

[28] Consult chart 16.
[29] Remember that a 'self-conception' is defined as a 'consistency or inconsistency between the *ideal*-self, with regard to an attitude, and the corresponding *actual*-self, including the *subconscious* part.'

own self-esteem. Note that an individual may respond to an inconsistency without his realising it; he may be ignorant of its existence or of the tension resulting from it, or even of the action taken to resolve the inconsistency.[30] When the individual in some way perceives a discrepancy, he may modify his attitudes or distort his perception of the reference group or institution. Brock and Blackwood[31] have shown that the tendency to choose the second alternative is very strong. We add that it will be even stronger when the individual has to protect his own central self-conceptions. Consequently, he will feel himself always more isolated and alienated from the reference group or from the religious community. It is in this way that one can understand, at least partially, the loneliness observed by Greeley[32] among American priests and considered to be an important factor in leaving the priesthood. Potvin and Suziedelis[33] make analogous observations with regard to American seminarians. The results of their research indicate that 'withdrawal is more strongly related to subjective views of the seminary and the priesthood than it is to objective factors such as seminary quality'.

2) The results presented in point 4 of p. 132 indicate that some tenets of general social psychology are also applicable to subjects who enter the religious life or priesthood: a) values may be less central, less influential than self-conceptions upon one's motivation;[34] b) it is easier to change behavior than to change attitudes which matter.[35] The gradual process of leaving vocation may be seen in the light of these tenets and findings. In the same framework, one can understand the trend of the vulnerable SI-II to persist after entrance[36] as well as its debilitating influence on vocational effectiveness.

3) The results presented throughout this book, particularly

---

[30] Tannenbaum, 1967, 1968; Brock, 1968; McGuire, 1960; Cohen, Greenbaum and Mansson, 1963, etc.
[31] Brock and Blackwood, 1962; Brock, 1965.
[32] Greeley, 1972 and NORC, 1971.
[33] Potvin and Suziedelis, 1969, p. 126.
[34] Cf. Rokeach, 1973, and other authors quoted by him.
[35] Freedman, Carlsmith and Sears, 1974, review the literature on this point.
[36] Chapter 8.

in charts 10 and 11, seem to offer good support for the basic elements of the five 'propositions' of the theory of vocation put forward in this book. The conscious self-ideal-in-situation (SI-II) of values and, to a lesser degree, of attitudes is the psychological force which disposes an individual to enter religious life (propositions I, II and III). This SI-II will remain the psychological pivot of the future life in vocation provided that it is not to a great degree the expression of central unconscious inconsistencies between needs and vocational attitudes and/or values. If these inconsistencies prevail over the central consistencies, then vocational perseverance and effectiveness may be affected (proposition IV). Initially, there is a lowering of vocational attitudes, which may undermine basic vocational values (proposition V).

4) The findings of this book seem to indicate clearly that what many authors and researchers in the field of social psychology in general, and of depth psychology in particular, have repeatedly stated and proven, is also valid for religious and seminarians: namely, that self-reports alone are an unreliable means of understanding a person's motivation. Our data show that the values and attitudes consciously proclaimed at the time of entrance into religious life are quite at variance with the psychodynamics indicated by the index of vocational maturity.[37] Furthermore, these values and attitudes are far from corresponding to the predictable internalizing capacity and to the vocational perseverance of the entering vocationers.[38]

5) Our investigation studied entering vocationers who had not yet been exposed to the prolonged and direct influence of the vocational institution. Thus the more or less unrealistic role expectations of the SI-II, found among many of these vocationers, were not the result of contact with the institution but rather, elaborations of the individuals. They entered with unrealistic expectations which undermined their capacity to internalize vocational values and attitudes and led many of them to leave.

Whilst these individual dispositions cannot be attributed to

---

[37] Cf. chart 10.
[38] Cf. chart 11.

the vocational institution, the latter does have the responsibility
of helping vocationers develop their internalizing capacity during
their years of formation. After all, this internalizing capacity
may affect not only perseverance but also vocational effectiveness.
Unfortunately, it does not seem that vocational institutions take
into serious consideration what our data suggest: that centrally
inconsistent and subconscious self-conceptions are individual
dispositions which may exert an influence on perseverance and
effectiveness greater than that of the conscious values and
attitudes. Institutional reforms which do not help the vocationers to overcome these debilitating subconscious self-percep-
tions overlook a vital aspect of the formation problem.

6) Our results should not be interpreted in the sense that
all the people who drop out are more psychologically inconsistent than people who do not drop out.

Actually the opposite may be true: psychologically consistent people do not necessarily always stay in. Here two
possibilities may be considered: 1) some DO may be individuals
who entered vocation without really knowing what it entailed.
Their decision to enter, however, was not prompted by the conflictual wishful thinking or by the projections on the institution
of the inconsistent people, but rather by a lack of objective
knowledge. By acquiring the latter, they may discover that they
are not called to that type of life. 2) *Some* people may have
chosen the religious life whilst still inconsistent and because of
the conflictual needs present in them. Later on, they worked
out their subconscious conflicts and became aware of their not
really having a vocation; their departure was a mature, objective
decision.

The psychological improvement of these people can be the
result either of some professional help through psychotherapy or of
the solution of their subconscious conflict, which is *possible* if such
conflicts are preconscious rather than unconscious. In fact, the self-
analysis which takes place through a serious, repeated examination
of conscience or meditation *may* lead to the described psychological
improvement. Also, when the conflicts are starting to become conscious, the positive influence of a favorable environment can be
quite helpful. However, experience teaches that usually such an

141

improvement of *preconscious* conflicts is a rather slow process which takes many years of trial and error that do not favor full vocational effectiveness and that could be avoided if properly handled.[39]

Anyway, the present findings indicate greater inconsistencies among drop-outs than among non-drop-outs at the time of entering. In fact, the difference between these two groups is shown mainly in the vulnerable part of their psychodynamics, and here drop-outs show more inconsistencies than non-drop-outs. Furthermore, the convergent results of Chapter 8 point to the strong tendency these initial inconsistencies have to persist. Finally, hypothesis 6 of the last Chapter shows a change in attitudes and in vocationally dissonant values which occurs more rapidly in early than in late drop-outs.

In the light of the results, but bearing in mind the qualifications made at the beginning of this Chapter, we can conclude that the right question to be asked concerning the drop-outs is not why they leave, but rather what are the expectations, especially the subconscious ones, which influence their decision to enter. The *entire* psychodynamics of the person on entrance *may* affect very much his decision to leave.

---

[39] Rulla, 1971, p.158.

PART   THREE

EPILOGUE

CHAPTER 10

IMPLICATIONS OF THE FINDINGS

The theory formulated in Part One of this book is not bound in a special way to any particular school of psychology; rather, it tries to select what seems best from various psychological and psychosocial models. Consequently, the experimental results of Part Two are interpreted according to an eclectic frame of reference, which aims at a better understanding of the processes related to religious experience and vocation.

The present Part Three intends to offer some general considerations. They do not in every instance follow inevitably from our research results; they are not, however, inconsistent with these results. The convergence of the findings presented in Part Two, as well as the structural approach adopted in the research,[1] encourage us to suggest some generalizations, hoping that they are not merely impressionistic, but rather that they emerge from the interplay among different sets of findings.

Some of the issues considered here were already partially discussed elsewhere;[2] reference to this source will be made when necessary. Other issues are more related to the findings in the present book. Needless to say, we do not intend to offer an exhaustive, comprehensive discussion of these problems. Our aim is very limited: to present some questions as springboards rather than to offer solutions.

A. INTERNALIZING VOCATIONAL MOTIVATION: INCONSISTENCIES OR PSYCHOPATHOLOGY?

The theory and the findings suggest that personalities of

---

[1] Cf. Chapter 2.
[2] Rulla, 1971.

vocationers should be considered according to vocational psychodynamics which are not necessarily related to the psychopathological dynamics of psychiatric classification.

Any psychosocial conceptualization about social status requires that its core be explicitly identified. This is true also for priestly or religious vocation. Now, with regard to religious vocation, *one* of the aspects of its core is the capacity which each vocationer has to internalize religious values and attitudes.[3]

The theory and the findings discussed in this book allow one to consider the entering vocationers according to the perspective of a continuum which presents 14 possible patterns or types, when the intrapsychic dynamics of the individuals are considered, and 56 possible types when intra- and inter- personal dynamics are assessed together.

The 14 intrapsychic types present two characteristics:

a) They are based on a typology of variables (e.g. abasement, aggression, etc.) rather than of persons. In fact, they focus upon the central *vocational* consistencies and inconsistencies of each individual. Note that the changing influence of the environment is also taken into consideration in this intrapsychic perspective because the consistencies/inconsistencies are assessed also according to the perception each individual has of his environment.

b) This perspective of consistencies and/or inconsistencies salient in each individual points to the interaction among the various parts of his self rather than to the behaviors according to which he may be described. It is therefore a perspective which stresses behavior as the end result of *processes,* of interactions among systems of the self, rather than behavior as a set of description patterns.

There follow several practical implications. First of all, the presented *psychodynamic* typology is not a typology of traits or of symptoms. In fact, it cuts across the normal or less normal traits as well as across the symptoms of the heterogeneous behaviors described by psychiatric psychopathology. This does not exclude the possibility that in *some* cases the inconsistent vocational psychodynamics may have their roots in the psychopathology of underlying neuroses, personality disorders, borderline cases, etc. However, people may be vocationally inconsistent because of psychodynamics which do not depend on or do not

---

[3] Cf. Chapters 7 and 9.

obviously appear as psychiatric psychopathology. Consequently, vocationers can be seen according to a vocational perspective which is different from the one of psychopathology. Actually, they should *also* be seen according to this different psychosocial perspective because it touches a core aspect of vocation: the capacity to internalize religious values and attitudes, at least the five values proper to any religious experience and the 14 attitudes/ needs widely accepted by scholars as significantly, even though not exhaustively, representing human motivation (cf. Chapter 1).

Another set of practical implications can be stressed. A particular kind of external behavior in a vocationer does not necessarily stem from a corresponding kind of underlying psychodynamic. In other words, similar external behaviors may be motivated by different psychodynamics and, vice versa, different external behaviors can be motivated by similar psychodynamics. As has been discussed elsewhere,[4] these possibilities make it difficult for superiors to assess the suitability of their subjects for religious vocation, the possibility of helping and improving them, the appropriateness of allowing the stress of specific apostolic activities, etc. More will be said later on with regard to this point.

The *possible* separation of vocational psychodynamics from psychopathology should be distinguished from another relevant issue: the relationship between spiritual growth and psychological growth. If we consider entrance, perseverance and growth in religious vocation as a socialization process, the issue to be discussed now is a common topic in the depth psychology literature. It suffices to mention Hartmann's and Erikson's ego-psychology formulations concerning the links between developmental stages and processes of social adaptation.

B. SPIRITUAL AND PSYCHOLOGICAL GROWTH: THEIR INTER-DEPENDENCE AND CONVERGENCE

The literature concerning this issue has increased notably in recent years. Many valuable contributions could be quoted, but few have called attention to the relevance of subconscious motiva-

---

[4] Rulla, 1971, pp. 152-160.

tion and perhaps none has offered any research support.

When speaking of spiritual growth or sanctification, one should distinguish it from the presentation of the means of sanctification. The latter may be called apostolic effectiveness and described as the visible manifestation and/or the social communication of the values of Christ. In turn, apostolic effectiveness should be distinguished from apostolic efficiency. Efficiency focuses upon means, effectiveness is concerned with the ends, i.e. the terminal values of union with God and imitation of Christ. Thus, for instance, to be an 'efficient' teacher or administrator does not necessarily mean to be 'effective' as a religious or as a priest. Of course, this does not exclude the fact that efficiency has its importance as a means to foster the desired effectiveness.

Another distinction is pertinent here: the one between subjective and objective holiness or spiritual growth. Subjective holiness is related to the use a person makes of the possibilities, of all the supernatural and spiritual 'talents' God has given to him personally. Objective holiness depends upon the availability to the action of God which a person has *de facto*.

What influence may the subconscious factors relevant to psychological growth have upon apostolic effectiveness, upon subjective and objective holiness? The elements in these interdependencies are extremely complex and we can bring in here only a few glimpses into what is involved.

First of all, it can be stated that subjective holiness does not depend on one's psychological growth or degree of developmental maturity. Holiness, that is, the presence of sanctifying grace and infused virtues in their cooperation with human will, does not depend 'intrinsically' on the psychological dispositions of the individual, provided that his freedom is not completely eliminated; in fact, God alone can sanctify souls who do not refuse his fully gratuitous action. Therefore, provided a minimum of freedom is present in the individual, the sanctifying action of God may grow by means of the sacraments and acts of supernatural virtues, regardless of the psychosocial elements influencing the person.

Perfection, in its essence, has no relationship with measurable quantity, and its possibility of growth in each individual is primarily related to the utilization of the possibilities which are given to each individual person. Therefore, it is related neither

148

primarily nor comparatively to the possibilities and realizations of someone else.[5]

Whilst the subconscious psychosocial elements of the developmental or affective maturity do not exert an influence on subjective holiness because they do not touch the sanctifying action of God or the *conscious* and *free correspondence* of man to this action, they do affect both the objective holiness and the apostolic effectiveness; the first indirectly or extrinsically, the second directly or intrinsically.

In fact, these subconscious psychosocial elements may affect the *subconscious* and *unfree availability* of the person to the action of God and thus, within the limits of this influence, they condition objective holiness. In other words, given an equal supernatural action of grace, these elements may limit the margin of freedom within which the person may correspond to God's action. God may overcome these subconscious limitations of the person, but this 'healing' influence of God does not seem to be a common, frequent event; in fact, it seems to be more the exception than the rule.

Two elements seem to confirm this conclusion. First of all, the findings (especially in Chapters 7, 8 and 9) indicate the interdependence between developmental maturity and vocational maturity. They indicate the relationship of the vocational maturity directly, and indirectly of the developmental maturity, with the predictable capacity of the individuals to internalize vocational attitudes and values. They show that this capacity is influenced more by unconscious than by conscious or preconscious factors and that the subconscious factors tend to persist, etc. All these results suggest that God respects the freedom of man and his personality.

Secondly, a logical argument consists of the following. As Einstein said: God is not capricious; so it is difficult to believe that God does not *usually* follow the natural psychodynamic laws which he himself has made operative in a person.

What we have just said for the interdependence between spiritual and psychological elements with regard to objective holiness is even more true with regard to apostolic effectiveness.

As was discussed at length in the publication of 1971, other things being equal, priests or religious would be more 'effective' if they did not have shortcomings stemming from subconscious

---

[5] Rahner, 1964.

inconsistencies of aggression, dependence, etc. As instruments in the hand of God, they would be more fitting both for the goals for which they work and for the aims of him who uses them.

Again, the findings of the present book are in this line; it is enough to recall the ones concerning the influence of sub-conscious inconsistencies on the predictable capacity to inter-nalize vocational values and attitudes. If a person has serious difficulty in internalizing the self-transcendent values of religious commitment, he will be hampered in his attempts '. . . to free himself from those obstacles which might draw him away from the fervor of charity and the perfection of divine worship'.[6] His basic attitudes tend to follow personal needs rather than self-transcendent ideals. His capacity to objectively listen to and to transmit the word of God, his messages through scripture, liturgy, institutions and the deep meaning of reality will be notably jeopardized. He will have difficulty in transcending himself, in losing himself in the unselfish surrender of love.

These possible negative influences of subconscious psycho-logical elements upon objective holiness and apostolic effective-ness suggest a corollary.

One of the ideals of Ignatian spirituality has been expressed in the formula of Fr Nadal: to be a contemplative in action. Without going into the historical-exegetical interpretation of this formula, one may say that its core message is well expressed by Ignatius' oft-reiterated phrase of 'finding God in all things' as well as by his other statement '. . . loving God in all creatures and all of them in him, in conformity with his holy and divine will'.[7]

As we have just seen, it will be rather difficult for a person with a poor capacity for internalizing self-transcendent ideals, to be a contemplative in action according to these Ignatian perspec-tives. Interestingly enough, the Ignatian statement 'loving God in all creatures and all of them in him' is the conclusion of number 288 of the 'Constitutions' in which Ignatius presents in his words a distinction suggested by contemporary social psycho-logy; we have formulated this distinction in terms of compliance, internalizing or non-internalizing identification and internalization

---

6   Vatican Council II, *Lumen Gentium*, no. 44.
7   The Constitutions of the Society of Jesus, no. 288; translated by
    G. E. Ganss, 1970.

(cf. introduction to Chapter 7). Let us quote the text of St Ignatius:

'. . . they should always aim at serving and pleasing the Divine Goodness for its own sake and because of the incomparable love and benefits with which God has anticipated us (*internalization*), rather than for fear of punishments or hope of rewards (*compliance*), although they ought to draw help also from them. Further, they should often be exhorted to seek God Our Lord in all things, stripping off from themselves the love of creatures to the extent that this is possible (*internalizing or non-internalizing identification*) in order to turn their love upon the Creator of them, by loving Him in all creatures and all of them in Him, in conformity with His holy and Divine will' (*internalization*).

These statements call to mind the analogous ones which C. S. Lewis[8] wrote about what God had taught him during his conversion: 'The commands were inexorable, but they were backed by no "sanctions". God was to be obeyed simply because he was God. Long since, through the gods of Asgard, and later through the notion of the Absolute, he had taught me how a thing can be reversed not for what it can do to us but for what it is in itself.'

Spiritual growth is not dichotomous, but continuous with psychological growth; they are convergent processes strictly interdependent.

C. THE 'DISCERNMENT OF SPIRITS': SOME NEW PERSPECTIVES

The two preceding issues have indicated that the vocational intrapsychic dynamics are both different from psychopathology, even though not necessarily so, and the result of two interdependent and convergent sets of forces, spiritual and psychological.

The present third issue intends to bring a limited contribution by furthering the analysis of these forces, considering some of the possible interactions between them. The 'Rules for the Discernment of Spirits' proposed by St Ignatius in the first and second weeks of his *Spiritual Exercises* will be taken as a frame of reference for this analysis. It is assumed that the reader is familiar with the *Spiritual Exercises* of St Ignatius.

---

[8] C. S. Lewis, 1955, p. 185.

God aims at bringing back to himself his creatures, men, in a transforming union. But what are the means God uses to direct human beings to himself? According to Buckley,[9] three different and complex answers have been given historically to this question. Schematically, they may be presented as follows: 1) through preternatural influences of personalities or realities: saints, devils, angels, in the terminology of Ignatius, 'good spirit' and 'evil spirit'; 2) through human processes of intellection or of imagination; 3) through human attractions of affectivity. Seldom does one of these three factors predominate to the total exclusion of the other two. Ignatius in his 'Discernment of Spirits' has offered a unique coordination of all the foregoing three critical factors of religious experience. Note that in the Ignatian scheme, the evil spirit of the first week of the Spiritual Exercises appears to be what it is, evil, whilst in the second week it is disguised as a seeming good.

Two recent contributions have introduced new possible perspectives according to which the Ignatian outline can be interpreted. The first contribution comes from depth psychology. As authors like Beirnaert[10] and Meissner[11] have pointed out, the religious conducts which Ignatius attributed to the influence of the good or evil spirit may be the consequence, at least in part, of unconscious motivations. It is interesting to note that Ignatius himself had already realised that psychological determinants other than the preternatural 'good spirit' could be at work in 'consolation'.[12]

Particularly important is the second contribution, by a theologian,[13] which has the merit of offering a structural approach. According to this author, the Ignatian schematization offers a structural matrix of causalities, of vectors in the discernment of 'spirits'. This basic matrix is presented in the first week (rules 1 to 4 and the second part of rule 5) and reformulated in the second week (rules 1 to 4) of the Spiritual Exercises.

The aspect of Buckley's presentation most relevant is the *two-way* causal interaction which exists among the three factors of religious experience described by Ignatius: preternatural influences of good and evil spirits, 'thoughts' or 'ideals' or human

---

9   Buckley, 1973.
10 Beirnaert, 1954.
11 Meissner, 1964.
12 Cf. *Spiritual Exercises*, no. 336, eighth rule of the second week.
13 Buckley, 1973.

intellection or imagination, and human affectivity. These three vectors *causally* can move either downward, i.e., from good or evil spirits to thoughts to affectivity, or upwards, in which case affectivity can spontaneously generate commensurate thoughts: 'the thoughts that spring from consolation (*que salen de la consolación*) are contrary to the thoughts which spring from desolation (*que salen de la desolación*)'.[14] These thoughts almost mechanically place one under the influence of the evil spirit: 'As the good spirit guides and consoles us in consolation, so in desolation the evil spirit guides and counsels. Following the counsels of this latter spirit, one can never find the correct way to a right decision.'[15]

The foregoing two contributions convergently stress an important fact: the 'affectivity' factor in the structure proposed by Ignatius has a causal influence much greater than that usually attributed to it by writers considering the Ignatian 'Rules for the Discernment of Spirits'.

But there is more. We would like to add a few considerations which may help towards a further understanding of Ignatius' causal schematization.

In the *first week* of the Spiritual Exercises, affectivity is qualified by the moral worth of the attraction, i.e., by the obvious terms of its direction. This affectivity exists in the two states of 'consolation' and of 'desolation'. It is consolation if the person is drawn towards God and desolation if he is drawn towards evil. Note that consolation and desolation are not synonymous with pleasure and pain. Thus, 'Consolation is any interior movement of human sensibility — irrespective of the cause — whose direction is God, whether the movement be one of exuberant emotion or quiet peace, whether its presence is experientially present or not.'[16]

However, 'affectivity' plays a basically different role in the two types of men which Ignatius considers in the first or in the second week of his Spiritual Exercises: the man of the first week is drawn 'strongly and openly' towards obvious evil; the man of the second week generously looks for the will of God.[17] Furthermore, the 'consolation' of the first man is the sign of the

---

14   *Spiritual Exercises,* no. 317.
15   *Ibid.,* no. 318.
16   Buckley, 1973, p. 29.
17   Cf. Annotations 9 and 10.

'good' spirit', whilst the consolation of the second man is ambiguous, equivocal.

In fact, in the *second week* Ignatius considers two kinds of consolation: 1) the consolation without cause (*consolación sin causa*), which is from God 'without any previous perception or knowledge of any object from which such consolation might come to the soul through its own acts of understanding and will'.[18] This consolation is not characterized by its suddenness nor by its engulfing qualities, but rather by the absence of any preceding intentionality proportional to the drawing of affectivity into God;[19] 2) the consolation with cause (*consolación con causa*), present when there is some preceding cause.

Now, the apparent good, which the man of the second week looks for, is really genuine and thus draws to God only when the feelings of peace and tranquillity which he enjoyed at the beginning *persist* over time, i.e. when this man's consolation has a historical peristence throughout his past-present-future.[20]

These distinctions and considerations of Ignatius may be seen according to the theory and findings presented in this book. The man of the first week, strongly pulled towards obvious evil, hopefully should not be frequently found among the people entering the priestly or religious vocation. We say 'hopefully' because in the mind of Ignatius these people — irrespective of the spiritual or psychological origin of their poor dispositions — will have little or no chance of properly discerning spirits unless these dispositions are changed.

In this regard, many texts could be quoted from the Directories for the Spiritual Exercises which St Ignatius gave to Fr Victoria. The reader can find them in *Directoria Exercitiorum Spiritualium*.[21] For instance, listing the conditions to be found — or not — in the person who is to be invited to the Exercises, we read that the subject 'should be able to decide about his person' (*que pueda determinar de su persona*), and 'should not be so attached to things that it would be difficult to lead him to set himself in a position of balance in front of God, or even more, he should be in some way worried (*angustiado*) by the

---

18 *Spiritual Exercises*, no. 330; note that for Ignatius 'soul' means the person, the self (Ganss, 1970, footnote 10, pp. 77-78).
19 Rahner, 1964.
20 *Spiritual Exercises*, no. 333 of the second week and no. 177 of the third time of election; also no. 336 of the second week.
21 *Directoria Exercitiorum Spiritualium*, 1955.

desire to know what he should do with himself, and he should be doubtful (*ambiguo*)'.[22]

Later on, speaking of the first week, we read that for 'those who enter the Spiritual Exercises with some designs and intentions (*disegnos y intentos*), it is very useful diligently to take care that they untie themselves from this imperfection, because it is a moth which corrodes the precious fabric of true vocation, and it does not allow one in any way to know truth (*y no dexa conocer por ninguna manera la verdad*). The person who is known to be very obstinate (*muy pertinaz*) in this before entering the Exercises should not be incited to make them nor be admitted to them until he has become more mature (*más maduro*) by means of frequent confessions' or of spiritual conversations.[23] How can the foregoing 'designs and intentions', which prevent the knowledge of truth, be overcome when their psychological source is unconscious? Since 1954, Beirnaert has called attention to this important point, but — it would seem — without too much success. Ignatius gave advice proper to the knowledge of his time, that is, when the possible deep psychological causalities were unknown.

However, the interest of our research has been rather in the man of the second week, that is, for vocationers who have good values and are generously looking for the will of God. But Ignatius cautions that their good disposition, their 'consolation' or 'affectivity' may be genuinely or only deceptively oriented towards God. These good people are not so much tempted by the obvious evil, but by the obvious good. However, this latter is far more destructive than the former, precisely because its true nature is temporarily disguised and may overtly appear only later on in the life of the subject, i.e. when it is more difficult for him to reconsider vocational commitments previously taken.

In the framework of the present book, the genuine affectivity described by Ignatius as having the characteristics of historical consistency throughout the past-present-future of the person, may be translated in terms of internalizing psychodynamics. In fact, the people more able to internalize can be seen as the subjects with genuine consolation, that is, as the persons drawn towards God and self-transcendence. These 'internalizers' are more

---

22 *Ibid.*, p. 90.
23 *Ibid.*, pp. 99-100.

consistent people than the 'non-internalizers'.[24]   Therefore they enjoy the persistent, underlying peace and tranquility which Ignatius presents as a sign of genuine consolation, of right inclination for God and his greater glory.   Their psychological consistency disposes to their historical consistency of peace and tranquility throughout their past-present-future.   This historical consistency is not present for the 'non-internalizers', i.e. for the people characterised by greater vocational inconsistencies; thus the 'consolation' felt by these people is not genuine but deceptive.

In addition to a persistent peace and tranquility, the 'internalizers' or consistent people present nine other aspects of their personality which may be helpful in discerning a genuine 'consolation' from a deceptive one.[25]   Of course these people feel a tension of renunciation, but they do not have a tension of frustration.   In fact, as the nine aspects of personality just cited indicate, their vocational performance is not affected.   Actually, the tension of renunciation can be useful for the growth of their personality and of their vocational commitment.[26]

Chart 14 diagrammatically represents the view presented here regarding the basic structural matrix of causalities, of vectors *only* for the *upward* interaction in 'The Discernment of Spirits'.   The downward causalities have been described in the text.   The last column recalls the psychodynamic elements of the theory[27] which may be seen as related to the causal matrix.

A look at the chart may help one to see the prudence and the skill of Ignatius in qualifying the appropriateness and the *usefulness* of the Spiritual Exercises not only for the man of the first week but also for that of the second week.   In spite of the good intentions which the man of the second week has, his internalizing or non-internalizing psychodynamics are a crucial factor in making the discernment of spirits profitable for him. The same can be said of the three 'occasions' or 'times' of election discussed in nos. 175-177 of the Spiritual Exercises.   In fact, the first 'occasion' of election may correspond psychologically with the 'consolation without cause' of the discernment of spirits, whilst the second and third occasions are parallel to

---

24   The reader is urged to review the concepts discussed in Chapters 7 and 9.
25   Cf. Rulla, 1971, pp. 145-149.
26   *Ibid.,* pp. 143-145.
27   Cf. Chapter 1 and chart 1.

CHART 14

STRUCTURAL MATRIX OF UPWARD CAUSALITIES IN "THE DISCERNMENT OF SPIRITS"

Evil Spirit	Good Spirit	Preternatural Influences	Self- or non self-transcendent ideals (values and attitudes)
"Thoughts" or "ideals"	"Thoughts" or "ideals"	Processes of intellection or of imagination	Consistencies or inconsistencies of needs with vocational attitudes and/or values
Desolation	Consolation	Processes of affectivity	Consistencies dispose to self-transcendence, to self-fulfillment, and to effectiveness, and thus they foster persistent, underlying "peace and tranquility"

(from God; however, in time, unconscious factors may interfere too)*

— without cause

— with cause { — internalizing or genuine / — non-internalizing or deceptive

* Spiritual Exercises, n. 336.

the discernment of spirits related to consolation-desolation or to the 'consolation with cause'.

What does St Ignatius tell us in terms of depth psychology? First of all, that people with non-internalizing psychodynamics i.e. the men of the first week, strongly and openly drawn towards evil as well as the men of the second week drawn towards the apparent good, cannot make a useful discernment of spirits or a profitable election. In spite of the absence of psychopathology, the subconscious inconsistencies of these men seriously undermine their efforts at decisions. Of course, as discussed at length in the 1971 publication,[28] these subconscious inconsistencies may affect the *growth* of the vocational commitment, but do not affect its *existence*. However, to give to these people the rules for the discernment of spirits in the first and/or second week without disentangling their subconscious inconsistencies is dangerous.[29] Why? Because it implies treating psychodynamically inconsistent people as though they were consistent. This is harmful to the individuals. In fact, their inconsistent psychodynamics will prevent a proper internalization of vocational values and instead will perpetuate the process of non-internalizing identification which, as we have seen, leads to false expectations. Thus these people will be prevented from understanding the proper implications and applications of these rules to themselves.

In the long run, these people will come out more subconsciously self-deceived and disoriented than properly enlightened and guided. This is particularly true for the individuals who present a deceptive consolation of seemingly good intentions: their initial joyful commitment to the renunciations implied in christian life will become in time a source of disturbing frustrations, originating from their false expectations concerning such a life. A mature, long-lasting commitment is possible only if the person has developed a sufficiently consistent psychodynamic capable of internalizing vocational values and attitudes. A proper help, also in the realm of depth psychology, should be offered to these people to make their discernment of spirits or their election in the Spiritual Exercises a profitable one.

The many convergent findings of the present book show that the foregoing cautions of Ignatius are valid and pertinent

---

28 Pp. 186-190.
29 Cf. e.g. *Spiritual Exercises*, **Annotation 9.**

also for those entering vocation. One should ask whether, without a proper discernment of spirits and a proper election, the Spiritual Exercises are profitable. Among the findings which are relevant to these issues, let us recall the high percentage of poor internalizers (60-80%) found also among those who showed no apparent signs of psychopathology; the lack of significant change shown by the vocationers after four years of formation which included the Spiritual Exercises of St Ignatius; the high frequency of transferences in religious life, that is, the frequent presence of resistances to change; the high drop-out rate, which is related to the poor predictable capacity to internalize vocational values and attitudes; the prevalent influence of the vulnerable part of the self which also leads to dropping out and which makes a proper discernment and election difficult since it is characterized by *unconscious* forces; the two facts that self-conceptions show greater motivational strength than the accepted values, and that people may more easily change behavior than important attitudes; the lack of face-value credibility of the ideals proclaimed by those entering religious life. All these results call to mind St Augustine's statement: 'For it is one thing to see the land of peace from a wooded ridge . . . and another to tread the road that leads to it.'[30]

To some extent there is a parallel between the man of the first week of the Spiritual Exercises and the man of the second week on the one hand, and our findings on the other hand.

Analogous to the man of the first week, we found that vocationers with rather poor religious values need to be helped to grow precisely in this area of personality, in order to be able to seriously consider a vocational commitment. Our sample of seminarians corresponds to this situation, at least in the sense that their ascetical ideals were not as high as those of the religious males and females. The first step is to be able to appreciate the appeal of religious values, as Ignatius says.

Our sample of religious males and females corresponds to the man of the second week. They proclaimed high religious values, but beneath this proclamation there existed for many of them a poor capacity to live according to these proclaimed values, as was indicated by the contrast between DO and NDO for the predictable internalizing capacity. The spiritual quest of individuals with low predictable internalizing capacity may

---

[30] *Confessions*, VII, 21.

be easily undermined with the passage of time; historical consistency or stability is undermined by psychological inconsistency.

Thus, an understanding of this psychological inconsistency may become another sign for the discernment of spirits, as is the historical consistency suggested by Ignatius. The predictable internalizing capacity indicates the possibility of historical consistency; the subconscious perspective complements the conscious one.

On the basis of the above findings as well as of our observations of several hundreds of additional vocationers, we believe that 60 to 80% of entering vocationers present, in differing degrees, one of the following two possibilities: either — like our seminarians — they did not acquire to a high degree the proper religious values, or — like a substantial majority of our religious males and females — they do not have a sufficient capacity to internalize these values. The helps offered by the traditional spirituality will make up for the first type of deficiency but will not usually or significantly touch the second type, which has its roots in subconscious layers of personality. A proper discernment of these two types of vocationers and corresponding helps are part of a sound programme of formation.

Of course, God can supply for all these deficiencies. However, it seems that in these areas too, he *usually* respects the human personality and builds on it. It should be clear that we do not intend to diminish in any way either the possibility for grace to influence the inner recesses of the unconscious, nor the imperative need to offer supernatural and spiritual helps. As we have said previously, subjective sanctification does not depend intrinsically on psychological dispositions, and the growth in the spiritual and psychological dimensions are interdependent. However, precisely because of this interdependence, *both* dimensions should be taken into serious account. Ignatius reminds us that the discernment of spirits is profitable for people who have a good degree of maturity and freedom and that the Spiritual Exercises are intended for this kind of person. In turn, contemporary depth psychology calls attention to the fact that maturity and freedom of human decisions towards a greater good may be really affected by *subconscious* non-internalizing 'affectivity'.

As Buckley[31] says, 'Only when affectivity is ordered can

---

[31] Buckley, 1973.

it in turn become the clue to the direction in which one should go within the myriad good options which surround one's life.' However, as the many convergent results of this book show, such an ordered, internalizing affectivity is a condition which is rather hard to find. It would therefore rarely be prudent to take *felt* affectivity as the sole criterion for important decisions, unless a discernment of its subconscious and non-internalizing elements has been properly made.

Without a doubt, conversion or spiritual progress is not so much a matter of doing differently, as of being different, and this being different is the result of a long, slow process of becoming different.

The findings and considerations concerning the individual's discernment prompt some comments about community discernment. First of all, if 60-80% of the vocationers, even after four years of formation, present the many signs of difficulties in discernment shown by the results of this book, it is unrealistic to believe that the same difficulties will disappear in a community discernment. After all, the findings of Kennedy and Heckler[32] and of Baars and Terruwe[33] indicate analogous difficulties for 'formed' priests and religious.

Secondly, as discussed at some length in the 1971 publication, group participation in making decisions should not be judged with the attitude of a wholesale condemnation or deification. Rather, as pertinent literature shows, it is important to consider the mediating conditions, that is, the properties of individuals and of situations which shape the effectiveness of community discernment. Here it suffices to mention two points.

For deliberations concerning structural changes of a vocational institution, a vicious circle may easily develop: ' . . . The internalizing psychodynamics prevailing in a religious Order may determine the potentials for internalization inherent in a structural change promoted by its representatives as individuals or as a group (or cliques), for instance in the general chapters. In turn, the effectiveness of this change is contingent on the psychodynamics predominant among the members and the groups. The crucial variable in the vicious circle is the internalizing psychodynamics of individuals and of groups. The one prevailing in the order will influence both the establishment and the imple-

---

[32] Kennedy and Heckler, 1971.
[33] Baars and Terruwe, 1971.

mentation of institutional changes.[34]   In such a case, the communal discernment concerning ideals *may* become a factor of entrenched immobility rather than of innovative growth.

For decisions concerning persons, one can recall the interesting recent findings of the research by Lieberman, Yalom and Miles[35] on 'encounter groups'. Judgements were asked about the changes in personality which had been noticed in the participants to group encounters six months after the ending of this educational experience. The evaluations were obtained from different kinds of judges: each participant, his co-participants, the leaders, the social networks, i.e. the friends and relatives of the participants. Evaluations of benefit obtained from the different perspective of these judges were found to be at variance with each other and friends and relatives noticed change in as many participants, as in controls who did not participate in the encounter groups.

Community discernment is more a point of arrival than of departure, more an end, an ideal, a sign of achieved maturity than a means to it.   In general, a long, in-depth background work with individuals should be done to prepare them for it.

D. THE FUNCTIONS OF PSYCHOLOGY IN VOCATIONAL TRAINING

Perhaps the most important implications which emerge from our findings are those related to the issue of the contribution of psychology to vocational training.

At least the following five functions seem to be relevant:

1) and 2) — A *pedagogical* function as distinguished from a *psychotherapeutic* one: the contribution of psychology should be oriented especially towards the pedagogical function of fostering the individuals' capacity to internalize vocational values and attitudes rather than only towards solving problems of overt or covert psychopathology.

3) — A *preventive* function as opposed to a reparative one. Our results indicate that when individuals enter the vocational settings, it is already possible to detect the difficulties which each

---

[34] Rulla, 1971, p. 335.
[35] Lieberman, Yalom and Miles, 1973.

one will have in the future in internalizing vocational values and attitudes. Why do we wait many years and allow these difficulties to grow and to generate stressful situations which often cannot be handled anymore? Would it not be more charitable to offer an *early* help which could lower the rate of onset of these frustrations? Of course, this help should take into consideration the limitations of both the individuals and the institutions.

4) — An *integrative* function as substantially different from one which implies a dichotomy. Here we are referring to the strict interdependence and convergence which exists between the spiritual and psychological growths. The discussion presented in the foregoing points 2) and 3) of this Chapter has underlined the fallacy of a training programme which allows a dichotomy between spiritual and psychological growth.

5) — A *selective* function of screening candidates before they enter vocation.

Let us elaborate briefly on some aspects of the above five functions.

The training, the formation of young vocationers should avoid a dichotomy between spiritual and psychological growth. Consensus on this point is increasing among those responsible for such a formation.

However, whilst an agreement for reaching this end of an integration of spirituality and psychology does exist, there remains nevertheless, the trend to keep a rather sharp separation between the means to reach this end. The spiritual and the psychological helps are offered to the vocationers as if the spiritual and psychological dimensions of man were completely separate. Actually, sometimes one of these two dimensions is inappropriately accentuated almost to the point of excluding the other. Thus, for instance, a point of view common among religious educators holds that psychology should serve especially or only the two functions of screening candidates and of treating people who present psychopathological problems.

On the basis of the findings of this book, we believe that these diagnostic-predictive and psychotherapeutic functions are relevant, but less salient than the pedagogical function of helping the individuals to increase their capacity to internalize vocational values and attitudes through a gradual growth in their developmental and vocational maturities. As spiritual direction should not aim primarily at solving difficulties, but at a progressive

163

education in the discernment of spirits, so the contribution of psychology should not be primarily diagnostic or therapeutic, but pedagogical.

Similarly, we believe that the means offered in formation should *continuously* integrate the interdependent spiritual and psychological growth. These means should also take into serious account the *subconscious* factors which, according to our findings, may notably affect the capacity to internalize values and attitudes as well as the capacity for a proper discernment of spirits and election.

Here again, St Ignatius had some interesting foresights. When advising how to counteract the influence of the 'evil spirit', he uses three images: the angry woman, the false lover, the commander of an army.[36] These three images point to the three means to be used: strength and determination which originates from union with God; openness with a confessor or spiritual director, which implies interpersonal guidance and points to a need for a preventive, early intervention; persistent and perceptive *self-knowledge* which is also related to a good *self-mastery*. The parallel between this last point and the relevance of an objective and free self-ideal-in-situation shown by our findings seems to be quite marked.

A programme of formation which intends to be effective should offer means to grow in all these three dimensions. This would not seem to be the case at present in the settings of vocational training. A systematic discussion of this topic is beyond the purpose of the present book. Some considerations have been offered in the 1971 publication.[37] They discuss the insufficiency of the helps offered at present by the vocational institutions. Furthermore, they offer suggestions specifically geared to the aim of increasing the capacity of the vocationers to internalize vocational values and attitudes. Among the issues discussed there, one can mention: *two new kinds of educators;* behavioral signs which may be indicative of underlying consistent or inconsistent psychodynamics; basic characteristics of the experiences which should be offered to people in formation; some principles which may be helpful in the institutionalization of the changes; systems of leadership and types of structure of vocational organizations, which may foster the capacity of members to internalize

---

[36] *Spiritual Exercises,* nos. 325, 326, 327.
[37] E.g., pp. 130-131, 145-149, 214-224 and 322-363.

values and attitudes; the limitations of the type of experience found in encounter groups or in group dynamics for inducing a real growth in the personality of the participants.

With regard to this last topic, a recent review of the pertinent literature[38] has shown that 'there is a dearth of carefully designed and executed research, a plethora of anecdotal and exhortative-descriptive pieces'. Croghan[39] also stresses the 'need for a scientific investigation of the effects of the growth group experience. Lieberman, Yalom and Miles have filled this need with their 1973 work, *Encounter Groups: First Facts*'. This recent, extensive research with normal college students brings a further support to the considerations formulated by Rulla in his 1971 publication. In their final Chapter, Lieberman, Yalom and Miles discuss the confusion of liking with learning which can derive from the experience of group dynamics. Here are some of their statements: 'Leaders (of encounter groups) value spontaneity, expressiveness, openness and self-disclosure and work from theoretical propositions from which they derive that these are the mechanisms *par excellence* which can induce learning or growth in the participants. The findings presented in (their) Chapter 12 clearly suggest that the expressions of strong positive or negative feeling, a great amount of self-disclosure in and of itself and the experience of intense emotional events are not mechanisms that uniquely maximize member learning. They are, however, vivid, intense experiences in the participants' minds, and thus the leaders whose techniques are oriented towards producing them come to believe that they are 'right on'. Perhaps both members and leaders have contributed to the construction of an elaborate mythology which specifies that where there is stimulation (or expressivity, or self-disclosure) there will also be learning: a mythology for which there is evidence, not of learning, but of involvement, of liking what is happening.'[40]

More specifically related to the content of the present book are the research conclusions which Lieberman, Yalom and Miles offer, concerning who would learn and who would falter in educational experiences like the encounter groups: 'What a person enters with tells us something about what kind of experience he will have in an encounter group.'[41] The real differences

---

38 Reddy and Lansky, 1974, p. 477.
39 Croghan, 1974, p. 443.
40 Lieberman, Yalom and Miles, 1973, pp. 451-452.
41 *Ibid.*, p. 334.

among the high learners, moderate changers, negative changers, casualties and drop-outs from encounter groups were '. . . not in their experiences in the groups but in what they were like when they entered, and how they anticipated the experience before they got started in it'.[42] Our findings of Chapter 9 are in complete concordance with these results of the above authors. In the same line are their data concerning the changes resulting from the encounter group experiences: '. . . One third of those who participated in the groups benefitted from them, a little over one third remained unchanged, and the remainder experienced some form of negative outcome: dropping out from the group for psychological reasons, making negative changes, or experiencing psychological decompensation.'[43] These percentages are very similar to the ones found in our research and in similar investigations among religious and priests[44]: between 60-80% of these people show signs of psychological underdevelopment which can seriously affect their improvement.

Throughout this book, the relevance of *subconscious* factors for growth in vocation has been stressed and supported by many convergent results. This relevance may be diagrammatically represented by chart 15, which reproduces the Johari window, the brain-child of Joseph Luft (Jo) and Harrington (Hari).

CHART 15

THE JOHARI WINDOW

	Known to Self	Not Known to Self
Known to Others	Public Self	Blind Self
Not Known to Others	Hidden Self	Unknown or Undeveloped Potential

In chart 15, one's public self is that part known to both oneself and to others; the hidden self represents what is known

---

[42] *Ibid.,* p. 334.
[43] *Ibid.,* p. 129.
[44] Cf. Chapters 7 and 8.

to oneself but not to others; the blind self is a part known to others but not to oneself; and one's undeveloped potential is unknown to both others and oneself.

The results presented in this book indicate that the 'unknown', subconscious area of the self related to central vocational inconsistencies is present in at least two-thirds of the vocationers. Furthermore, the same results show that these subconscious factors have a significant, negative influence which prevents internalization of vocational values and attitudes. Now, the help usually offered in vocational institutions in this area of unconscious processes is not proportionate to the nature of the problem. As discussed elsewhere,[45] two new categories of educators and appropriate centers of training for them are an impelling need. Charity towards the vocationers and the greater glory of God would require this.

These two new categories of educators should be able to perceive the existence of (first type of educator) and to handle (second type of educator) the following four kinds of vocational difficulties which seem to be the most common:

1) problems of a 'spiritual' nature: e.g. doubts of faith, morals, etc;

2) problems resulting from the usual developmental difficulties; these should be significantly solved by the time the individual has reached the chronological age of about 27 years, provided a proper existential experience has been possible for him;

3) the subconscious vocational inconsistencies which do not give signs of and are not directly related to psychopathology; these inconsistencies have been the topic of the findings in the present book;

4) the difficulties coming from the psychopathological dynamics of psychiatric classification.

Note that the first two kinds of vocational difficulties may be independent of, i.e. not related to the problems described under 4) and especially under 3). If this is the case, the first two sets of problems usually do not present serious difficulty in being handled. Supernatural means, time, experience, proper help by spiritual directors, counselors, superiors, etc. will gradually improve the situation.

However, the case is quite different if the 'spiritual' and

---

[45] Rulla, 1971, pp. 216-219.

'developmental' difficulties are in reality the *expression* of sub-conscious vocational inconsistencies or of psychopathology. Let us emphasize that the cases of subconscious vocational inconsistencies without signs of psychopathology are usually considered as 'normal' by superiors. Still, on the one hand, as the results of this present book show, they are very frequent. On the other hand, for these subconscious vocational inconsistencies, existential experience, time, counselors, group dynamics, spiritual directors, etc. will not be helpful or not meaningfully so, especially if the unconscious or deeply preconscious problems are not properly handled. New types of educators are necessary for these subconscious difficulties.

Note that, after all, the function of these new types of educators is no different from the one exerted by the present 'spiritual advisors' or directors or formators, except in the following crucial aspect: to the helps offered to a person for his conscious life, the new educators would *add and integrate* the helps necessary to disentangle the negative effects of his subconscious life. Thus meditation, examination of conscience, etc. would more easily reach the subconscious roots of attitudes and habits which jeopardize the person's apostolic effectiveness and growth in *objective* holiness. Furthermore, these new educators would have solved for themselves the third or fourth kinds of the above-mentioned problems of vocation. Therefore they would avoid the deleterious influence coming from the subconscious projection of their own unsolved vocational difficulties onto the group or some of its members.

The high frequency of inhibiting *subconscious inconsistencies* presented by the entering vocationers is the most relevant reason for helping them *also* in this aspect of their vocational growth. In fact, a person is free only if his motivational affirmations are consistent with the structures of his self;[46] man is free when his choices are the product of full awareness of his operative needs and actual constraints. If these needs and constraints are buried in the unconscious, they engender irrationalities which remain invulnerable behind masks of rationality. Our data repeatedly confirm this fact. Now, the removal of these masks allows men to know what they truly want and what they can truly have; this truth does not make men free, but makes freedom *possible.*[47]

---

[46] Weigel, 1960.
[47] Kaplan, 1957.

After all, truth is the root of freedom. In turn, freedom — or lack of it — may affect one's being disposed to supernatural grace.

E. THE GROWTH IN VOCATIONAL COMMITMENT: EXPERIENCING ROLES OR INTERNALIZING VALUES?[48]

One of the most intriguing problems of social psychology in general[49] and of vocational commitment in particular, concerns the various factors which influence the behavior of an individual in his growth. If we limit our considerations just to the two sets of individual and situational determinants of behavior, two difficult questions arise: What is the relative importance of the person's assigned *and conceived* roles as a member of a group in comparison with his internal and entire psychodynamics? What is the relevance of the experiencing of roles in comparison with the internalizing of vocational values and attitudes?

Our purpose here is not to answer exhaustively these extremely complex questions. We will only offer first some speculative considerations, then the findings of our research relevant to these considerations will be recalled. Finally, some practical suggestions will be presented for problems concerning spiritual life, professional-occupational involvement of priests and religious, and planning of programmes of training for vocational growth.

If there is some common definition of role of which we speak, it is that role is the set of prescriptions defining what the behavior of a group member should be.[50] Some roles are not chosen, e.g. being a man or a woman, infant, adult or old. But some roles *are chosen,* e.g. professional and vocational roles. Such a choice implies values, in the general sense defined by Rokeach:[51] enduring abstract ideals about ideal modes of conduct and ideal end-states of existence.

One can in principle distinguish two possibilities: either the role *itself* is chosen as a kind of ideal end-state, or else the

---

48 We would like to thank B. Kiely, S. J. for his very valuable contribution to this section.
49 Cf., for example, Zigler and Child, 1969; Secord and Backman, 1974.
50 Thomas, 1968.
51 Rokeach, 1968.

169

role is chosen for the sake of values beyond itself. In the former case one can speak of role-orientation, and in the latter case of value-orientation.

If role-orientation in this sense is in question, then there are no motives beyond the role for remaining in or for working in the role. Perseverance and effectiveness appear to be conditioned by role-satisfaction. The gratification of the individual's needs found in the role then becomes central.

Where value orientation is in question, however, the main reason for choosing the role will not be the gratification which it offers, but the 'ideal modes of conduct' which the role makes possible, and which serve to reach the 'ideal end-states of existence', i.e. the role-transcendent values on account of which the role is chosen. Any treatment of the priestly role which makes no explicit provision for such an orientation is basically inadequate.

Secondly, it must be conceded that any role whatsoever entails some renunciation of satisfactions. This is true in its own way of the priest's and the religious' role. Hence a part of the matter of value-orientation is the question of whether the individual's values are so held as to permit the necessary price to be paid. On the other hand, when values are not clearly introduced into the discussion, vocational outcome (perseverance/dropping out) can only be conceived in terms of a 'balance of payments' mode, or of role conflict; that is, of role-orientation.

In other words, by role-orientation we mean a way of using the role as an end in itself rather than using the role as a means to realize values which are both role-transcendent and self-transcendent.

Returning now to a consideration of the consequences to be expected when such a value-orientation is not effective in the individual's life, that is, when role-orientation prevails: it can be seen that because of the motivational forces involved, certain consequences in terms of perseverance and effectiveness in the role can be anticipated.

Perseverance is threatened by the prevalence of non-internalizing identification and compliance[52] over internalization or internalizing identification, as ways in which the role is interpreted and sustained. Behavior maintained on account of compliance or of non-internalizing identification *is dependent on*

---

[52] These terms of Kelman are applied to vocation in Chapter 7, pp. 67 ff.

the persistence of external factors: reward or punishment in the case of compliance, a satisfying self-defining relationship with another or others (including a profession, a vocation) in the case of non-internalizing identification. Note that to the extent to which the *part* of the self gratified by the role relationship cannot be integrated with objective vocational values, to the same extent this role relationship will lead to compliance or at least away from internalization (non-internalizing identification). Perseverance, being thus conditional, is precarious.

The behavior of a person maintained on account of internalization depends on the worth of a value (e.g. imitation of Christ) for its own sake, rather than for the person's sake. To the extent that a role relationship with others gratifies a part of the self that may be integrated with objective vocational values, to that extent the identifying relationship will lead towards the internalization of vocational values and attitudes (internalizing identification).

Kelman[53] tested his ideas in a context of induced opinion-change. In general, conditions inducing role-orientation produced identification, whilst value-orientation conditions led to internalization. Whilst the situations examined in Kelman's research are somewhat remote from that of a priestly or religious vocation, the validation of his ideas in the one situation suggests that they may also be valid in the other.

Thus, in so far as one is role-oriented in the sense explained above, the more one's perseverance and effectiveness are undermined. It is also to be expected that in so far as role-orientation prevails, time spent in a role by no means guarantees growth in the direction of value-orientation. What counts is not time, but the way in which the role is used, that is, the underlying motivation. When role-orientation prevails, one can expect compliance or non-internalizing identification; when value-orientation prevails, one can expect internalization or internalizing identification.

The results of the research presented in this book are in line with these considerations.

First of all, in the vocational commitment there is initially a conscious emphasis on values and appropriate attitudes which

---

53 Kelman, 1961.

the individual professes and desires to realize.[54] Such a conscious emphasis differentiates all three groups of vocationers (seminarians, female and male religious) from their lay controls. Whilst this may not seem surprising, it does go to confirm an earlier assertion made above: to omit any explicit consideration of personal role-transcendent ideals is to approach the question of vocation with a systematic oversight.

On the other hand, another seemingly obvious but important implication follows from the fact that a conscious emphasis on values and attitudes does not guarantee perseverance, as shown by the majority of all three groups of vocationers having left within four to eight years. If the traditional kind of seminary or religious formation seemed to operate on the assumption that values initially professed, plus time spent in role-enactment was sufficient provision for the vocation to be 'grown into' then, in the light of our results, this policy appears to be inadequate.

The factors which principally serve to differentiate drop-outs from non-drop-outs (hypotheses 2 to 5 of Chapter 9) are not accessible via self-reports alone: central subconscious inconsistencies and consistencies are very relevant elements. This indicated that to rely solely on self-reports constitutes a serious systematic limitation in the investigation of vocational outcome; self-reports based on questionnaires readily permit a defensive style of answering.

Verification of the sixth hypothesis of Chapter 9 shows a trend towards the undermining of vocational attitudes and towards an increase in vocationally dissonant values prior to the actual moment of leaving the vocation. Seeing that this is a manifestation of the vulnerability of the ideals proclaimed and remembering that this vulnerability is rooted mainly in vocationally dissonant subconscious needs which will cause the individual frustration when these needs are not satisfied, we find support for the idea of the *vicious circle* described in Chapter 9 (cf. p. 137). This vicious circle is diagrammed in chart 16. The findings of hypothesis 6 (an actual change in attitudes and vocationally dissonant values, occurring more rapidly in early drop-outs) indicates movement rather than a static balance-

---

[54] Hypothesis 1 of Chapter 9.

172

CHART 16

THE VICIOUS CIRCLE OF MANY ENTERING VOCATIONERS

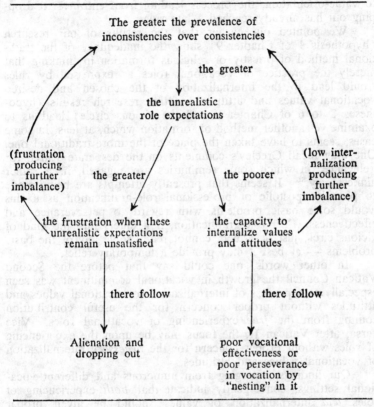

The greater the prevalence of
inconsistencies over consistencies

the greater

the unrealistic
role expectations

(frustration
producing
further
imbalance)

the greater

the poorer

(low inter-
nalization
producing
further
imbalance)

the frustration when these
unrealistic expectations
remain unsatisfied

the capacity to
internalize values
and attitudes

there follow

there follow

Alienation and
dropping out

poor vocational
effectiveness or
poor perseverance
in vocation by
"nesting" in it

of-forces. The vicious circle is an interpretation of such movement.

We can now translate this scheme in terms of value-orientaton and role-orientation as described above. In so far as frustrations/satisfactions experienced in the role become functionally significant or, in other words, in so far as the individual is in effect using the role in the search of gratification of needs dissonant with vocational values, rather than as a means toward

173

realizing and internalizing role-transcendent values, his perseverance in vocation is being undermined. Furthermore the findings
would suggest that by the time that role-satisfaction has reached
the conscious level, i.e. the status of a rival purpose with respect
to value-orientation, the process leading from entrance to dropping out has already reached a late stage.

We pointed out earlier that the results of our research
(hypothesis 1 of Chapter 9) show the inadequacy of the traditional method of priestly or religious formation in thinking that
merely the practice of vocational roles as expressed by rules
would lead to the internalization of the chosen and desired
vocational values and attitudes. Other research results (hypotheses 2 to 6 of Chapter 9 and the vicious circle) lead us to
examine yet another method of formation which, at least in some
cases, seems to have taken the place of the more traditional one.
One may recall Greeley's comments on the desperate search for
'relevance' in which some seminaries are engaged, in a rather
aimless way.[55]   It seems that presently attempts are being made
to provide apostolic or professional role-gratification as if this
would solve basic problems with regard to perseverance and
effectiveness.   Yet role-gratification, if it enters into the kind of
vicious circle just described, cannot really solve any of the basic
problems — at best it may provide a temporary relief.

In other words, one could say that before the Second
Vatican Council the growth in vocational commitment was seen
especially as a process of internalization of vocational values and
attitudes without proper concern for the useful contribution
coming from the *free* experiencing of vocational roles. Vice
versa, after Vatican II, the focus may be upon the experiencing
of roles without proper concern for the *necessary* internalization
of vocational values and attitudes.

Our findings, emerging from numerous and different vocational settings, convergently indicate that *both* experiencing of
roles *and* internalization of values should be given proper
consideration. However, the *possibility* of internalizing values
and attitudes resulting from the conscious and unconscious
intrapsychic dynamics is a necessary *pre*requisite for making the
experiencing of roles profitable.   To expect growth in vocational
commitment only or especially through these role-experiences may
lead to stressful frustrations for the individuals and to painful

---

[55]   Greeley, 1972, p. 31.

failures in their vocational growth. In fact, roles may be an expression of vocationally inconsistent needs rather than of vocational values. The psychodynamics of individuals should be adequately free and thus capable of internalizing vocational attitudes and values *before* the experiencing of roles, so that they may have a positive influence upon the growth in vocational commitment. Otherwise, such role-experiencing may have a negative, destructive influence.

Interestingly enough, in the last presentation of his extensive research and theorizing concerning moral development, Kohlberg[56] suggests similar conclusions: role-taking opportunities lead only to conventional morality, whilst the movement from the conventional to the mature, principled morality is one which must be considered a matter of personal choice and is a *free choice of a self*.

Some relevant practical suggestions, then, follow. First of all, should our *spiritual life* be directed rather by an interior focus of prayer or of meditation *or* by an exterior involvement in social activities and relationships? Should our spirituality be characterized by the *role*-experiences of active life with people and for people or by the *role*-experiences related to interiority?

To overemphasise one type of role to the detriment of the other would mean overlooking two important facts: first, that roles as such have a highly ambivalent power; according to the way in which they are used, roles may lead towards or away from internalization. Secondly, it would mean overlooking the determining influence of the psychodynamics of each individual in this ambivalence. If the prevailing psychodynamics of a person is one of central vocational inconsistencies, the roles either of the 'interior' life or of the 'exterior' life will be subconsciously used not so much as a means to actualize and to internalize the spiritual values of a genuine self-ideal, but rather as a means to gratify or to defend oneself against conflictual needs.[57]

On the one hand, for the 'interior' roles, chastity may become a means of narcissistic self-centeredness, poverty and penance a source of masochistic dependency, obedience the occasion to develop a conforming symbiosis. On the other hand, for the 'exterior' roles, to be with people and for people may become for the individual either a means of giving in order to

---

56 Kohlberg, 1973.
57 Cf. Chapters 6 and 7.

get, or of being continuously and masochistically a sacrificed victim, or of fighting for social justice in all sorts of activities subconsciously moved by deep feelings of personal abasement or by strong needs of rebellion against authority.

We do not wish to indicate a preference for either of the two tendencies. We must recognize the primacy of supernatural means such as love of one's neighbor. The crucial point, however, is that it is necessary in both interior and exterior roles that the individual be able to choose his ideals (values and attitudes) both freely and objectively.

What has been said about spirituality can be applied to *two other recent trends* in vocational life. First, for people who have been in vocation for some time (e.g. people in temporary vows or theology students), there is the trend to overstress involvement in professional or academic roles before a sufficient help for the growth in vocational commitment has been offered. Secondly, there is the trend to train, to form *entering* vocationers by engaging them immediately and prevailingly in role-experiences of external apostolic activities. Again, for both situations, the prevailing psychodynamics of each individual is a crucial factor, because it determines whether or not vocational values will be internalized by means of those roles the individual enacts.

If, as the several findings quoted in Chapters 7 and 8 indicate, from 60-80% of the vocationers may present central subconscious inconsistencies which tend to persist, a premature emphasis on choosing and exercising role opportunities will tend to be rather destructive than constructive for vocational commitment. In fact, even though the conscious motivation of the individual is for a genuine commitment, the underlying subconscious orientation may not be integrating, i.e. not defining, informing and moulding the roles the individual plays at different times according to that conscious motivation. His behavior in each one of these different roles may represent an important *part* of the individual and be regarded as such by him, but it will tend to be isolated from the *rest* of his value-system. Actually — in extreme cases — this part 'may be encapsulated and function almost like a foreign body within the person'.[58]

In such cases, the experiencing of roles will not lead towards internalization of values. This outcome is highly probable if the institution does not provide the conditions which help the

---

[58] Kelman, 1961, p. 71.

members overcome the vocational inconsistencies with which they entered.[59]

However, let us recall that growth in vocation can also be fostered if the role experience offered fulfill at least the four following conditions: they are existential, integrating, proportionate, and supported. These four conditions are all necessary during the training period of the priest or religious. Later on, the level of 'psychological' age, as distinguished from the 'chronological' age, reached by the individual will determine the extent to which each one of them will be needed and useful.

Existential experience means that the young vocationer is offered the possibility of *testing himself* in substantially different kinds of tasks, in various types of social situations which require personal initiative and decisions. In fact, if the individual has to develop an internal and internalized basis for self-evaluation and self-direction, he must have the experiences that confront him with his own self. These experiences should challenge as much as possible his real self, his abilities, values, underlying needs and should expose him to failure, to frustration and to a sense of loneliness. Only in this way does he have the 'possibility' of knowing and accepting his real self into the depths of his being; only so can he achieve the joy of being himself and thus have the joy of giving himself to others. The period of training is particularly favorable for this existential experience. The individual is not required to make any permanent commitment and thus the continuous opportunity to test himself in various spheres of activity does not make his failures catastrophic and does not catalyze his successes into premature commitments.

Integrating experience is required by the fact that man is a differentiated existing unity . . . his psychic life includes the three levels of psycho-physiological, psychosocial and spiritual functions and potentialities. It is true that these three dimensions of the human psyche are inextricably mingled in every act of man; however, every human act may be initiated independently in any one of the three levels. After the initial inducement, the functions of the starting new level should be integrated, should be adjusted to the other levels in order to have consistency and internalization with the unifying value system. It follows that any member of vocational institutions should be repeatedly confronted with the challenge to perform these integrating, adjusting endeavors. The three vows of poverty, chastity and obedience offer, among many other factors, the occasions inducing these challenges of integration. Thus the possibility to practice them should be offered to every member. Any success in this integration process will mean a strengthening of the capacity of the self for internalization.

Proportionate experience is a very delicate aspect of the con-

---

[59] A discussion of these conditions is not possible here; the interested reader is referred to the 1971 publication, pp. 322-384.

tinuous learning process of religious members. The functions and potentialities of the self improve as they are performed with success in increasingly challenging situations. The issue is a delicate one because these situations should fulfill two requirements: on the one hand, they should be a step ahead of the developmental stage reached by the individual so that he may learn new patterns of integration; on the other hand, they should not be so difficult or anxiety-arousing that he is forced to make use of primitive, childish, immature defensive devices. It follows that the growth of the self is hampered both by authoritarian and by laissez-faire regimes of training. Authoritarian or overprotective systems do not give the functions and potentials of the self the chance for exercise; laissez-faire or permissive systems, through an excessive stimulation of needs, of impulses, with consequent anxiety may put too heavy a strain upon the self, and lead to a regression to immature feelings and behavior. The relevance of these considerations is brought to the fore if two elements are recalled: 1) the differences in psychodynamic consistency possible among members of vocational institutions (as indicated by the findings); to deal with all the members as if they had the same 'psychological' age is both unrealistic and not according to charity; 2) the frequent possibility for some members to find other people inside or outside the vocational institution who will respond to and support unconsciously the shaky psychodynamics of the individual by positive or negative reciprocation, transferences of subconscious, conflictual patterns, whether these are dependent, submissive, passive-resistant or rebellious. Blocking of growth or regression to infantile patterns rather than new developmental learning will follow; non-internalizing identification or compliance rather than internalization of vocational values and attitudes will be the end result.

Supported experience is demanded by the need which every member has to develop objective and free ideals if internalization of vocational values and attitudes is to take place. Let us recall the vulnerability of these ideals especially because of subconscious factors.[60]

The findings of the present book all converge to substantiate the foregoing vulnerability and its trend to persist especially because of the influence of *subconscious* factors.

In spite of the fact that people are well intentioned about their vocational commitment and willing to question their previous cherished but less appropriate personal attitudes, it is gratuitous to assume (actually the opposite is proven), that all or even the majority of them has a high degree of self-awareness. They may be open in specific areas, but closed, frozen in others, in which the *readiness for learning* may be seriously jeopardized. In these aspects of their personality they may be subconsciously searching more for safety or gratification than for genuine growth. Actually these subconscious

---

[60] Rulla, 1971, pp. 324-326.

areas may be or may become *dominant* in the equilibrium of their total psychodynamics. It is true, people should be free to learn through trials and errors, free to be wrong. But they should also be free to be *not* wrong; that is, able to recognize, to accept errors and free to 'really' change, free not to fall into the same mistakes. If this self-awareness and this freedom are not present, they should be helped; if they are not able to learn through experience, they should be supported. More precisely, help should be offered, and if this 'offering' is not reaching its aims, people should be invited to reconsider their situation with regard to their commitment. To allow the perpetuation of an incapacity to learn through experience without offering the proper help, (especially for the subconscious hindrances), is against charity towards the individual and the other members of the community.[61]

Regarding the last statements, the reader is invited to recall what has been said in the present Chapter when discussing the functions of psychology in vocational training. The importance of the pedagogical function emerges from these statements. We should not pretend that subjects become 'perfect' prior to and without personal experience (as was assumed frequently in the past). But we should not betray our duty to *properly* help them personally in establishing new attitudes and values, before throwing away their previous ones, in integrating new inner controls, before loosening the longstanding ones of previous experience, in taking important decisions before rejecting altogether the support of past identities. The accent here is on the individual person and on personal help to him. Great numbers and concomitant structured group formation of the past are unrealistic, i.e. not existential; but the laissez-faire policy of the present is not existential either. The idea that to change structures and to give freedom in experiencing roles will automatically be followed by improvement of individuals is simply naive.

F. VOCATIONAL DEVELOPMENT AND THE CHALLENGE OF SEXUALITY[62]

Several reasons can be indicated for focusing on the issue of celibacy, chastity, and the whole area of sexuality in priestly and religious life. The major focus and impact of our research was not directed to this area. However, a few considerations

---

[61] *Ibid.*, pp. 326-327.
[62] This section is being expanded on the basis of further empirical

seem appropriate when confronting the data analyzed and presented in this work, with a set of data obtained from the same subjects concerning their sexual behavior and attitudes.

These data were collected by means of the depth interview and partially from the biographical inventory. Such data are analyzed in detail, but are reported here only indirectly and in summary form.

An analysis of the available data suggest the following considerations:

1) Weaknesses in chastity like masturbation, hetero- and homosexual manifestations are present in individual vocationers with different personality traits and disorders. Our data are in line with the empirical findings and scientific tenets of the authorities in this field:[63] sex shows a great plasticity and ubiquitousness. Sex should not be seen only or especially as a biological, developmental instinct; rather it is a psychological need with a social direction or orientation. As such, it may be related to *many* different personality traits or disorders; i.e. *any* personality trait or disorder may use sexual manifestations as an outlet or as a defence. Thus a serious approach to religious chastity should take into consideration the *entire* personality of the vocationer.

2) This conclusion that sexual identity and sexual weaknesses are related to the entire personality, emerges also from the results of other researches, and has interesting connections with the issue of perseverance.

Numerous recent studies concerning ordained priests of the regular and secular clergy have indicated that the dissatisfactions of the clergy in the Western world arise from conflicts centered around institutional work roles and values.[64]

According to these studies, the foregoing conflicts concerning institutional roles and values lead to a sense of self-dissatisfaction, of loneliness, of alienation and isolation from the vocational

---

investigations which are in course.

63 Cf., for example, the review of the pertinent literature in Schmidt, Meyer and Lucas, 1974; Emmerich, 1973.

64 The following investigations are relevant: Greeley, 1972 and NORC, 1971, for the priests of the USA; Schmidtchen, 1973, for the clergy of West Germany; Olabuenaga for the Spanish milieu (1970, and Pro Mundi Vita, 1971); Stryckman, 1971, for the Quebec area; Schallert and Kelley, 1970, for American priests who had left the active ministry.

institutions. In turn, this sense of self-dissatisfaction leads to the desire to marry. In the nationwide investigation by the National Opinion Research Center for the American priests,[65] a desire to marry is the strongest predictor of plans to leave the priesthood, and the principal reason for the desire to marry is loneliness.[66]

Our research did not consider ordained priests, but young vocationers, and studied their personality as soon as they entered their vocational settings therefore, before they were exposed to the influence of the vocational institutions. Our data indicate that, at entrance, people who will leave vocation in a span of 6-8 years, already show personality characteristics which, in time, will develop in them a sense of alienation from the institution, a sense of loneliness, and concomitantly in some the desire to marry as the foregoing quoted studies suggested.

It is interesting that future 'dropouts' of vocation already present at entrance a capacity to internalize vocational values and attitudes which is significantly lower than the one of people who remain in vocation. Thus, the roots of a future sense of alienation from the vocational institution, of a future sense of loneliness, are already present at entrance and they are related to *dispositions* which characterize the entire personality.

3) According to our research data, the shortcomings of the *entering* personality produce and sustain in time false expectations concerning the roles which the individuals look forward to playing in their vocational life. Since these expectations are unrealistic, it is not surprising that frustrations can be felt in vocation and that these frustrations may seek some outlets in sexual phenomena. In this regard, a comparison between sexual weaknesses at entrance and after 4 years revealed certainly no hint of improvement. This result was true for male religious, female religious and for seminarians.

4) Furthermore, our results indicate that some tenets of general social psychology are valid also for entering vocationers: a) the values a person proclaims may be less influential upon his motivation than what he considers central for his self-

---

[65] NORC, 1971.
[66] Greeley, 1972.

concept;[67] b) it is easier to change behavior than attitudes which matter.[68]

In this regard, an important point of clarification comes from our findings: some people succeeded in overcoming their sexual weakness during the first 1-2 years of vocational formation; later on, after only 4 years of vocational life, these weaknesses gradually reappeared and sometimes increased. The deep roots of these problems had not been sufficiently influenced by the formation.

5) Another consideration seems to be appropriate. As the research findings have indicated, the personality of entering vocationers already presents the elements which may lead to future shortcomings in the vocational commitment in general, and in the handling of sexual phenomena in particular. These short-comings are mostly of a subconscious nature. Thus, in the light of the foregoing findings, an institutional, role or behavioral approach alone would not seem to offer the *most* helpful intervention towards integration in the area of sexual identity.

Here the results obtained by NORC[69] on the marital adjustment of priests who left the ministry are important in suggesting that a mere change of status — in this case from celibate to married — is no guarantee that the individual will find the resources to resolve his personality shortcomings because of changed circumstances.

In this sociological investigation, Greeley and his associates distributed a questionnaire to priests who had resigned from the ministry. They obtained 873 responses on several issues including information about marital relationships. Such information constitutes a measure of 'marriage adjustment'[70] articulated in three indices: the index of marital tension, the index of marital sociability, and the index of marital companionship. By combining the first index with the other two taken together, a marriage adjustment balance scale was obtained, expressive of a level of marital satisfaction. Chart 17 reports these findings according to year of resignation from the ministry, in comparison with the scores obtained by a sample of college-educated males. Note that the lower the score, the better is the adjustment.

---

[67] Rokeach, 1973, who quotes other authors.
[68] See the discussion of the pertinent literature in Freedman, Carlsmith and Seers, 1974.
[69] NORC, 1971.
[70] Bradburn, 1969; Orden and Bradburn, 1968, 1969.

CHART 17

MARITAL ADJUSTMENT BALANCE SCALE SCORES
OF RESIGNED PRIESTS AND COLLEGE-EDUCATED MALES

Resigned priest (by year of resignation)	Mean Scores
1970	6.9
1969	6.6
1968	6.2
1967	5.8
1966	4.9
1964-65	5.0
TOTAL	6.1
College-education males (by age): *	
26-35	5.5
36-45	5.4
46-55	6.4

* Data from NORC Happiness Study, 1963.

The overall mean score on the marriage adjustment balance scale for all resignees is better than that of American college-educated males between 26 and 45. However, for priests, with the passing of time, this good level of marriage adjustment progressively reached a point worse than that of college-educated males. 'Whatever the explanation, former Roman Catholic priests do seem to experience greater tensions in marriage than the typical college-educated American male, and these tensions increase as the resignation date recedes into the past.'[71]

Somewhat in the same line of reasoning, our data have shown that for both boys and girls, the experience of steady dating *before* entering the vocational institutions has no influence upon the degree of developmental and vocational maturity. Advantages and disadvantages of dating have been discussed by different authors and researchers.[72] More information is required to reach definite conclusions, but perhaps we can advance the hypothesis that the experience of steady dating

---

[71] NORC, 1971, p. 298.
[72] Kobler, Rizzo, and Doyle, 1967; Mietto, 1968; Vergote, 1968; Godin, 1975.

before entering vocation may well offer useful opportunities for acquisition of social roles and skills in the area of interpersonal competence and in the area of sexual identity *when* the *only* problems are those of normal developmental growth. However, the situation is different when the individuals have *central* inconsistencies coming from unconscious conflictual needs. The usefulness or harmfulness of the role-opportunities, like the ones offered for sex-identity in the experiences of dating, should be carefully considered. The reader is referred for this discussion to the previous topic of this Chapter, keeping in mind that data of several researches indicate that conflictual needs are present in 60-80% of vocationers.[73]

After all, friendship between a man and a woman is different in many aspects from the one between two persons of the same sex. Providence has disposed a complementarity of roles which entails complementarity of needs. Therefore, role-enactment in heterosexual *interaction* puts into motion *new* powerful forces. Now, if a person presents subconscious central inconsistencies, the vicious circle described in chart 16 may become operative and thus seriously undermine the vocational commitment. As already mentioned, it is the prevailing psychodynamics which will make the relationship constructive or destructive.

6) The *Guide to Formation to Priestly Celibacy*,[74] quoting Paul VI,[75] states that 'every candidate for the priesthood must know himself thoroughly, his physical, psychological, moral, religious and emotional dispositions, so that he can answer the call of God with a creative, responsible and considered decision', (n. 50).

Speaking of the training in celibacy, the Guide also indicates that 'while the motives for choosing celibacy are particularly personal to each candidate, through his developing relationships with God and others, these motives are *subject to a process of growth*. It is *here* that attention should be paid more than in trying to evaluate the initial motivation.'[76]

In the light of these statements, the question arises as to what is being done concretely towards the goal outlined above, keeping in mind the presence of the subconscious inconsistent

---

[73] Cf. Chapters 7 and 8.
[74] S. Congregation of Education, 1974.
[75] Encyclical, *Sacerdotalis Caelibatus, Acta Apostolicae Sedis,* 1967, 59, p. 682.
[76] *Ibid.,* n. 48; our italics.

components in the personalities of the people in vocational training. Our research has convergently indicated that these subconscious components are frequently present and do affect the capacity to grow.

Again, we are reminded at this point of the previously discussed functions of psychology, particularly of the pedagogical one, but also of the suggestions concerning *new* types of educators. Their contribution appears to be strongly needed if an 'enlightened direction' is to be offered which 'can notably facilitate the overcoming of this kind of crisis' (developmental and personality imbalances in the area of sexual identity) and 'securely assure the integral development of the personality of the young.'[77]

Of course, this does not intend to diminish the importance of taking into consideration also the spiritual, supernatural factors. However, *'unum facere et aliud non omittere'* ('it is these you should have practised, without neglecting the others-Mt 23:23). Spiritual and psychological elements of the vocationers are not dichotomous, as we have emphasized earlier, but strictly interdependent and convergent for the final purpose to 'form that perfect man who is Christ come to full stature.'[78]

G. WHY HAVE SO MANY PEOPLE LEFT VOCATION SINCE VATICAN II?

Leaving aside the influence deriving from the new policy of the Church for dispensation, a tentative answer to this question would require a long discussion which cannot be made here. The interested reader may find some pertinent considerations in the 1971 book,[79] discussing the influences coming from the changes in the Church after Vatican II, as well as the ones emerging from the impact of the socio-cultural factors of our time. All these influences explain the phenomenon of massive dropping out in terms of social forces external to the organism. But what about the influence of internal psychodynamics?

The findings of the present book suggest that the intra-psychic dynamics which dispose to dropping out have not changed

---

[77] *Ibid.,* no. 36.
[78] Eph 4:13.
[79] Pp. 194-212, 137-140, and indirectly in pp. 266-321.

after Vatican II: people were and are undermined in their vocational commitment by central, subconscious vocational inconsistencies.[80] Our approach to the influence of intrapsychic factors is a structural one and as such prescinds from the norms which characterize a vocational group or institution, as well as from the ones proper to a particular socio-cultural milieu or historical period.[81] Thus, our approach is somehow trans-situational, transtemporal.

Apart from the influence of supernatural or spiritual factors, more people leave because their subconscious vocational inconsistencies *more frequently and more deeply* may affect their commitment. Why more frequently and more deeply? Referring the reader to the above quoted discussion of the 1971 publication for more comprehensive considerations, here we will answer by schematically pointing out three sets of possible influences.

a) As our data indicate, about 2/3 of the vocationers present central inconsistencies, i.e. rather shaky psychodynamics in which *subconscious* needs are inconsistent or dissonant, with the objective vocational values of imitation of Christ or union with God, and of the three evangelical counsels. However, as explained on pages 34-5, inconsistent people may be distinguished as psychologically inconsistent (PsI) or as socially inconsistent (SoI): the former have attitudes which are consonant with the objective vocational values, whilst the latter have attitudes which are consonant with the needs of the individual. Thus, psychologically inconsistent people may be called 'uniformists' since they are socially adjusted to their vocational institutions, but psychologically maladjusted because of their vocationally dissonant needs. Socially inconsistent people may be called 'rebels' because they are both socially *and* psychologically maladjusted. Thus the vocational perseverance and effectiveness of the 'rebels' is worse than that of the 'uniformists'; as a consequence, defections or poor vocational effectiveness are greater among the 'rebels'.

Now, before Vatican II, the type of leadership prevailing in vocational institutions was somehow oriented towards forced compliance with the norms of the institution. After Vatican II the prevailing orientation in leadership is not towards such forced compliance; structures are not fixed and rigid; actually, they are sometimes almost non-existent. The first, a rigid orientation,

---

[80] Cf. Chapter 9.
[81] Cf. Chapter 2.

tends to favor the development of 'uniformists'; the second, a permissive orientation, leads rather to the emergence of 'rebels'.

In fact, both uniformists and rebels have unconscious needs which are dissonant with objective values. But 'when dissonance is present, in addition to trying to reduce it, the person will actively avoid situations and information which would be likely to increase the dissonance'.[82] Thus:

> 1) When the environment is somewhat oriented towards forced compliance of attitudes and of not-directly vocational values, the religious vocationer cannot avoid many such dissonant situations and information. However, he can reduce his inner dissonance between his subconscious needs and vocational values by accepting the attitudes and the not-directly vocational values and by warding off the latter dissonance by means of the mechanisms of defense: such vocational inconsistency is the one previously described as the psychological inconsistency of the 'uniformist'.

> 2) The situation is different when the environment is not oriented towards compliance through attitudes and not-directly vocational values, but subconscious needs conflicting with vocational values are present in the individual. In fact, in such a case, especially if the general atmosphere of the environment is towards indiscriminate freedom, the individual or some of the peers in the institution can try to reduce the dissonance by favoring *new* situations and information, i.e. by choosing attitudes which are consonant with the subconscious needs but are dissonant with vocational values, and by warding off such dissonance by means of defense mechanisms: this vocational inconsistency is the one we have called the social inconsistency of the 'rebels'.[83]

Needless to say, here we are not stating that, because central social inconsistencies are vocationally worse than psychological inconsistencies, we should go back to the 'holy uniformity' ideas and methods which we have seen in the past; just the opposite. Both social and psychological inconsistencies are compromises rather than genuine coping with the underlying persistent conflicts between vocational values and subconscious inconsistent needs; both are detrimental to healthy personality growth and real internalization of vocational values and attitudes.[84] We do not remedy one mistake by making another!

However, the point may be made that the rigid, fixed structures of the pre-Vatican II situation were offering some help to the shaky psychodynamics of the *inconsistent* people and keeping them in, with the defensiveness of the 'uniformists'. Still, this was a

---

[82] Festinger, 1957, p. 3.
[83] Rulla, 1971, p. 139.
[84] Cf. the findings of Chapter 9.

very artificial help as has been shown by the massive dropping out in the post-Vatican II period. It was enough that the crutches of the structures more or less compliantly accepted were taken away, for the inconsistent psychodynamics of the individual to fall apart, leading to his defection.

b) Some considerations have been presented elsewhere[85] concerning the changes brought about by Vatican II with regard to the ideas, functions and structures related to priestly and religious vocation. Also discussed[86] was the influence of recent theological and sociocultural patterns upon leadership in the Church (e.g. the questioning of belief in prior knowledge or of any normative standard, the uncertainty about previous frames of reference).

What are the possible effects of all these changes upon the individuals' psychodynamics? For the purpose of our discussion we can limit ourselves to mention one among many others: the functional relationship of the three significant operative forces of psychodynamics — values, attitudes and needs (conscious and subconscious) — has been changed. In fact, the power of the values *may be* more easily weakened; attitudes are less subject to the influence of institutional structures which have been more or less loosened; the needs of the individuals, conscious and especially unconscious, remain the same. Thus, the functional relationship between values, attitudes and needs tends towards less strength for the first two elements, and a 'relatively' greater influence of the last, especially in the inconsistent people. There follows a greater influence of the *subconscious* elements in the psychodynamics of inconsistent people. Such a greater subconscious influence is felt also in creating one's ideals which hence may more easily become less objective and free, may more easily be *pseudovalues*. The greater relative strength of subconscious needs makes them more influential than values upon attitudes; as a consequence, the attitudes will tend to coincide with the needs rather than the values. Concretely, this means that social inconsistencies become more frequent than psychological inconsistences. And since social inconsistencies are worse than psychological inconsistencies for both vocational perseverance and effectiveness, more frequent defections and vocational maladjust-

---

85 Rulla, 1971, pp. 195-199.
86 *Ibid.*, pp. 293-321.

ment are the consequences. Note that the relationship between values and subconscious factors may become a two-way street: decrease in spiritual life makes possible greater negative influence of subconscious elements and vice versa; increase in subconscious factors may affect spiritual life.

c)   As was previously mentioned,[87] before Vatican II growth in vocational commitment was seen primarily as a process of internalization of vocational values and attitudes without proper concern for the useful contribution coming from the *free* experiencing of roles. Vice versa, after Vatican II, the focus is upon experiencing roles without proper concerns for the *necessary* internalization of vocational values and attitudes.

However, as discussed in part E of this Chapter, role-enactment may not lead to internalization of vocational values and attitudes. This is true at least for the centrally inconsistent people. Actually, for them the role orientation may be in opposition to the value orientation and role-enactment may initiate the vicious circle described in chart 16. As a consequence, people may drop out.

All the three sets of factors described, point to the relevance of the intrapsychic dynamics in the process of dropping out *when* such psychodynamics are centrally inconsistent. Social forces external to the individual's personality may have a strong negative influence on this process. However, it would seem that people who are vocationally consistent have the strength both to stand this influence and to overcome it by creatively, constructively acting upon these social forces, whilst people undermined by central inconsistencies more easily fail in their vocational endeavors. After all, man may and in fact does 'code' all the social messages he receives. Among these one can include the messages from spiritual sources like readings, conferences, constitutions of religious institutions, etc. The findings of our Chapters 5-9 are all indicative of this.

The same three sets of factors point also to the gap between the healthy ideas of freedom, responsibility and initiative proposed by Vatican II on the one hand, and the capacity of individuals to implement them on the other. To give greater personal freedom does not automatically make people free; to give responsibility does not necessarily make people responsible; to foster initiative does not inevitably lead to a mature use of it.

---

[87]   P. 130.

Before the Second Vatican Council, institutional structures offered some help to the shaky psychodynamics of the *inconsistent* people. It was a precarious help because it fostered more compliance or non-internalizing identification than genuine internalization of vocational values and attitudes. Now that, after the Council, the precarious help of the structures is no longer there, some new help should be offered to increase the internalizing capacity of individuals.

> If we want to, and we should (in order not to perpetuate previous mistakes), implement the new ideas of Vatican II about personal freedom, responsibility, initiative, functions, etc. *then we should have more mature subjects, and educators who can help them to become so.* To implement the ideas without having prepared the subjects and the educators will lead to more problems than solutions, as the experience of recent years has shown. Freedom and responsibility are useful in a degree proportionate to the personality psychodynamics of each individual, and therefore the psychodynamics should be prepared in order to profit from this usefulness, otherwise more harm than help will result.[88]

H. ARE THERE PSYCHOLOGICAL LAWS OF PRIESTLY AND RELIGIOUS VOCATIONS?

Let us qualify the meaning of the proposed question. The findings of this book did not necessarily consider the whole man, especially his superior activities of the spiritual level.

Our results, first of all, tend to show some elements (needs, values and attitudes) and the 'psychological' relations of consistency-inconsistency among them; secondly, they indicate how both the elements and their *structural* relations act as *dispositions* to the self-transcendent action of the spiritual and of the supernatural factors in the processes of vocational entrance, perseverance and effectiveness.[89]

As such, many of our data do not fall *directly* under the influence of freedom and of spiritual dynamism. The French philosopher Ricoeur[90] assigns to the foregoing dispositions the function of a 'material cause' of human behavior:

> Ce peut être le même potentiel affectif qui alimente la sexualité enfantine et la moralité de l'adulte. L'origine de la 'matière' affective

---

88 Rulla, 1971, p. 216.
89 For 'structural approach', see Chapter 2.
90 Ricoeur, 1949, p. 380.

et le *sens* de la 'forme' intentionelle posent deux problèmes radicale-
ment différents. Il n'y a rien de scandaleux à ce que le psychanalyste
retrouve à la racine de la série discontinue des valeurs parcourues par
la conscience, depuis le vital jusqu'au sacré, l'unité d'une meme
matière affective . . .

It is the 'affective charge' (*potentiel affectif*) which Ricoeur
mentions, that may dispose individual priests or religious in different ways and degrees to the action of the spiritual and supernatural forces on their entrance, perseverance and effectiveness in
vocation.

It is with the foregoing connotations in mind that we speak
of affective dispositions as psychological laws in vocation. In
fact, as our findings indicate, the strength of these affective dispositions may be considerable. After all, supernatural grace
builds on nature and brings it to completion (it is the '*gratia
perficit naturam*' of Thomas Aquinas).

In spite of the differences among individuals, the structural
consistencies/inconsistencies are basic, *common* processes which
dispose them to the action of self-transcendent and *objective*
values. Seen in this perspective, the vocational 'laws' found in
our research point to the fallacies inherent in approaches to an
understanding of and dealing with vocation which follow one of
the following two views of man: the deterministic-pessimistic view
of classical Freudian psychoanalysis (to be distinguished from
'Ego-psychology') and the subjectivistic-optimistic view of the
self-fulfillment, self-actualization model of man expressed by authors like C. Rogers, A. Maslow and some of the existentialists.

According to the first view, man is a product or effect of a
chain of diverse causes. The human person is a phenomenon
whose essence can be grasped as if it were a fully conditioned and
wholly predictable thing among and like other things. Now, as
our research confirms, it is true that we may try to predict the
dynamics of the human psyche. But man is more than psyche:
man is spirit and thus he has the chance of changing. Note that
we admit the fact that man has 'dispositions', but — against the
strictly deterministic view — we uphold that man may dispose of
his dispositions;[91] i.e. man is not responsible for some of his
dispositions, but he is responsible for the attitude he takes to do
or not to do something in order to change them, e.g. to seek or

---

[91] Frankl, 1949.

not to seek help in fostering his vocational perseverance and effectiveness.

This idea of 'responsibility' leads us to comment on another concept common to the two schools of thought just mentioned. As Frankl[92] has shown, both Freudian psychoanalysis and the self-actualization models imply a subjectification of values; for both, values are not 'objective', but a mere self-expression of the subject himself. But this excludes self-transcendence as an inherent characteristic of the human person. In the words of Frankl:

> If meaning and values were just something emerging from the subject himself — that is to say, if they were not something that stems from a sphere beyond man and above man — they would instantly lose their demand quality. They could no longer be a real challenge to man, they would never be able to summon him up, to call him forth. If that for the realization of which we are *responsible* is to keep its obligative quality, then it must be seen in its objective quality.[93]

The same holds for the concepts of 'happiness' of psychoanalysis and of 'peak-experiences' of Maslow; in fact, they are the same, irrespective of the experiences which cause them. But: 'It is obvious that dealing with the uniform forms of experiences rather than with their different contents presupposes that the self-transcendent quality of human existence has been shut out.'[94]

Both 'happiness' and 'self-actualization' point to fulfillment of the self, or self-actualization, rather than to the fulfillment of self-transcendent values and meanings. But:

> Self-actualization is not man's ultimate destination. It is not even his primary intention. Self-actualization, if made an end in itself, contradicts the self-transcendent quality of human existence. Like happiness, self-actualization is an effect, the effect of meaning fulfillment. Only to the extent to which man fulfills a meaning out there in the world, does he fulfill himself. If he sets out to actualize himself rather than fulfill a meaning, self-actualization immediately loses its justification.[95]

With regard to the self-actualization model, it should be noted that this view of man has been fairly widely accepted in vocational institutions after Vatican II, but not necessarily because of any empirical substantiation. In the words of Berkowitz: 'Basically

---

[92] Frankl, 1967, 1969.
[93] Frankl, 1967, p. 64 with footnote 4.
[94] Frankl, 1969, p. 39.
[95] *Ibid.*, p. 38.

. . . the self-actualization thesis is a romantic throwback to the eighteenth-century notion of the "noble savage". Based more on wishes of what man should be like than on actual hard fact . . . this growth-through-gratification doctrine has a dubious scientific and philosophic status, both as a motivational theory and as a formula for bringing up the young.'[96] We have already quoted some analogous conclusions of Lieberman, Yalom and Miles[97] who considered the application of the self-actualization model to the experience of the 'encounter groups'.

The inherent characteristic of man for self-transcendence rather than for self-actualization, self-fulfillment, is valid not only for priestly and religious vocations, but for any form of christian commitment. Such a vital characteristic has been proclaimed by Christ: 'I tell you, unless a grain of wheat falls on the ground and dies, it remains just one grain. But if it dies, it yields a great harvest.' (Jn 12:24) Again: 'Whoever gains his life will lose it, and whoever loses his life for my sake will gain it.' (Mt 10:39) Our results of Chapters 5, 6 and 9 indicate that in the call to religious vocation, God seems to underline self-transcendence rather than self-actualization.

I. SOME FINAL CONSIDERATIONS

The following general messages seem to emerge from the results and discussion of our study.

Every human life is a vocation, is a mission. Every mission is a person before being a work; a man must be before he acts, he must be entirely himself with his humanity redeemed by Christ before he offers himself for the work of the Kingdom. It is this priority in time of the person over his mission, over his work-roles, that is underscored by the findings of the present book.

A second message: Vocation is usually begun with ideals which are seemingly evangelical, i.e. unselfishly self-transcendent. But, whilst in some instances these initial ideals develop genuinely and are christianly germinative, in others they present already in themselves the roots not only of self-transcendence but also of *prevailing* self-centeredness. In time, the person may identify

---

[96] Berkowitz, 1969, p. 87.
[97] Lieberman, Yalom and Miles, 1973.

more and more with the latter and make of himself and of his apostolic activities an absolute, which has no freedom to transcend itself in the gift of unselfish love. In these frequent instances, blocked in himself, in his needs, the vocationer consequently has to create his own expectations which meet his needs but which are often at variance with the evangelical message.

The self-detachment, the self-transcendence proclaimed by Christ as the royal road to the love of God and of neighbor is replaced by self-fulfillment. Accordingly, the person will feel more and more alienated and isolated; his vocational perseverance and/ or effectiveness will gradually be undermined. The person will be prompted to try different roles, but this will hardly change the foregoing absolute, which he has created himself and which stands as a strong impediment to his freedom for vocational growth.

A third message: the presentation and the internalization of the vocational ideals offered by the traditional methods of spirituality should be complemented in most instances by an appropriate help offered by the methods of *depth*-psychology to uproot the self-centered elements which may seriously impair both a mature election of and a growth in the self-transcendent commitment of christian vocation.

After all, if the divine inspiration depends on God, the way of receiving and implementing it depends also on the *whole* man. As Laplace[98] says, a decision is as valuable as the man who takes it. The empirical findings of this book say the same, and point to an important distinction: the perception of a call coming from a set of values is different from the capacity to internalize it. A proper help to vocationers should offer spiritual food, but should also assure an adequate capacity to assimilate it. Actually, there should be some correspondence between the spiritual values offered and the capacity the person has to assimilate them, to internalize them; otherwise, the ideals proposed will become sources more of frustration than of growth. As we have repeatedly seen, depth psychology has a lot to contribute in increasing such a capacity to assimilate, to internalize the proposed ideals. Any dichotomy between spiritual and in-depth psychological help is most likely to be more harmful than helpful.

This is particularly true now, after Vatican II, if the healthy principles of individual responsibility and initiative proposed by

---

[98] Laplace, 1972.

the Council are to be implemented: there should be a correspondence between these ideals and the capacity to actualize them. But, as our very recent findings concerning vocationers of 1974 confirm, the man, the vocationer of post-Vatican II is still the same fragile vessel as the one of pre-Vatican II. For him too, chronological age does not necessarily coincide with psychological age; for him too, having opportunity for experiences does not necessarily mean learning and growth; at least this is true for 60-80% of the vocationers. Individual responsibility, freedom and initiative are a challenge which the vocationer of post-Vatican II has to meet, without the crutches of rigid institutional structures. It is our serious duty to replace these precarious supports from without with more mature personality structures from within.

From this follows the fourth message: the need for new educators. Two types of educators were previously described in this Chapter and — at greater length — in the 1971 publication. Here we would like only to explain what we hope could be somehow 'new' in them.

First of all, these educators should be able to perceive the deep, underlying psychodynamics of the vocationers and help them to avoid the 'tunnel syndrome'. An example will illustrate what is meant by this expression. Recently, a superior stated that the formation program of his religious community was very good at the novitiate level; people would come out of the novitiate with promising signs of real growth. But then he added, 'Our program does not seem to function when individuals are in their college studies or in their first experiences of the apostolate'. As had happened before Vatican II, so now after the Council, in all good faith, vocationers go through the first years of their religious life and formation almost as one would go through a tunnel: many aspects of their personality *seem* to have changed, but in fact they were only covered up or ignored. Unfortunately, especially when deeply subconscious inconsistencies are present, reality will catch up with these persons later on. In such cases — which also in the words of the same superior seem to be quite frequent — it is not the later but rather the earlier program of formation which did not function because it did not touch the depths of the personality. The findings of this book indicate that this is what seems to happen.

Secondly, these educators should be able to avoid projecting some of their own unsolved personality problems on to their

195

vocationers and/or falling into some of the inordinate demands which the latter may make subconsciously. In both instances, charity is not served. These educators should have worked out their own 'tunnel syndrome'. Aware of their inner strivings, they should be able to love unselfishly, to give without getting.

This leads to the fifth message: As previously discussed, the integration of spiritual and psychological helps should offer especially the pedagogical support, as distinguished from the ones of psychotherapy and screening; i.e. this integration should aim at fostering the growth of vocationers in their capacity to internalize vocational values and attitudes, rather than at solving problems of overt or covert psychopathology (which, however, should not be overlooked).

As was seen in Chapter 9, this capacity is related to structural rather than to content properties of the personality of the individuals. Therefore it transcends the content of the value system (excluding the five basic values indicated in Chapter 1) and that of attitudes proposed in different vocational situations. Thus it helps the educators overcome a dilemma in which they frequently find themselves: siding with the institution or with the subjects, with the 'establishment' or with the 'reformers'. What is at stake in the pedagogical help is the combined effort of everyone involved — subjects, representatives of the institution, and educators — to search for truth and for growth in the capacity to live it. This effort should be made not only by the educators, but also and especially by the interested subjects *and* the legitimate representatives of the institution. The educators, paradoxically, should be at the service of neither one nor the other of the two interested parties, but of *both*. They should serve neither one nor the other, but both the parties in so far as they ask to be helped to grow in their capacity to internalize the basic vocational ideals which *they* profess. After all, the obligation for this personal growth is valid for the educators, for the superiors, and for the other members of the community.

Of course, many may resist the dismantling of the false expectations they may have created; thus the new educators may be disliked by both the right and the left wings, even though the opposite may also be true. Anyway, the new educators should be ready to pay the price asked by self-transcendent love: to profess in themselves and to help others to 'profess the truth in love' and thus to 'grow to the full maturity of Christ, the head' (Eph 4:14).

196

APPENDICES

APPENDICES

APPENDIX A

INSTRUMENTS

A-1 MAI: MODIFIED ACTIVITIES INDEX

Symbols	Scales
Sc 1	Abasement
Sc 2	Achievement
Sc 3	Humility (as opposed to defendance and infavoidance), Adaptability
Sc 4	Affiliation
Sc 5	Aggression
Sc 6	Change, novelty
Sc 7	Conjunctivity, planfulness
Sc 8	Counteraction
Sc 9	Deference
Sc 10	Dominance
Sc 11	Ego Achievement, striving for social action
Sc 12	Emotional Expressiveness
Sc 13	Energy, effort
Sc 14	Exhibition
Sc 15	Fantasied Achievement
Sc 16	Harm Avoidance
Sc 17	Humanities and Social Science
Sc 18	Impulsiveness
Sc 19	Narcissism
Sc 20	Nurturance
Sc 21	Not Superstitious
Sc 22	Order
Sc 23	Pleasure Seeking, Play
Sc 24	Practicalness
Sc 25	Reflectiveness
Sc 26	Science
Sc 27	Sensuality, sentience
Sc 28	Supplication, succorance
Sc 29	Understanding
Sc 30	Chastity
Sc 31	Conscientiousness in observance of rules (poverty)
Sc 32	Piety
Sc 33	Mortification
Sc 34	Responsibility to Studies and Work
Sc 35	Obedience

199

N.B. Of the 35 variables described above, 14 may be correlated with the same variables obtained from the classification of the TAT and Rotter ISB.

The 14 variables are: Abasement, Achievement, Affiliation, Aggression, Avoid censure, Chastity, Counteraction, Dominance, Exhibition, Harm avoidance, Knowledge, Nurturance, Order, Succorance.

In relation to the 5 values indicated in Chapter 1, these 14 variables are divided as follows into vocationally *dissonant* and vocationally neutral:

Vocationally dissonant variables:

Abasement, Aggression, Avoid censure, Chastity (the name given to the need for sexual gratification), Exhibition, Harm avoidance, Succorance.

Vocationally neutral variables:

Achievement, Affiliation, Counteraction, Dominance, Knowledge, Nurturance, Order.

A-2   MODIFIED GENERAL GOALS OF LIFE INVENTORY

General Goals of Life

A. Serving God, doing God's will.
B. Achieving personal immortality in heaven.
C. Self-discipline . . . overcoming my irrational sensuous desires.
D. Self-sacrifice for the sake of a better world.
E. Doing my duty.
F. Peace of mind, contentment, stillness of spirit.
G. Serving the community of which I am a part.
H. Having fine relations with other people.
I. Self-development . . . becoming a real, genuine person.
J. Finding my place in life and accepting it.
K. Living for the pleasure of the moment.
L. Getting as many deep and lasting pleasures out of life as I can.

M. Promoting the most deep and lasting pleasures for the greatest number of people.
N. Making a place for myself; getting ahead.
O. Power; control over people and things.
P. Security . . . protecting my way of life against adverse changes.
Q. Being able to 'take it': brave and uncomplaining acceptance of what circumstances bring.
R. Realizing that I cannot change the bad features of the world and doing the best I can for myself and those dear to me.
S. Survival, continued existence.
T. Handling the specific problems of life as they arise.
U. Developing my mind so that I am knowledgeable and effective in intellectual endeavor.

A-3 ROTTER AND THEMATIC APPERCEPTION TEST

Definitions of Emotions

Anxiety, Overt: public, unconcealed anguish, marked and continuous apprehension.
Anxiety, Covert: concealed anguish, marked and continuous apprehension of evil.
Sadness (Depression), Overt: Unconcealed inaccessibility to stimulation, low initiative, gloom.
Sadness (Depression), Covert: concealed inaccessibility to stimulation, low initiative, gloom, feeling of abandonment and frustration.
Pride: Paranoid thinking: lack of objectivity in the form of exaggerated ideation (Cameron, 1963).
Guilt, overt: unconcealed, manifest sorrow or anxiety for ethical or moral or psychological wrong performed. Expectation of retribution.
Guilt, covert: concealed, manifest anxiety or apprehension for ethical, moral or psychological wrong performed or vicari-

ously performed in thought, with expectation of retribution.

ROTTER AND THEMATIC APPERCEPTION TEST

Definitions of Needs
(Murray's)

Abasement: to submit passively to external force. To accept injury, blame, criticism, punishment. To surrender. To become resigned to fate. To admit inferiority, error, wrongdoing, or defeat. To confess and atone. To blame, belittle, or mutilate the self. To seek and enjoy pain, punishment, illness and misfortune.

Achievement: to accomplish something difficult. To master, manipulate, or organize physical objects, human beings, or ideas. To do this as rapidly and as independently as possible. To overcome obstacles and attain a high standard. To excel oneself. To rival and surpass others. To increase self-regard by the successful exercise of talent.

Acquirement: to gain possession and property, to get goods or money for oneself.

Affiliation: to draw near and enjoyably cooperate or reciprocate with an allied other (another who resembles the subject or likes the subject). To please and win the affection of a cathected object. To adhere and remain loyal to a friend. (Two-way relationship. See succorrance) Negative schizoid.

Aggression: to overcome opposition forcefully. To fight. To revenge an injury. To attack, injure or kill another. To oppose forcefully or punish another.

Autonomy: to get free, shake off restraint, break out of confinement. To resist coercion and restriction. To avoid or quit activities prescribed by domineering authorities. To be independent and free to act according to impulse. To be unattached, irresponsible. To defy convention.

Avoid Censure or Failure: defendence — to defend the self

against assault, criticism or blame. To conceal or justify a misdeed, failure or humiliation. To vindicate the ego. *Passive* conformity, or Infavoidance — to avoid humiliation. To quit embarrassing situations or to avoid conditions which may lead to belittlement: the scorn, derision, or indifference of others. To refrain from action because of the fear of failure.

Change (Novelty): to change, to alter his circumstances, environment, associations, activities, to avoid routine or sameness.

Knowledge (Curiosity): to know, to satisfy curiosity, to explore, to acquire information or knowledge.

Submission (Deference): to admire and support a superior. To praise, honor or eulogize. To yield eagerly to the influence of an allied other. To emulate an exemplar. To conform to custom. *Active* conformity.

Domination: to control one's human environment. To influence or direct the behavior of others by suggestion, seduction, persuasion, or command or enticement. To dissuade, restrain or prohibit.

Excitement: to be easily aroused, stimulated, excited or agitated.

Exhibition: to make an impression. To be seen and heard. To excite, amaze, fascinate, entertain, shock, intrigue, amuse or entice others.

Avoid Injury (Harm avoidance): to avoid pain, physical injury, illness and death. To escape from a dangerous situation. To take precautionary measures.

To Nurture (Nurturance): To give sympathy and gratify the needs of a helpless object: an infant or any object that is weak, disabled, tired, inexperienced, infirm, defeated, humiliated, lonely, dejected, sick, mentally confused. To assist an object in danger. To feed, help, support, console, protect, comfort, nurse, heal.

Organization (Order): to put things in order. To achieve cleanliness, arrangement, organization, balance, neatness, tidiness, and precision.

Playfulness (Play): to act for 'fun' without further purpose. To like to laugh and make jokes. To seek enjoyable relaxation of stress. To participate in games, sports, dancing, drinking parties, cards. Daydreaming.

Recognition (Social Approval): to gain prestige, to win honors, to get praise and recognition.

203

Sexual Gratification: to form and further an erotic relationship. To have sexual intercourse.

Succorance: to have one's needs gratified by the sympathetic aid of an allied object. To be nursed, supported, sustained, surrounded, protected, loved, advised, guided, indulged, forgiven, consoled. To always have a supporter. *One* way relationship.

Counteraction: to strive persistently to overcome difficult, frustrating or humiliating or embarassing experiences and failures versus avoidance or hasty withdrawal from tasks or situations that might result in such outcomes.

THEMATIC APPERCEPTION TEST

Definitions of Defenses

Compensation: Attempts to make up for real or imagined deficiency in personal characteristics or status by exaggerated striving in fantasy or action.

Denial: Painful aspects of external reality are unconsciously handled by denying (negation or unawareness of) their existence.

Displacement: Attaches affects to other than their proper objects.

Identification: Transfers and attaches to his own personality the qualities or traits of another.

Parentification: Attempts to utilize individuals as if they are mother or father.

Intellectualization: (rationalization) — concocts plausible reasons for his opinions or actions which he believes to explain them, thereby avoiding recognition of less acceptable motivations which are the real underlying source.

Isolation: Avoids threatening affective arousal by selectively confining his attending and reporting to the cognitive, causal, unemotional or depersonalized aspects of an underlying wish or impulse.

Projection: (To be used only when a person in the story (not the hero) is the object of the projection).
 A) *Supplementary:* Avoids recognition of own unacceptable impulses by attributing them to others.
 B) *Complementary:* Ascribes to others motives that explain one's distress.

Reaction Formation: Shows behavior or thought which is opposite in form or manifest direction to the underlying impulse.

Regression: Handles intrapsychic conflict or external frustration by reverting to earlier, primitive, infantile patterns of impulse expressions.

Repression: Excludes psychic contents (ideas or impulses) from consciousness in the interest of anxiety-avoidance, either with (suppression) or without (repression) awareness of doing so.

Undoing: Performs activity unconsciously intended to 'cancel out' or 'render undone' some other action.

ROTTER AND THEMATIC APPERCEPTION TEST

Conflict Descriptions
(Erikson, 1950, 1959)

1. Trust-mistrust:
 (a) A disposition to trust others, a capacity to receive from others and to depend on them.
 (b) The opposite.
2. Autonomy-shame, doubt:
 (a) Capacity to self-assertion and self-expression, an ability to maintain self-control without loss of self-esteem;
 (b) lack of self-esteem reflected in shame, and lack of self-confidence implied in self-doubt (Note: this version of autonomy is less rebellious and aggressive than on MAI scale 37, and the Murray TAT description).

3. Initiative-guilt:

    (a) Sense of responsibility, capability, and discipline — capacity to direct energies toward goals (ego);

    (b) harsh, rigid, moralistic, self-punishing superego (guilt superego). Sexual conflict.

4. Industry-inferiority:

    (a) Capacity to *maintain* the directed energies until the goal is achieved or the task completed;

    (b) fear of failure or inability to compete with others.

5. Identity-role diffusion:

    (a) Confident sense of ability to maintain inner sameness and continuity, and solidarity with a realistic system of values as embodied in social or cultural contexts;

    (b) uncertainty about self-image and no commitment to a system of values.

6. Intimacy-isolation:

    (a) Capacity to relate intimately and meaningfully with others in mutually satisfying and productive interactions;

    (b) opposite of that as a failure to realize secure and mature self-acceptance. (Note: In contrast to 1, this implies both acceptance of self and other).

7. Generativity-stagnation:

    (a) Concern with, and capacity for the utilization of productive capabilities for the welfare of others;

    (b) the absence of expression of productive capabilities, or the use of such capabilities in a self-centered way.

8. Ego integrity-despair:

    (a) Acceptance of oneself and all the aspects of life, and the integration of these elements into a stable pattern of living;

    (b) lack of acceptance of oneself and one's life, associated with self-contempt and fear of death.

TAT STORIES

SCORER'S SHEET

	1	2	3	4	5	6	7	Rotter

Emotions

Anxiety < overt / covert

Sadness < overt / covert

(Depression)

1 Pride

Guilt < overt / covert

Abasement
Achievement
2* Acquirement
Affiliation
Aggression
Autonomy
3 Avoid Censure
or Failure
4* Change
(Novelty)
5* Knowledge
(Curiosity)

---

* = Not on Murray's List.
1   Pride: Paranoid thinking; lack of objectivity in the form of exaggerated ideation (Cameron, 1963).
2* Acquirement: to gain possessions and property, to get goods or money for himself.
3   Avoid censure or failure (defendance or infavoidance).
4* Change (Novelty): to change, to alter circumstances, environment, associations, or activities, to avoid routine or sameness.
5* Knowledge (Curiosity): to know, to satisfy curiosity, to explore, to acquire information or knowledge.

Submission
  (Deference) —— —— —— —— —— —— —— ——
Domination —— —— —— —— —— —— —— ——
Excitement —— —— —— —— —— —— —— ——
Exhibition —— —— —— —— —— —— —— ——
Avoid Injury —— —— —— —— —— —— —— ——
To Nurture —— —— —— —— —— —— —— ——
Organization
  (Order) —— —— —— —— —— —— —— ——
Playfulness —— —— —— —— —— —— —— ——
6* Recognition
  (Social
  Approval) —— —— —— —— —— —— —— ——
Sexual
  Gratification —— —— —— —— —— —— —— ——
Succorance —— —— —— —— —— —— —— ——
Counteraction —— —— —— —— —— —— —— ——

TAT STORIES

SCORERS' SHEET

Defenses	1	2	3	4	5	6	7	Rotter
Compensation (in fantasy or action)	——	——	——	——	——	——	——	——
Denial (external)	——	——	——	——	——	——	——	——
Displacement (symbolization)	——	——	——	——	——	——	——	——
Identification	——	——	——	——	——	——	——	——
Intellectualization (rationalization)	——	——	——	——	——	——	——	——
Isolation	——	——	——	——	——	——	——	——

6* Recognition (Social Approval): to gain prestige, to win honors, to get praise and recognition.

Parentification ——— ——— ——— ——— ——— ——— ——— ———

Projection ——— ——— ——— ——— ——— ——— ——— ———
Reaction
    Formation ——— ——— ——— ——— ——— ——— ——— ———

Regression ——— ——— ——— ——— ——— ——— ——— ———

Repression ——— ——— ——— ——— ——— ——— ——— ———
(suppression)
Undoing ——— ——— ——— ——— ——— ——— ——— ———
Conflict by
Erikson ——— ——— ——— ——— ——— ——— ——— ———

———————

A-4 EXTRACT FROM THE BIOGRAPHICAL INVENTORY

The following questions concern your family life before entering the novitiate/seminary.

Please circle the appropriate number in each of the following rows, considering each row to refer to an aspect of the way your mother was towards you.

Extreme		*Extreme*
Affectionate	0 1 2 3 4 5 6 7 8 9	Unaffectionate
Strict	0 1 2 3 4 5 6 7 8 9	Lenient
Trusting	0 1 2 3 4 5 6 7 8 9	Distrustful
Consistent	0 1 2 3 4 5 6 7 8 9	Inconsistent
Self-Preoccupied	0 1 2 3 4 5 6 7 8 9	Generous
Understanding	0 1 2 3 4 5 6 7 8 9	Unsympathetic
Punitive	0 1 2 3 4 5 6 7 8 9	Supportive
Critical	0 1 2 3 4 5 6 7 8 9	Forgiving
Envious	0 1 2 3 4 5 6 7 8 9	Appreciative
Open-Minded	0 1 2 3 4 5 6 7 8 9	Close-Minded
In Conflict	0 1 2 3 4 5 6 7 8 9	In Harmony
Independent	0 1 2 3 4 5 6 7 8 9	Dependent
Overpowering	0 1 2 3 4 5 6 7 8 9	Gentle
Pushy	0 1 2 3 4 5 6 7 8 9	Relaxed
Trustworthy	0 1 2 3 4 5 6 7 8 9	Untrustworthy

N.B. The same fifteen dimensions served also to describe the relationship with the *father*, with *brothers*, with *sisters* and the relationship between the parents.

A-5   FAMILY DYNAMICS INTERVIEW

No Communication   Great Communication
   Father   1 2 3 4 5
   Mother   1 2 3 4 5
No Affection   Great Affection
   Father   1 2 3 4 5
   Mother   1 2 3 4 5
No Interactional Conflict   Great Interactional Conflict
   Father   5 4 3 2 1
   Mother   5 4 3 2 1
Usual Role   5 4 3 2 1 Role Reversal
No Parental
   Conflict   5 4 3 2 1 Great Parental Conflict

Psychopathology in Family:
   Father ....
   Mother ....
   Siblings ....
   Others ....

Personal Characteristics:
   Insecurity   1   2   3
   Rapport   1   2   3
   Defensiveness 1   2   3

A-6   OUTLINE FOR DEPTH INTERVIEW

1. Skim through family interview results plus most relevant information of the Biographical Inventory.
2. Interpretation of the most important data in the profile con-

figurations of the MMPI for the three testing periods.
3. Check the data of the Intuitive Analysis for the three testing periods and cluster them according to clinical and dynamic significance.
4. Questionnaire guided interview following the Depth Interview Supplements.
5. More unstructured depth interview about the conflictual aspects of the personality in order to discriminate the conscious from the subconscious elements of personality.
6. Inquiry about the psychogenesis of the main conflict.
7. Inquiry about sex life.
8. Final investigation about the degree of developmental maturity at the beginning, during the first two years of life in religious settings (or Novitiate), and during the third and fourth years.
9. Subject is asked if he has something to discuss, to object to, or to clarify.
10. Fill up the items in 'TAT stories' according to the result of the interview.
11. Rank the developmental stages or conflicts described by Erikson found in the interview.
12. Write a summary with psychopathological, dynamic and psychogenetic evaluations.

A-7 DEPTH INTERVIEW SUPPLEMENT

Interaction in the novitiate:

No Communication			Great Communication
Father master 1	2	3	
Assistant 1	2	3	
Peers 1	2	3	

Strict			Lenient (Autonomy)
Father master 1	2	3	
Assistant 1	2	3	
Peers 1	2	3	

211

Psychological Structure and Vocation

Inconsistent				Consistent
Father master	1	2	3	
Assistant	1	2	3	
Peers	1	2	3	

Cold				Warm
Father master	1	2	3	
Assistant	1	2	3	
Peers	1	2	3	

In Conflict				In Harmony
Father master	1	2	3	
Assistant	1	2	3	
Peers	1	2	3	

Personality Variables

Guilt	1	2	3
Hostility (rage; uncoopera-tiveness)	1	2	3
Tension	1	2	3
Pride	1	2	3
Depression	1	2	3
Affection	1	2	3

APPENDIX B

TABLES

TABLE I

ORIGINS OF THE SUBJECTS ANALYZED IN THIS BOOK

Institutions, formation centers and corresponding groups; Years of entry; age range and mean of the subjects, with indication of the experimental procedures used: questionnaires, projective tests, interviews (in footnote).

TABLE. I

RELIGIOUS, SEMINARIANS AND CONTROL GROUPS
BY INSTITUTION AND SETTING

MALES[2]				
RELIGIOUS OR SEMINARIANS [1]Age range 18-24 mean 18.3			LAY CONTROL [1]Age range 18-20 Mean 18.2	
Institution I		Institution II [3]	Institution I	Institution II
Setting 1	Setting 2	Setting 3		
Group A (1963) Group B (1964) Group C (1965) Group D (1966) Group E (1967)	Group A (1965) Group B (1966) Group C (1967)	Group A (1966)	Group A (1966)	Group A (1967)
FEMALES[2]				
RELIGIOUS		[1]Age range 18-21 Mean 18.1	LAY CONTROL [1]Age range 18-20 Mean 18.2	
Institution I		Institution II	Institution I	Institution II
Setting 1	Setting 2	Setting 3		
Group A (1963) Group B (1964) Group C (1965) Group D (1966)	Group A (1963) Group B (1964) Group C (1965)	Group A (1963) Group B (1964) Group C (1965) Group D (1966)	Group A (1966)	Group A (1967)

---

[1] Testings
For religious and seminarians: with the exception of Group A in setting 3, composed of seminarians who were tested only twice (on entrance and after two years), all were tested three times: on

(Cont'd on page 214)

entrance (the year is indicated in parenthesis), after *two* years, and after *four* years.

It is important to note that in this book we study only the results of the *first* testing, of the family interview (4 months after entrance), and of the depth interview.

For the control groups: there were only two testings: on entrance, and after four years.

2 *The instruments used* (tests, family interview and depth interview) were always the same: they are dealt with in Chapter 3.

In the first series of tests, we did not use the modified version of the activities index (MAI) for the following groups:

For male religious, groups A and B of Institution I, Setting 1.

For female religious, groups A and B of Settings 1, 2 and 3.

3 Another group of 39 seminarians beginning theology (age range 21-24, mean 22.1), described in Chapter 7, who were studied only on entrance (1974), does not appear in this table.

TABLE II

MEAN SCORES OF THE PREDICTABLE INTERNALIZING CAPACITY FOR DROP-OUTS (DO) AND NON-DROP-OUTS (NDO)

VARIABLES	SEMINARIANS		FEMALE RELIGIOUS		MALE RELIGIOUS		MALE CONTROLS (N=52)	FEMALE CONTROLS (N=50)
	DO (N=21)	NDO (N=19)	DO (N=77)	NDO (N=18)	DO (N=57)	NDO (N=39)		
INCONSISTENCIES:								
Abasement	7.38	5.14	6.61	4.46	3.21	2.32	4.24	6.68
Aggression	7.00	5.00	7.61	7.90	6.50	4.08	3.77	4.93
Chastity	3.33	3.00	3.08	2.25	3.40	3.75	1.50	3.50
Defendence	.66	7.43	5.06	3.10	4.92	5.58	5.52	7.14
Exhibition	—	—	3.50	—	7.00	—	5.33	—
Harm Avoidance	3.50	8.00	4.60	5.33	1.75	1.50	1.75	3.66
Succorance	5.44	2.20	8.29	5.17	3.89	2.32	3.25	3.65
Achievement	3.91	3.81	3.82	3.20	3.26	3.54	3.11	—
Affiliation	2.77	5.11	4.88	5.18	4.03	3.40	3.28	—
Counteraction	7.00	9.76	6.70	7.23	11.72	11.65	10.45	5.67
Dominance	5.55	4.27	7.54	8.00	3.71	4.52	3.63	7.34
Nurturance	4.36	4.85	6.60	4.80	4.36	5.43	5.17	5.30
Order	5.35	4.10	4.36	5.30	4.20	3.13	3.45	4.95
Understanding	4.06	4.72	3.29	4.09	3.94	3.33	4.71	5.37
CONFLICTS:								
Abasement	2.40	3.50	6.07	5.00	3.06	2.67	3.07	3.71
Aggression	1.00	1.00	5.50	1.67	3.60	2.33	4.23	1.00
Chastity	1.66	7.50	2.53	3.00	4.43	2.00	2.71	2.61
Defendence	3.00	4.66	5.93	4.87	3.82	5.69	3.10	6.33
Exhibition	3.20	4.00	3.50	4.00	3.08	4.20	4.80	3.80
Harm Avoidance	3.50	3.87	4.51	4.08	2.61	2.25	2.07	3.80

TABLE II (*continued*)

VARIABLES	SEMINARIANS DO (N=21)	NDO (N=19)	FEMALE RELIGIOUS DO (N=77)	NDO (N=18)	MALE RELIGIOUS DO (N=57)	NDO (N=39)	MALE CONTROLS (N=52)	FEMALE CONTROLS (N=50)
Succorance	5.00	4.57	4.86	4.80	4.35	3.00	3.85	3.43
Achievement	3.83	2.57	4.50	3.50	3.88	3.69	3.21	4.60
Affiliation	3.50	6.75	3.12	3.50	3.16	3.17	3.82	4.92
Counteraction	7.14	4.00	4.45	6.67	3.12	6.33	8.36	3.30
Dominance	—	1.00	4.75	3.67	3.20	3.57	3.83	3.33
Nurturance	7.71	9.12	5.48	3.00	6.17	4.91	5.90	6.84
Order	4.33	5.16	4.50	6.00	3.78	4.67	4.00	5.66
Understanding	5.00	3.85	4.62	4.00	4.92	4.64	2.88	6.50
CONSISTENCIES:								
Abasement	1.50	1.33	5.50	—	—	—	5.00	—
Aggression	4.84	2.66	2.33	2.40	3.17	1.33	1.78	2.38
Chastity	—	—	3.60	3.30	3.72	3.28	3.60	4.90
Defendence	—	—	5.00	—	—	—	6.00	—
Exhibition	6.25	8.22	6.75	6.43	7.15	7.14	5.65	7.88
Harm Avoidance	4.12	8.44	4.65	4.33	4.37	3.64	4.81	3.41
Succorance	4.00	4.66	9.00	2.00	—	3.50	3.50	2.00
Achievement	—	—	—	—	—	—	—	—
Affiliation	—	—	—	—	—	—	—	—
Counteraction	—	—	—	—	—	—	—	—
Dominance	—	—	—	—	—	—	—	—
Nurturance	—	—	—	—	—	—	—	—
Order	2.33	3.66	5.20	0.00	4.14	2.87	3.00	5.25
Understanding	—	—	—	—	5.00	—	—	—

Case No. —————————————

SUMMARY CHART
FOR INDIVIDUAL PSYCHODYNAMIC EVALUATION

Inconsistencies

1. Abasement —————
2. Aggression —————
3. Chastity —————
4. Defendence —————
5. Exhibition —————
6. Harm Avoidance ———
7. Succorance —————
8. Achievement —————
9. Affiliation —————
10. Counteraction —————
11. Dominance —————
12. Nurturance —————
13. Order —————
14. Understanding —————
SUM ———

Defensive Consistencies

1. Abasement —————
2. Aggression —————
3. Chastity —————
4. Defendence —————
5. Exhibition —————
6. Harm Avoidance ———
7. Succorance —————
8. Achievement —————
9. Affiliation —————
10. Counteraction —————
11. Dominance —————
12. Nurturance —————
13. Order —————
14. Understanding —————
SUM ———

Conflicts

1. Abasement —————
2. Aggression —————
3. Chastity —————
4. Defendence —————
5. Exhibition —————
6. Harm Avoidance ———
7. Succorance —————
8. Achievement —————
9. Affiliation —————
10. Counteraction —————
11. Dominance —————
12. Nurturance —————
13. Order —————
14. Understanding —————
SUM ———

Consistencies

1. Abasement —————
2. Aggression —————
3. Chastity —————
4. Defendence —————
5. Exhibition —————
6. Harm Avoidance ———
7. Succorance —————
8. Achievement —————
9. Affiliation —————
10. Counteraction —————
11. Dominance —————
12. Nurturance —————
13. Order —————
14. Understanding —————
SUM ———

SUM TOTAL = ———

217

APPENDIX C (*cont'd*)

A. DEGREE OF COMPLIANCE $= \dfrac{\text{Sum Incons.} + \text{Sum Defens. Consist.}}{\text{Sum Total}} = \dfrac{}{100}$

B. DEGREE OF IDENTIFICATION $= \dfrac{\text{Sum Conflicts}}{\text{Sum Total}} = \dfrac{}{100}$

C. DEGREE OF INTERNALIZATION $= \dfrac{\text{Sum Consistencies}}{\text{Sum Total}} = \dfrac{}{100}$

D. INDEX OF ADAPTATION $= \dfrac{C - A}{A + C} =$

E. INDEX OF POSSIBLE GROWTH $= \dfrac{B}{200} =$

F. INDEX OF VOCATIONAL MATURITY $= D + E =$

GLOSSARY

Adaptation: Index of: a measurement devised to express the relative weight and therefore the prevalence of the tendency toward internalization over the tendency toward compliance.

Assessment: 1) a loose general term for measurement; 2) a complex measuring procedure in which several subjects are observed in a sequence of unstructured and structured activities — lasting for hours or days — and are rated by trained observers.

    Assessment 'of': the evaluation of the psychodynamics of entering vocationers emphasizing the 'understanding' of the mechanics of the entering process.

    Assessment 'for': the evaluation of the psychodynamics of entering vocationers emphasizing its 'predicting' aspects or its influence upon future vocational perseverence or effectiveness.

    Multidimensional model or strategy: based on quantitative variation of dimensions or variables.

    Typological model or strategy: based on a qualitative patterning of variables.

Attitude: a mental and neural state of readiness to respond, organized through experience, exerting a directive and/or dynamic influence on mental and physical activities. An attitude includes a cognitive, affective and conative component, and may have the following 4 functions:

    1) *Utilitarian function* of an attitude is present when a particular attitude is adopted because of its specific utility — reward or punishment — to the adopting subject.

    2) *Ego-defensive function:* is present when an attitude is adopted in order to defend the subject's self from a conscious or subconscious threat.

    3) *Cognitive function:* is present when an attitude is adopted to satisfy the desire to know reality.

    4) *Value-expressive function:* is present when an atti-

tude is adopted in view of realizing the values held by the subject.

Normative vs. preferential: see under VALUE.

Examples of specific attitudes are e.g. 'taking the blame for something done by someone I like'. Specific attitudes can be grouped to indicate general attitudes like 'self-depreciation versus self-confidence', etc. (cf. Appendix A-1)

Centrality: a structural quality of a consistency or inconsistency indicating the functional significance of the same consistency or inconsistency for the psychodynamics of the individual. Three factors contribute to the definition of centrality: a) relevance of a self-attribute for the achievement of one's goals; b) centrality of the same self-attribute for maintaining a positive self-conception or self-esteem; c) adequacy or inadequacy of the person's coping mechanisms in handling the same self-attribute toward the achievement of his goals.

Compliance: the process of accepting influence from a social agent on the basis of reward or punishment.

Conflict: In general, the state of an individual who is prompted to respond simultaneously in different and incompatible ways. Specifically, in this work, three patterns on the intra-actual self-consistency/inconsistency continuum (cf. Chapter 3, c., nn. 3, 4, 5) have been designated as 'conflicts'. In this sense, they constitute rather preconscious inconsistencies as opposed to consistencies and to unconscious inconsistencies.

Conscious: the normal field of consciousness that the individual has of himself and things actually present.

Consistency: is present when an individual is motivated by needs in accordance with vocational values.

Social consistency (SC): when a need, conscious or subconscious, and its corresponding attitude is consonant with vocational values.

Psychological consistency (PsC): when a need, conscious or subconscious is consonant with vocational values but is not consonant with the corresponding attitude.

Type of: the pattern taken by the relationship between need, attitude and value. Basically, two types were considered, psychological (PsC) and social (SC) consistency; see, however, TYPOLOGY.

Level of: the fact that a consistency is found at the

conscious, preconscious or unconscious level of personality.

Degree of: a quantitative expression of the amount of congruence among the relevant subsystems of the self.

Construct: a formal concept, a concept that has been systematically defined, delineated, and perhaps related to other constructs.

Correlation: the degree of relationship or association between two variables. It is most commonly expressed by a coefficient, like e.g. the Pearson product-moment.

Data combination: a basic component of assessment, distinct from data collection, indicating the way in which the data were organized in the assessment procedure.

Clinical combination: when the data are organized largely by the cognizing activity of a clinician.

Statistical combination: when the combining of the data is made by a statistician or a computer.

Data Collection: see MEASUREMENT.

Defense: a subconscious psychodynamic process which serves to protect the person against danger arising from his impulses or affects.

Depth Interview: an assessment technique used with the subjects of this study after about four years of training. Its procedures are described in Chapter 3.

Depth Psychology: the psychology relating to the realm of the subconscious, in contradistinction to the psychology of the conscious part of the mind.

Developmental Maturity, Index of: a measurement devised to express the degrees of compliance, identification and internalization of an entering vocationer as they can be inferred by his/her capacity to handle, to control his/her major core conflicts.

Discriminant Function Analysis: a statistical technique which, providing a partial control for variable intercorrelation, allows a consideration of the magnitude of each variable's contribution to the discrimination between two groups.

Effectiveness (Vocational): the visible manifestation and/or social communication of the terminal values, union with God and imitation of Christ.

Family Dynamics Interview: a relatively structured type of interview aimed at clarifying major family conflicts, major familial influences on the subjects and the degree of insight

221

of the subject concerning family dynamics. Its procedures are described in Chapter 3.

Frequency: the number of cases, persons or events in a given distribution or group.

Fulfillment: the process of realization of the potentialities as well as of the ideals of an individual.

Functional Significance: of a consistency/inconsistency: see CENTRALITY.

Germinative Self-Ideal-in-Situation: the extent to which the self-ideal of individual vocationers is open to growth toward self-transcendence. Concretely, it is the extent to which the self-ideal-in-situation shows a prevailing consistency with the actual-self of the vocationer.

Goal: any object appraised as suitable or unsuitable for action. See VALUE.

Identification: the process of accepting influence from a social agent or referent, based on the self-defining value of the relationship with the social agent, person of group.

> *Internalizing identification:* when the process of identification leads to the process of internalization, because the part of the self which is defined is consistent with the values to be internalized.

> *Non-internalizing identification:* when identification does not lead to internalization because the part of the self which is defined is not consistent with the values to be internalized.

Inconsistency: is present when an individual is motivated by needs that are dissonant with vocational values.

> *Social inconsistency* (SoI): when a subconscious need is dissonant with values but consonant with its corresponding attitude.

> *Psychological inconsistency* (PsI): when a subconscious need is dissonant with values and with its corresponding attitude.

> *Type of:* the pattern taken by the relationship between need, attitude and value. Basically, two types were considered, psychological (PsI) and social (SoI); see however TYPOLOGY.

> *Level of:* the fact that an inconsistency is found at the conscious, preconscious or unconscious level of personality.

> *Degree of:* a quantitative expression of the amount of discrepancy among relevant subsystems of the self.

Interjudge Reliability: the generalizability of a procedure over raters or judges, determined from the correlation between their ratings.

Internalization: the process of adopting a way of behaving or thinking because it is congruent with one's value system.

Internalizing Capacity, Predictable: the more or less unrealistic Self-Ideal-in-Situation (SI-II) of expectations of the individual about his future vocational roles. This unrealistic Self-Ideal-in-Situation stems from the imbalances between the central inconsistencies and consistencies of needs vs. homonymous attitudes. The unrealistic Self-Ideal-in-Situation may influence vocational perseverence and effectiveness because it influences the capacity to internalize vocational values and attitudes.

Inventory: a paper-and-pencil test of personality with verbal content, usually measuring more than one variable and implying inclusiveness of coverage.

Measurement: the assigning of a quantitative ordering to objects in accordance with certain rules. In a more specific way, it is the assigning of scores or indices to persons on the basis of their responses as elicited by a standard procedure.

Need: action tendency resulting from a deficit of the organism or from natural inherent potentialities which seek exercise or actuality. For examples, see Appendix A-3; e.g.: ABASEMENT, ACHIEVEMENT, etc.

Operational Definition: the empirical measurement or set of measurements taken to express a theoretically relevant concept or construct.

Possible Growth, Index of: a measurement which is an elaboration of the Degree of Identification and is intended to express the weight of the internalizing identification on the psychodynamics of the individual.

Predictive validity: the correlation between a criterion measure, generally obtained at a later point in time, and a specific test or set of tests.

Psychodynamics: the constellation of motivational forces operating within the person which may be expressed by the external behavior.

223

Psychopathology: the branch of science dealing with morbidity or pathology of the mind.

Overt or manifest: when there is evidence of open symptoms, like in schizophrenia or the neuroses.

Covert or latent: in the absence of clear symptoms, like in character disorders or central vocational inconsistencies.

Questionnaire: a paper-and-pencil personality test. Its content are questions or implied questions.

Reliability: the extent of the agreement between two or more sets of measurements when essentially the same precedure has been used.

Role: the set of prescriptions defining what the behavior of the position member should be.

Role concept: the perceptions or beliefs of the subjects about his own role, which society offers to him.

Role expectation: the perceptions of a role as held by others in society and offered to an individual for assimilation. These perceptions are organized as social expectations, societal demands or professional requirements.

Role concept: the perceptions or beliefs of the subjects itself (rather than using the role as a means to realize values which are both role-transcendent and self-transcendent; see, in contrast, VALUE orientation).

Score: a number assigned to a subject and based on the subject's response to one or several items, usually of a test.

Self or personality: the way the person interacts with the world outside him and the world within him.

Ideal-Self: a) as *Institutional Ideal* are the perceptions one has of the ideals his vocational institution values for its members; the individual's role concept (indicated in this work by II); b) as *Self-Ideals* are the ideals a person values for himself, e.g. what he would like to be or do.

Actual-Self: a) as *Present Behavior* or the manifest self-concepts, e.g. the subject's cognitions about his own present behavior (indicated in this work by PB; b) as *Latent-Self:* or the personality characteristics revealed by projective-type instruments. It is assumed that this type of instruments reveals what characteristics, conscious or subconscious, a person actually possesses not merely those which he thinks he has or would like to have (In this work is indicated by LST — prevailingly unconscious — and LSR — prevailingly preconscious).

Self-Attribute: a specific dimensional content (e.g. aggression, succorance) assessed in this study in function of its structural qualities, like centrality, type, level and degree of consistency/inconsistency.

Self-Conception: A consistency or an inconsistency of the ideal-self for attitude with the corresponding actual-self, including its subconscious part.

Sentence Completion Test: a semi-unstructured test in which the subject is provided with a series of sentence beginnings which he has to finish in some way.

Stability: the generalizability over time estimated from the correlation between scores on a test administered at two different times.

Structural Approach: a way of considering man as a composite of a definite number of structures, of subsystems of the self: the actual-self, the ideal and their components. The subsystems are distinct but dynamically related among themselves by qualitative patterns. This approach allows one to obtain results which may be trans-situational and trans-temporal, i.e. valid for people of different cultures, social milieux and vocational institutions.

Subconscious: encompasses the field of psychic experience which is not present to the actual consciousness of the individual and may be:

   Preconscious: when the memories can be recalled to consciousness through ordinary rational methods, like reflection, examination of conscience, introspection, meditation etc.

   Unconscious: comprehensive of those psychic contents which can be brought to consciousness only through professional intervention, like for instance, psychotherapy.

Test: a measuring device consisting of a standard set of operations.

   Structured: also called objective, when the subject is presented with a structured, organized, specific situation to which to respond.

   Unstructured: also called projective, when the subject is

225

presented with a relatively unstructured, ambiguous situation to which he responds.

Transference: the process of feeling and behaving toward a person in the same way as one did toward important figures of the past, generally parents, relatives or educators.

  Positive: when there is a friendly, attractive attitude toward the other person.

  Negative: when there is an unfriendly, hostile attitude toward the other person.

Typology: the placing of each subject or variable in one of two or more qualitatively different. types within a psychometric model.

  Typology of variables: the patterns in which a specific variable can appear in the personal psychodynamics.

  Typology of individuals: the patterns of individual intra-psychic dynamics. Only functionally significant vocational consistencies or inconsistencies are considered. (cf. Chapter 3)

Validity: the extent to which a test or set of tests measure the variable(s) they are intended to measure.

Value: enduring abstract ideals of a person, which may be ideal end-states of existence (*terminal* values or ends) or ideal modes of conduct (*instrumental* values or means). A terminal value may be the 'Imitation of Christ'; instrumental values may be the three vows of Poverty, Chastity and Obedience or the ones listed in Appendix A-2, pages 200-1.

  Norm value to Preference value: a continuum ranging from mandatory to preference based on a matter of taste.

  Value orientation: the adopting and use of behaviors or roles as means toward the realization of values or the expression of the same values.

Variable: a quantity that varies; in this work it is used as a general term for a dimension or aspect of personality that varies over people.

  Vocationally dissonant: a specific variable which, for its content, is particularly relevant to vocational values (cf. Appendix A-2).

  Vocationally neutral: a specific variable which, for its

content is not particularly conducive or opposite to vocational values (cf. Appendix A-1).

Vocational Maturity, Index of: a measurement which aims to express the total psychodynamics of the individual in terms of the structural qualities of his consistencies/inconsistencies. It is obtained by finding the algebraic sum of the Index of Adaptation and the Index of Possible Growth.

Vocational Problems: different types of impairment in the personality of vocationers: 1) spiritual problems; 2) developmental difficulties; 3) vocational subconscious and latent (the individual appears normal) inconsistencies; 4) more or less manifest non vocational psychopathology.

Vulnerable Self-Ideal-in-Situation: the extent to which the Self-Ideal of individual vocationers is undermined by subconscious conflicts or inconsistencies.

BIBLIOGRAPHY

Adams, J. F. (Ed.). *Contributions to the understanding of adolescence.* Rockleigh, N.J.: Allyn and Bacon, Inc., 1968.

Allen, V. L. Role theory and consistency theory. In R. Abelson et al., *Theories of cognitive consistency: A sourcebook.* Chicago: Rand McNally and Co., 1968, pp. 201-209.

Allport, G. W. Attitudes. In C. Murchison (Ed.), *Handbook of social psychology.* Worcester, Mass.: Clark University Press, 1935, pp. 798-884.

—— Attitudes in the history of social psychology. In G. Lindzey, (Ed.), *Handbook of social psychology,* Vol. I. Reading, Mass.: Addison-Wesley Publishing Co., 1954, pp. 43-45.

—— *Patterns and growth in personality.* New York: Holt, Rinehart and Winston, Inc., 1961.

Arnold, M. B. *Emotion and personality.* 2 vols. New York: Columbia University Press, 1960.

Aronson, E. Dissonance theory: progress and problems. In R. Abelson et al., *Theories of cognitive consistency: A sourcebook.* Chicago: Rand McNally and Co., 1968, pp. 5-27.

Arrupe, P. 'Y, a-t-il encore des Jésuites? Réponse à quelque questions. *Dossier des Informations Catholiques Internationales,* 1972, 419, 11-28.

Baars, C. W. and Terruwe, A. *How to treat and prevent the crisis in the priesthood.* Chicago, Ill.: Franciscan Herald Press, 1972.

Bandura, A. and Walters, R. H. *Social learning and personality development.* New York: Holt, Rinehart and Winston, Inc., 1963.

Becker, R. J. Religion and psychological health. In M. P. Strommen (Ed.), *Research on religious development.* New York: Hawthorn Books, 1971, pp. 390-421.

Becker, S. L. and Mittman, A. Student perceptions of SUI, Report No. 1. Unpublished manuscript, 1962.

Becker W. C. Consequences of different kinds of parental discipline. In M. L. Hoffman and L. W. Hoffman (Eds.), *Review of child development research.* New York: Russel Sage Foundation, 1964, pp. 169-208.

Beier, E. G. The effects of induced anxiety on flexibility of intellectual functioning. *Psychological Monographs,* 1951, 65, No. 9.

Beirnaert, L. (S.J.). Discernement et psychisme. *Christus,* 1954, 4, 50-61.

Berkowitz, L. *The development of motives and values in the child.* New York: Basic Books Inc., 1964.

—— Social Motivation. In G. Lindzey and E. Aronson (Eds.). *The Handbook of Social Psychology,* Vol. III Reading Mass. Addison — Wesley Publishing Co., 1969, pp. 50-135.

Berkun, M., Bialek, H., Kern, R., and Yagi, K. Experimental studies of psychological stress in men. *Psychological Monographs,* 1962, 76, 1-39.

Bier, W. C. (S.J.) (Ed.) *Psychological testing for ministerial selection.* New York: Fordham University Press, 1970.

Bock, D. R. Multivariate analysis of variance of repeated measurements. In C. W. Harris (Ed.), *Problems of measuring change.* Madison: University of Wisconsin Press, 1963.

Bordin, E. S., Nachmann, B., and Segal, S.J. An articulated framework for vocational development. *Journal of Counseling Psychology,* 1963, *10,* 107-117.

Bradburn, N.M. *The structure of psychological well-being.* NORC monographs in social research, no. 15. Chicago: Aldine-Atherton, Inc., 1969.

Brehm, J. M. and Cohen, A. R. *Explorations in cognitive dissonance.* New York: John Wiley and Sons, Inc., 1962.

Brock, T. C. Effects of prior dishonesty on postdecision dissonance. *Journal of Abnormal and Social Psychology,* 1963, *66,* 325-331.

—— Commitment to exposure as a determinant of information receptivity. *Journal of Personality and Social Psychology,* 1965, *2,* 10-19.

—— Dissonance without awareness. In R. Abelson et al. (Eds.), *Theories of cognitive consistency: A sourcebook.* Chicago: Rand McNally and Co., 1968, pp. 408-416.

Brock, T. C. and Blackwood, J. E.   Dissonance reduction, social comparison and modification of other's opinions.   *Journal of Abnormal and Social Psychology,* 1962, *65,* 319-324.

Brock, T. C. and Grant, L. D.   Dissonance, awareness and motivation.   *Journal of Abnormal and Social Psychology,* 1963, *67,* 53-60.

Bronfenbrenner, U.   Some familial antecedents of responsibility and leadership in adolescents.   In L. Petrullo and B. M. Bass (Eds.), *Leadership and interpersonal behavior.* New York: Holt, Rinehart and Winston, Inc., 1961, pp. 239-271.

Buckley, M. J. (S.J.).   The structure of the rules for the discernment of spirits.   *The Way,* Supplement 20, Autumn 1973.

Byrne, D. and Blaylock, B.   Similiarity and assumed similiarity of attitudes between husbands and wives.   *Journal of Abnormal and Social Psychology,* 1963, *67,* 636-640.

Campbell, A., Converse, P. E., Miller, W. E., and Stokes, D. E.   *The American voter.* New York: John Wiley and Sons, Inc., 1960.

Carroll, D. W.   A follow-up study of psychological assessment.   In W. C. Bier (S.J.) (Ed.), *Psychological testing for ministerial selection.* New York: Fordham University Press, 1970, pp. 159-189.

Cattell, R. B. et al.   *Sixteen Personality Factor Questionnaire.* Champaign, Ill.: Institute for Personality and Ability Testing, 1956.

Chickering, A. W.   Faculty perceptions and changing institutional press.   Goddard College (Mimeo), n. d.

Cohen, A. R., Greenbaum, C. W., and Mansson, H. H.   Commitment to social deprivation and verbal conditioning.   *Journal of Abnormal and Social Psychology,* 1963 *67,* 410-421.

Croghan, L. M.   Encounter groups and the necessity for ethical guidelines.   *Journal of Clinical Psychology,* 1974, *30,* 438-445.

Dahlstrom, W. G.   *Personality systematics and the problem of types.* From General Learning Press, Morristown, N.J., 1972, pp. 1-27.

D'arcy, P. F.   Bibliography of psychological, sociological and related studies on the Catholic priesthood and the religious life. In W. J. Coville, P. F. D'Arcy, T. N. McCathy, and J. J. Rooney, *Assessment of candidates for the religious life.* Washington, D.C.: CARA, 1968.

Darmanin, A. *Etude psychologique des séminaristes à travers le test de Rorschach.* Louvain, Centre de Psychologie da la Religion, Mimeo, 1973.

De Waelhens, A. *Sciences humaines, horizon ontologique et rencontre,* in *Existence et Signification,* Louvain: Nauwaelerts, 1958, pp. 233-261.

Directoria Exercitiorum Spiritualium (1540-1599). Ed. I. Iparraguirre. Rome: Monumenta Historica Societatis Jesu, 1955.

Dittes, J. E. Research on clergymen: Factors influencing decision for religious service and effectiveness in the vocation. *Religious Education* (Research Supplement), 1962, Vol. LVII, 141-165.

—— Psychological characteristics of religious professionals. In M. P. Strommen (Ed.), *Research on religious development.* New York: Hawthorn Books, Inc., 1971, pp. 422-460.

Dollard, J., Doob, L. W., Miller, N. E., Mowrer, O. H., and Sears, R. R. *Frustration and aggression.* New Haven, Conn.: Yale University Press, 1939.

Douglas, W. T. Response. In W. C. Bier (Ed.), *Psychological testing for ministerial selection.* New York: Fordham University Press, 1970, p. 190.

Douvan, E., and Kaye, C. Motivational factors in college entrance. In N. Sanford (Ed.), *The American college: A psychological and social interpretation of the higher learning.* New York: John Wiley and Sons, Inc., 1962, pp. 199-224.

Easterbrook, J. A. The effect of emotion on cue utilization and the organization of behavior. *Psychological Review,* 1959, *66,* 183-201.

Educational Testing Service. *General goals of life inventory.* Princeton, N.J.: 1950.

Emmerich, W. Socialization and sex-role development. In P. B. Baltes and K. W. Schaie (Eds.), *Life-span developmental psychology.* New York: Academic Press Inc., 1973, pp. 123-144.

Erikson, E. H. *Childhood and society.* New York: W. W. Norton and Co., Inc., 1950, 1963.

—— Identity and the life cycle. *Psychological Issues,* 1959, *1,* No. 1.

Essen-Möller, E. Individual traits and morbidity in a Swedish rural population. *Acta Psychiat. Scand. Suppl.,* 1956, 100.

Etzioni, A. Basic human needs, alienation and inauthenticity. *American Sociological Review,* 1968, *34,* 870-885.

Fairchild, R. W. Delayed gratification: A psychological and religious analysis. In M. P. Strommen (Ed.), *Research on religious development.* New York: Hawthorn Books, 1971, pp. 155-210.

Feldman, K. A., and Newcomb, T. M. *The impact of college on students.* San Francisco: Jossey-Bass Inc., Publishers, 1969.

Festinger, L. *A theory of cognitive dissonance.* New York: Harper and Row Publishers, Inc., 1957.

—— *Conflict, decision and dissonance.* Stanford, Calif.: Stanford University Press, 1964.

Finney, J. C. Development of a new set of MMPI scales. *Psychological Reports,* 1965, *17,* 706-713.

—— Factor structure with the new set of MMPI scales and the formula correction. *Journal of Clinical Psychology,* 1966, *22,* 443-449.

Fishbein, M. An investigation of the relationships between beliefs about an object and attitude toward that object. *Human Relations,* 1963, *16,* 233-239.

—— A consideration of beliefs, attitudes and their relationship. In I. D. Skinner and M. Fishbein (Eds.), *Current studies in social psychology.* New York: Holt, Rinehart and Winston, Inc., 1965, pp. 107-120.

Fisher, M. S. The relationship of satisfaction, achievement, and attention to anticipated environmental press. Unpublished M. A. thesis, Brigham Young University, 1961.

—— Environment, expectations, and the significance of disparity between actual and expected environment at the University of Utah. Unpublished doctoral dissertation, University of California, Los Angeles, 1966.

Fiske, D. W. *Measuring the concepts of personality*. Chicago: Aldine-Atherton, Inc., 1971.

Fouriezos, N. T., Hutt, M. L., and Guetzkow, H. Measurement of self-oriented needs in discussion groups. *Journal of Abnormal and Social Psychology*, 1950, *45*, 682-690.

Frankl, V. E. *Der Unbedingte Mesch*. Wien: Deuticke, 1959.

—— *Psychotherapy and existentialism*. New York: Washington Square Press, 1967.

—— *The will to meaning*. New York: The World Publishing Company, 1969.

Freedman, J. L., Wallington, S. A., Bless, E. Compliance without pressure: The effect of guilt. *Journal of Personality and Social Psychology*, 1967, *7*, 117-124.

Freedman, J. L., Carlsmith, J. M., and Sears, D. O. *Social psychology* (2nd Ed.). Englewood Cliffs, N.J.: Prentice-Hall Publishers, 1974.

Freedman, M. B. Personality growth in the college years. *College Board Review*, 1965, *56*, 25-32.

French, J. R. P., Jr. and Sherwood, J. J. Self-actualization and self-identity theory. *Paper No. 107*. Institute for Research in the Behavioral, Economic and Management Sciences. Purdue University, 1965.

Fratellière, F. A report presented at Lourdes. In *Préparation au Ministère presbytéral*. Paris: Centurion, 1972.

Ganss, G. E. (S.J.) (Trans.) *The Constitutions of the Society of Jesus*, by St Ignatius of Loyola. St Louis: The Institute of Jesuit Sources, 1970.

Ginzberg, E., Ginzberg, S. W., Axelrod, S. and Herma, J. L. *Occupational choice*. New York: Columbia University Press, 1951.

Godin, A. (S.J.) Psychologie de la vocation: un bilan. *Le supplément*, 1975, n. 113, 151-236.

Greeley, A. M. *Priests in the United States: Reflections on a survey*. Garden City, N.Y.: Doubleday and Co., Inc., 1972.

Harding, L. W. A value-type generalization test. *Journal of Social Psychology*, 1944, *19*, 53-79.

—— Experimental comparisons between generalizations and problems as indices of values. *Journal of General Psychology*, 1948, *38*, 31-50.

Harris, R. E. and Lingoes, J. C. Subscales for the MMPI: An aid to profile interpretation. Mimeographed. San Francisco: Department of Psychiatry, University of California, 1955.

Hartmann, H. Comments on the psychoanalytic theory of the ego. *Psychoanalytic Study of the Child*, 1950, *V*, 74-96.

—— The mutual influences in the development of the ego and id. *Psychoanalytic Study of the Child*, 1952, 7, 9-30.

—— Notes on the theory of sublimation. *Psychoanalytic Study of the Child*, 1955, *10*, 9-29.

—— *Ego psychology and the problem of adaptation.* New York: International Universities Press, 1958.

Harvey, J. La vie religieuse: présent incertain, avenir possible. *Relations*, 1973, 383.

Hathaway, S. R. and McKinley, J. C. *Minnesota Multiphasic Personality Inventory (MMPI)*. New York: The Psychological Corporation, 1951.

Henry, W. E. Guetzkow, H. Group projection sketches for the study of small groups. *J. Social Psychology*, 1951, *33*, 77-102.

Hilliard, A. L. *The forms of value.* New York: Columbia University Press, 1950.

Hoffman, M. L. Development of internal moral standards in children. In M. Strommen (Ed.), *Research on religious development*. New York: Hawthorn Books Inc., 1971, pp. 211-263.

Holland, J. L. *The psychology of vocational choice.* Waltham, Mass.: Blaisdell Publications, 1966.

Hollander, E. P. *Principles and methods of social psychology*, 2nd ed. New York: Oxford University Press, 1971.

Hollen, C. C. Value change, perceived instrumentality, and attitude change. Unpublished Ph. D. dissertation, Michigan State University Library, 1972.

Homant, R. Values, attitudes and perceived instrumentality.

Unpublished Ph. D. dissertation, Michigan State University Library, 1970.

Ignatius of Loyola, St   *The Constitutions of the Society of Jesus.* Trans. by G. E. Ganss, S.J. St Louis: The Institute of Jesuit Sources, 1970.

—— *Spiritual Exercises.* New York: Catholic Book Publishing Company, 1948; or Garden City, N.Y.: Image Books, Doubleday and Company, 1964.

Imoda, F. (S.J.). Sociometric status and personality in training centers for religious. Unpublished Ph. D. dissertation. The University of Chicago, 1971.

Jackson, D. N.   A sequential system for personality scale development. In C. D. Spielberger (Ed.), *Current topics in clinical and community psychology,* Vol. 2. New York: Academic Press Inc., 1970, pp. 61-96.

Janis, I. L., Mahl, G. F., Kagan, J. and Holt, R.   *Personality: Dynamics, development and assessment.* New York: Harcourt, Brace Jovanovich, Inc., 1969.

Kaplan, M. F.   Freud and modern philosophy. In B. Nelson (Ed.), *Freud and the 20th century.* New York: Meridian Books, 1957.

Katz, D.   The functional approach to the study of attitude change. *Public Opinion Quarterly,* 1960, *24,* 163-203.

—— Motivational basis of organizational behavior. *Behavioral Science,* 1964, *9,* 131-146.

Katz, D. and Stotland, E.   A preliminary statement to a theory of attitude structure and change. In S. Koeh (Ed.), *Psychology: A study of a science,* Vol. 3: *Formulations of the person and the social context.* Hightstown, N.J.: McGraw-Hill Book Co., 1959, pp. 423-475.

Kauffman, M.   Regard statistique sur les prétres qui quittent le ministère. *Social Compass,* 1970, (4), 495-502.

Kelman, H. C.   Compliance, identification and internalization: three processes of attitude change. *Journal of Conflict Resolution,* 1958, *2,* 51-60.

235

—— Effects or role-orientation and value-orientation on the nature of attitude change. Paper read to the Eastern Psychological Association, New York, 1960.

—— Three processes of social influence. *Public Opinion Quarterly,* 1961, *25,* 57-78.

Kelman, H. C. and Baron, R. M. Determinants of modes of resolving inconsistency dilemmas: a functional analysis. In R. Abelson, et al. (Eds.), *Theories of cognitive consistency: A sourcebook.* Chicago: Rand McNally and Co., 1968, pp. 670-683.

Keniston, K. The sources of student dissent. *Journal of Social Issues,* 1967, *23,* 108-137.

Kennedy, E. C. and Heckler, V. J. The Catholic priests in the United States: Psychological investigations. Washington, D.C.: United States Catholic Conference, 1971.

Kernan, J. B. and Trebbi, G. G. Attitude dynamics as a hierarchical structure. *Journal of Social Psychology,* 1973, *89,* 193-202.

Klinger, E. *Structure and functions of fantasy.* New York: John Wiley and Sons, Inc., 1971.

Kobler, F. J., Rizzo, J. V. and Doyle, E. D. Dating and the formation of the religious. *Journal of Religion and Health,* 1967, *6,* 137-147.

Kohlberg, L. The development of modes of moral thinking and choice in the years ten to sixteen. Unpublished Ph. D. dissertation, University of Chicago, 1958.

—— Development of moral character and moral ideology. In M. L. Hoffman and L. W. Hoffman (Eds.), *Review of child development research.* New York: Russell Sage Foundation, 1964, pp. 383-432.

—— A cognitive development of children's sex-role concepts and attitudes. In E. Maccoby (Ed.), *The development of sex differences.* Stanford, California: Stanford University Press, 1966.

—— Stage and sequence: The cognitive-developmental approach to socialization. In D. Goslin (Ed.), *Handbook of socialization theory and research.* New York: Rand McNally and Co., 1969.

—— From is to ought: How to commit the naturalistic fallacy

and get away with it in the study of moral development. In T. Mischel (Ed.), *Cognitive development and epistemology*. New York: Academic Press Inc., 1971a.

—— Continuities in childhood and adult moral development revisited. In P. B. Baltes and K. W. Schaie, *Life-span developmental psychology*. New York: Academic Press Inc., 1973, pp. 179-204.

Kohlberg, L. and Gilligan, C. The adolescent as a philosopher: the discovery of the self in a postconventional world. *Daedalus,* 1971b, *100,* 1051-1086.

Koval, J. P. and Modde, Sr. M. M. (O.S.F.). Women who have left religious communities: A study in role stress. Presented at the annual meeting of the Society for General Systems Research, January 29, 1975.

Laplace, J. Une expérience de la vie dans l'Esprit. Lyon: Chalet, 1972.

Lee, J. L. An exploratory search for characteristic patterns and clusters of seminary persisters and leavers. Unpublished Ph. D. dissertation, University of Michigan, 1968.

—— Toward a model of vocational persistence among seminarians: Part I. *National Catholic Guidance Conference Journal,* 1969a, *13*(3), 18-29.

—— Toward a model of vocational persistence among seminarians: Part II. *National Catholic Guidance Conference Journal,* 1969b, *14*(1), 33-43.

—— Toward a model of vocational persistence among seminarians: Part III. *National Catholic Guidance Conference Journal,* 1970a, *14*(2), 104-111.

—— Cognitive dissonance and seminary persistence. An unpublished final research report. University of Wisconsin, 1970b.

Lee, J. L. and Doran, W. J. Vocational persistence among seminarians. *National Catholic Guidance Conference Journal,* 1970, *15,* (2), 55-62.

—— Vocational persistence: An exploration of self-concept and dissonance theories. *Journal of Vocational Behavior,* 1973, *3* (2), 129-136.

Leighton, D. C., Harding, J. S., Mackling, D. B., Macmillan,

A. M. and Leighton, A. H. *The character of danger.* New York: Basic Books, 1963.

Levitt, E. E. *The psychology of anxiety.* Indianapolis: The Bobbs-Merrill Co., 1967.

Lewis, C. S. *Surprised by joy.* London: Collins, 1955.

Lieberman, M. A., Yalom, I. D., and Miles, M. B. *Encounter groups: First facts.* New York: Basic Books, Inc., 1973.

Loevinger, J. Models and measures of developmental variation. *Annals of the New York Academy of Sciences,* 1966a, *134,* 585-590.

—— The meaning and measurement of ego development. *American Psychologist,* 1966b, *21,* 195-206.

—— *Ego Development: Conceptions and Theories.* San Francisco: Jossey-Bass, 1976.

Loevinger, J. and Wessler, R. *Measuring ego development.* San Francisco: Jossey-Bass, Inc., Publishers, 1970.

Lovejoy, A. O. Terminal and adjectival values. *Journal of Philosophy,* 1950, *47,* 593-608.

Luft, J. *Group processes: An introduction to group dynamics.* Palo Alto, California: National Press, 1966.

Maddi, S. R. The pursuit of consistency and variety. In R. Abelson, et al. (Ed.), *Theories of cognitive consistency: A sourcebook.* Chicago: Rand McNally and Co., 1968, pp. 267-274.

Maddi, S. R. and Rulla, L. M. (S.J.). Personality and the Catholic religious vocation, I: Self and conflict in female entrants. *Journal of Personality,* 1972, *40,* 104-122.

Mahl, G. F. Basic concepts of conflict and defense. In I. L. Janis, et al., *Personality: Dynamics, development and assessment.* New York: Harcourt Brace Jovanovich, Inc., 1969, pp. 235-244.

Maslow, A. H. Self-actualizing people: A study in psychological health. In *Personality,* Symposium No. 1, 1950, pp. 11-34. Revised in A. H. Maslow, *Motivation and Personality,* New York: Harper and Row Publishers, Inc., 1954, Chapter 12.

McClelland, D. C. *The achieving society.* Princeton, N.J.:

Van Nostrand Reinhold Co., 1961.

McGuire, W. J. Cognitive consistency and attitude change. *Journal of Abnormal and Social Psychology,* 1960, *60,* 345-353.

—— The nature of attitudes and attitude change. In G. Lindzey (Ed.), *The handbook of social psychology,* Vol. II. Reading, Mass.: Addison-Wesley Publishing Co., 1969, pp. 136-314.

Meissner, W. W. (S.J.). Psychological notes on the Spiritual Exercises. *Woodstock Letters,* 1964, *2,* 165-191.

Mietto, P. *Maturità Umana e Formazione Sacerdotale.* Bologna: Dehoniane, 1968.

Milanesi, G. and Aletti, M. *Psicologia della religione.* Torino: Leumann Elle Di Ci, 1973.

Miller, D. R. The study of social relationships: situation, identity and social interaction. In S. Koch (Ed.), *Psychology: A study of a science,* Vol. 5: The process areas, the person, and some applied fields: their place in psychology and in science. New York: McGraw-Hill Book Co., 1963, pp. 639-738.

Modde, Sr. M. M. (O.S.F.). Study on entrances and departures in religious communities of women in the United States, January 1, 1972 — May 1, 1974. Chicago, Illinois: National Sisters Vocation Conference, 1974.

Mönikes, W. *Zur Analyse Von Rollen-konflikten Ehemaliger Priester der Römisch-Katholischen Kirche.* Unpublished Ph. D. dissertation, University of Bonn, West Germany, 1973.

Morgan, C. D. and Murray, H. A. A method for investigating fantasies: The Thematic Appreciation Test. *Archives of Neurological Psychiatry,* 1935, *34,* 289-306.

Murray, H. A. *Explorations in personality.* New York: Oxford University Press, 1938, pp. 152-226.

National Opinion Research Center (NORC). *American priests.* Chicago: University of Chicago, 1971.

Neal, M. A. The relation between religious belief and structural change in religious orders I: Developing an effective measuring. *Review of Religious Research,* 1970, *12* (1), 2-16; II: Some evidence. Ibidem, 1971, *12* (3), 153-164.

239

Newcomb, T. M. Interpersonal balance. In R. Abelson, et al., *Theories of cognitive consistency: A sourcebook.* Chicago: Rand McNally and Co., 1968, pp. 28-51.

Nuttin J. *Psychoanalysis and personality.* New York: Mentor Omega, Books, 1962.

Olabuenaga, J. I. *Los ex-sacerdotes y ex-seminaristas en España.* Cuernavaca, Mexico: Centro Intercultural (Cidoc), Son Deos, 73, 1970. Also in *Social Compass,* 1970, *17* (4), 503-516.

Orden, S. R. and Bradburn, N. M. Dimensions of marriage happiness. *American Journal of Sociology,* VTFR, 73, 715-731.

—— Working wives and marriage happiness. *American Journal of Sociology,* 1969, *74,* 392-407.

Osler, S. F. Intellectual performance as a function of two types of psychological stress. *Journal of Experimental Psychology,* 1954, *47,* 115-121.

Ostrom, T. M. The relationship between the affective, behavioral, and cognitive components of attitude. *Journal of Experimental Social Psychology,* 1969, *5,* 12-30.

Ostrom, T. M. and Brock, T. C. Cognitive bonding to central values and resistance to a communication advocating change in policy orientation. *Journal of Experimental Research in Personality,* 1969, *4,* 42-50.

Pace, C. R. *Preliminary technical manual: College and university environment scales.* Princeton, N.J.: Educational Testing Service, 1963.

—— When students judge their college. *College Board Review,* 1965-66, No. 58, 26-28.

—— Comparisons of CUES results from different groups of reporters. College Entrance Examination Board Report No. 1. Los Angeles, California: University of California, 1966a.

—— The use of CUES in the college admissions process. College Entrance Examination Board Report No. 2. Los Angeles, California: University of California, 1966b.

Paul VI. Encyclical letter, *Sacerdotalis Caelibatus,* Acta Apostolicae Sedis, 1967, 59.

Peek, P. F., and Havighurst, R. J. *The psychology of character development.* New York: John Wiley and Sons, Inc., 1960.

Pervin, L. A. Reality and nonreality in student expectations of college. *Journal of Psychology,* 1966, *64,* 41-48.

Piaget, J. *The moral judgement of the child.* Glencoe, Ill.: Free Press, 1948. (Originally published, 1932).

—— *The origins of intelligence in children.* New York: W. W. Norton and Co., Inc., 1963.

Potvin, R. and Suziedelis, A. *Seminarians of the sixties* (A national survey). Washington, D.C.: CARA, 1969.

Prelinger, E. and Zimet, C. N. *An ego-psychological approach to character assessment.* New York: The Free Press, 1964.

Pro Mundi Vita. *Le clergé et les séminaires en Espagne.* Bruxelles: Bulletin, 31, 1971.

Pro Mundi Vita. *Le prêtre de 1971 à la recherche de son identité.* Bruxelles: note spéciale, 18, 107-117.

Rahner, K. (S.J.). *The dynamic element in the Church.* Trans. by W. J. O'Hara. Freiburg: Herder and Herder, Inc., 1964.

——. Uber die evangelische Rate, *Geist und Leben,* 1964, *17,* 17-37.

Rashke, R. Evolution des attitudes envers le ministère pastoral. *Lumen Vitae,* 1973, *28*(4), 617-634.

Reddy, W. B., Lansky, L. M. The group psychotherapy literature: 1973. *International Journal of Group Psychotherapy,* 1974, *24,* 477-517.

Ricoeur, P. *Philosophie de la volonté,* Tome I. Paris: Aubier, 1949, pp. 380, ff.

Ridick, S. J. (S.S.C.). Intrapsychic factors in the early dropping out of female religious vocationers. Unpublished Ph. D. dissertation, University of Chicago, 1972.

Roe, A. *The psychology of occupation.* New York: John Wiley and Sons, Inc., 1956.

Roe, A. and Siegelman, M. *The origin of interests.* Washington, D.C.: American Personnel and Guidance Association, 1964.

Rogers, C. R. A theory of therapy, personality, and interpersonal relationships, as developed in the client-centered framework.

241

In S. Koch (Ed.), *Psychology: A study of a science,* Vol. 3. New York: McGraw-Hill Book Co., 1959, pp. 184-256.

——— *On becoming a person.* Boston: Houghton Millin Co., 1961.

Rokeach, M. The nature of attitudes. In *International Encyclopedia of Social Sciences.* New York: The Macmillan Co., 1968a.

——— A theory of organization and change within value-attitude systems. *Journal of Social Issues,* 1968b, *24,* 13-33.

——— *The nature of human values.* New York: The Free Press, 1973.

Rooney, J. J. Psychological assessment in a community of teaching Sisters. *The Catholic Psychological Record,* 1966, *4,* 56-62.

——— Needed research on the psychological assessment of religious personnel. In W. J. Coville, et al., *Assessment of candidates for the religious life.* Washington, D.C.: CARA, 1968.

——— Psychological research on the American priesthood: A review of the literature. In E. C. Kennedy and V. J. Heckler, *The Catholic priest in the United States: Psychological investigations.* Washington, D.C.: United States Catholic Conference, 1972.

Rosenberg, M. J. Cognitive structure and attitudinal affect. *Journal of Abnormal and Social Psychology,* 1956, *53,* 256-261.

Rotter, J. B. *Social learning and clinical psychology.* New York: Prentice-Hall, Inc., 1954.

Rotter, J. B. and Rafferty, J. E. *The Rotter Incomplete Sentences Blank: Manual.* New York: The Psychological Corporation, 1950.

Rulla, L. M. (S.J.). Psychological significance of religious vocation. Unpublished Ph. D. dissertation. The University of Chicago, 1967.

——— *Depth psychology and vocation: A psycho-social perspective.* Rome: Gregorian University Press, and Chicago: Loyola University Press, 1971.

Rulla, L. M. (S.J.) and Maddi, S. R. Personality and the

Catholic religious vocation, II: Self and conflict in male entrants. *Journal of Personality,* 1972, *40,* 564-587.

Sacred Congregation of Catholic Education, *Guide to formation in priestly celibacy.* Rome: 1974.

Sampson, E. E.   Student activism and the decade of protest. *Journal of Social Issues,* 1967, *23,* 1-33.

Sampson, E. E. and Insko, C. A.   Cognitive consistency and conformity in the autokinetic situation. *Journal of Personality and Social Psychology,* 1964, *68,* 189-192.

Schafer, R.   *Aspects of internalization.* New York: International Universities Press, Inc., 1968.

Schallert, E. J. and Kelley, J. M.   Some factors associated with voluntary withdrawal from the Catholic priesthood. *Lumen Vitae* (English edition), 1970, 25 (3), 425-460.

Schmidt, C. W., Meyer, J. K., Lucas, J.   Sexual deviations and personality disorders. In J. R. Lion (Ed.), *Personality Disorders: Diagnosis and Management.* Baltimore: The Williams and Wilkins Co., 1974.

Schmidtchen, G.   *Priester in Deutschland.* Freiburg: Herder und Herder, Inc., 1973.

Scoresby, J.   A study to determine the relationship of anticipated and actual perceptions of college environment to attrition and persistence at Brigham Young University.   Unpublished M. A. thesis, Brigham Young University, 1962.

Sears, D. O.   The paradox of de facto selective exposure without preferences for supportive information. In R. Abelson, et al. *Theories of cognitive consistency: A sourcebook.* Chicago: Rand McNally and Co., 1968, pp. 777-787.

Secord, P. F. and Backman, C. W.   An interpersonal approach to personality. In B. A. Maher (Ed.), *Progress in experimental personality research,* Vol. 2.   New York: Academic Press Inc., 1965.

—— *Social psychology.* New York: McGraw-Hill Book Co., 1974.

Siegel, S.   *Non-parametric statistics.* New York: McGraw-Hill Book Co., 1956.

Silber, E., Hamburg, D. A. Coelho, G. V., Murphey, E. B., Rosenberg, M., and Pearlin, L. I.   Adaptive behavior in competent adolescents: coping with the anticipation of college. *Archives of General Psychiatry,* 1961, *5,* 354-365.

Simons, G. B. An existential view of vocational development. *Personnel and Guidance Journal,* 1966, *44,* 604-610.

Smith, M. B., Bruner, J. S., and White, R. W. *Opinions and personality.* New York: John Wiley and Sons, Inc., 1956.

Srole, L., Langer, T. S., Michael, S. T., Opler, M. K., and Rennie, T. A. C. *Mental health in the metropolis.* New York: McGraw-Hill Book Co., 1962.

Standing, G. R. A study of the environment at Brigham Young University as perceived by its students and as anticipated by entering students. Unpublished M. A. thesis, Brigham Young University, 1962.

Standing, G. R. and Parker, C. A. The College Characteristics Index as a measure of entering students' preconceptions of college life. *Journal of College Student Personnel,* 1964, *6,* 2-6.

Stern, G. G. *Preliminary Journal: Activities Index-College Characteristics Index.* Syracuse: Syracuse University Psychological Research Center, 1958.

—— Recent research on institutional climates: I. Continuity and contrast in the transition from high school to college. In N. C. Brown (Ed.), *Orientation to college learning — a reappraisal: report of a conference on introduction of entering students to the intellectual life of the college.* Washington, D.C.: American Council on Education, 1961, pp. 33-58.

—— Myth and reality in the American college. *American Association of University Professors Bulletin,* 1966a, *52,* 408-414.

—— Studies of college environments. U.S. Department of Health, Education, and Welfare Cooperative Research Project No. 378. Syracuse, New York: Syracuse University, 1966b.

—— *People in context.* New York: John Wiley and Sons, Inc., 1970.

Stryckman, P. *Les prêtres du Québec aujourd'hui,* Vol. I. Québec: Centre de Recherches au Sociologie religieuse (Univ. Laval), 1971.

Sullivan, C., Grant, M. Q., and Grant, J. D. The development of interpersonal maturity: applications to delinquency. *Psychiatry,* 1957, *20,* 373-385.

Sullivan, H. S. *The interpersonal theory of psychiatry.* New York: W. W. Norton and Co., Inc., 1953.

Super, D. E., Starishevsky, R., Matlin, W., and Jordaan, G. P. *Career development: Self-concept theory.* New York: College Entrance Examination Board, 1963.

Tannenbaum, P. H. The congruity principle revisited: Studies in the reduction, induction and generalization of persuasion. In L. Berkowitz (Ed.), *Advances in experimental social psychology,* Vol. 3. New York: Academic Press Inc., 1967, pp. 271-320.

—— Comment: Models of the role of stress. In R. Abelson, et al., *Theories of cognitive consistency: A sourcebook.* Chicago: Rand McNally and Co., 1968, pp. 432-436.

Thibaut, J. W., and Kelley, H. H. *The social psychology of groups.* New York: John Wiley and Sons, Inc., 1959.

Thomas, E. J. Role theory, personality and the individual. In E. F. Borgatta and W. W. Lambert, *A handbook of personality theory and research.* Chicago: Rand McNally and Co., 1968, pp. 691-727.

Tiedeman, D. V., and O'Hara, R. P. *Career development: Choice and adjustment.* New York: College Entrance Examination Board, 1963.

Vatican Council II. In W. M. Abbot, S.J. (Ed.). *The·documents of Vatican II.* New York: The America Press, 1966.

Vergote, A. Reflexions psychologiques sur le devenir humain et chrétien du prêtre. *Le Supplément,* 1969, *90,* 366-387.

Vroom, V. H. The effects of attitudes on perception of organizational goals. *Human Relations,* 1960, *13,* 229-240.

—— Organizational choice: A study of pre- and post-decision processes. *Organizational Behavior and Human Performance,* 1966, *1,* 212-225.

Wallace, J. An abilities conception of personality: some implications for personality measurement. *American Psychologist,* 1966, *21,* 132-138.

—— What units shall we employ? *Journal of Consulting Psychology,* 1967, *31,* 56-64.

Wallace, W. L. Peer groups and student achievement: the college campus and its students. Report No. 91. Chicago: National Opinion Research Center, University of Chicago, 1963.

Wallis, W. A. and Roberts, H. V. *Statistics: A new approach.* Glencoe, Ill.: The Free Press, 1956.

Webb, S. C. Eight questions about the Emory environment. Research Memorandum 2-63. Atlanta, Ga.: Testing and Counseling Service, Emory University, 1963.

Webster, H., Sanford, N., Freedman, M. B. *Research manual for Vassar College Attitude Inventory and Vassar College Figure Preference Test.* Vassar College, Mary Conover Mellon Foundation, 1957.

Weigel, G. (S.J.). Theology and freedom. *Thought,* 1960, *35,* 165-178.

Weisgerber, C. A. (S.J.). *Psychological assessment of candidates for a religious order.* Chicago: Loyola University Press, 1969.

—— Validity of psychological testing with religious. In Bier, W. C. (S.J.) (Ed.), *Psychological testing for ministerial selection.* New York: Fordham University Press, 1970.

Weiss, R. F. Student and faculty perceptions of institutional press at St Louis University. Unpublished Ph. D. dissertation, University of Minnesota, 1964.

Welsh, G. S. Factor dimensions A and R. In G. S. Welsh and W. G. Dahlstrom (Eds.), *Basic readings on the MMPI in psychology and medicine.* Minneapolis: University of Minnesota Press, 1956.

Wiggins, J. S. *Personality and prediction: Principles of personality assessment.* Reading, Mass.: Addison-Wesley Publishing Co., 1973.

Winch, R. F. The theory of complementary needs in mate-selection: a test of one kind of complementariness. *American Sociological Review,* 1955a, *20,* 52-56.

—— The theory of complementary needs in mate-selection: final results on the test of the general hypothesis. *American Sociological Review,* 1955b, *20,* 552-555.

—— *Mate-selection. A study of complementarity needs.* New York: Harper and Row Publishers, Inc., 1958.

Wood, P. L.   The relationship of the *College Characteristics Index* to achievement and certain other variables for freshman women in the College of Education of the University of Georgia.   Dissertation Abstracts, 1963, *24*, 45-58.

Wylie, R. C.   Some relationships between defensiveness and self-concept discrepancies. *Journal of Personality*, 1957, *25*, 600-616.

Wyss, D. *Psychoanalytic Schools from the Beginning to the Present*. New York: Jason-Aronson Press, 1973.

Zigler, E., and Child, I. L.   Socialization.   In G. Lindzey and E. Aronson (Eds.), *The handbook of social psychology*, Vol. III.   Reading, Mass.: Addison-Wesley Publishing Co., 1969, pp. 450-589.

INDEX OF AUTHORS

248

249

INDEX OF SUBJECTS

253

254

Riproduzione anastatica: 15 settembre 1995
Tipografia Poliglotta della Pontificia Università Gregoriana
Piazza della Pilotta, 4 – 00187 Roma

FROM THE SAME PUBLISHER

1990

AA. VV.: *Human Rights and Religions*. (Studia Missionalia, 39).
1990. pp. VIII-460.   ISSN 0080-3987.   L. 65.000

RULLA, Luigi: *Depth Psychology and Vocation. A Psychosocial Perspective*. Third Reprint.
1990. pp. 438.   ISBN 88-7652-374-X.   L. 42.000

1991

AA. VV.: *Effective Inculturation and Ethnic Identity*. (Inculturation, IX). Reprint.
1991. pp. XII-128.   ISBN 88-7652-572-6.   L. 20.000

AA. VV.: *Faith and Culture. The Role of the Catholic University*. (Inculturation, XI). Reprint.
1991. pp. XII-148.   ISBN 88-7652-604-8.   L. 15.000

AA. VV.: *Women and Religions*. (Studia Missionalia, 40).
1991. pp. VIII-368.   ISSN 0080-3987.   L. 65.000

ABELA, Anthony M.: *Transmitting Values in European Malta*. Coedizione con Jesuit Publications - Malta.
1991. pp. XXII-340.   L. 20.000

BATE, Stuart C.: *Evangelisation in the South African Context*. (Inculturation, XII).
1991. pp. XIV-118.   ISBN 88-7652-635-8.   L. 19.000

BIERNATZKI, William E.: *Roots of Acceptance: The Inculturation Communication of Religious Meanings*. (Inculturation, XIII).
1991. pp. VIII-188.   ISBN 88-7652-640-4.   L. 23.000

CONN, James J.: *Catholic Universities in the United States and Ecclesiastical Authority*. (Analecta Gregoriana, 259).
1991. pp. XVI-348.   ISBN 88-7652-639-0.   L. 45.000

DE FINANCE, Joseph: *An Ethical Inquiry*. (Translated and adapted by Michael O'Brien).
1991. pp. 576.   ISBN 88-7652-632-3.   L. 48.500

ROEST CROLLIUS, A. A. – NKERAMIHIGO, Theoneste: *What is So New about Inculturation?* (Inculturation, V). Reprint. 1991. pp. XI-54. ISBN 88-7652-608-0. L. 7.000

1992

AA. VV.: *Religious sects and movements.* (Studia Missionalia, 41).
1992. pp. VIII-392. ISBN 88-7652-650-1. L. 65.000

AA. VV.: *Cultural Change and Liberation in a Christian Perspective.* (Inculturation, X). Reprint.
1992. pp. XII-64. ISBN 88-7652-578-5. L. 12.000

MALPAN, Varghese: *A Comparative Study of the Bhagavad-Gītā and the Spiritual Exercises of Saint Ignatius of Loyola on the Process of Spiritual Liberation.* (Documenta Missionalia, 22).
1992. pp. 444. ISBN 88-7652-648-X. L. 48.500

VAN ROO, William A.: *The Christian Sacrament.* (Analecta Gregoriana, 262).
1992. pp. VIII-196. ISBN 88-7652-652-8. L. 25.000

1993

AA.VV.: *Theology of Religions.* (Studia Missionalia, vol. 42).
1993. pp. VIII-396. ISBN 88-7652-657-9. L. 65.000

HARTEL, Joseph Francis: *Femina ut Imago Dei. In the Integral Feminism of St. Thomas Aquinas.* (Analecta Gregoriana, 260).
1993. pp. XVI-354. ISBN 88-7652-646-3. L. 45.000

McDERMOTT, John M. (editor): *The thought of Pope John Paul II. A Collection of Essays and Studies.*
1993. pp. XXIV-244. ISBN 88-7652-656-0. L. 24.000

NECKEBROUCK, Valeer: *Resistant Peoples – The Case of the Pastoral Maasai of East Africa.* (Inculturation, XIV).
1993. pp. VI-86. ISBN 88-7652-663-3. L. 13.000

1994

AA.VV.: *Interfaith Dialogue.* (Studia Missionalia, vol. 43).
1994. pp. X-366.   ISBN 88-7652-669-2.   L. 65.000

AA.VV.: *Yunus Emre: Spiritual Experience and Culture.*
(Inculturation, XVI).
1994. pp. VI-102.   ISBN 88-7652-674-9.   L. 13.000

HENNESSY, Anne: *The Galilee of Jesus.*
1994. pp. X-78.   ISBN 88-7652-666-8.   L. 15.000

1995

RUESSMANN, Madeleine: *Exclaustration. Its nature and use
according to current law.* (Tesi Gregoriana, Serie Dirit-
to Canonico n. 1).
1995. pp. 550.   ISBN 88-7652-682-X. L. 52.000

STANDAERT, Nicolas: *The Fascinating God.* (Inculturàtion,
XVII).
1995. pp. X-154.   ISBN 88-7652-680-3.   L. 18.000

Orders and payments to:

EDITRICE PONTIFICIA UNIVERSITÀ GREGORIANA
Piazza della Pilotta, 35 – 00187 Roma – Italia
Tel. 06/678.15.67 – Fax 06/678.05.88
Conto Corrente Postale n. 34903005
Monte dei Paschi di Siena – Sede di Roma – c/c n. 54795.37